the essential guide to
GARDENING
TECHNIQUES

the essential guide to
GARDENING
TECHNIQUES

Susan Berry

THUNDER BAY
P·R·E·S·S

San Diego, California

Contents

Introduction

Gardening is without doubt one of the most pleasurable and rewarding pastimes you can enjoy, providing a feast for all the senses—beautiful colors and forms, a heady mixture of fragrances, delicious produce, and a wonderful panoply of sounds and textures.

Although gardening offers many rich rewards, it can seem daunting and confusing to those who are new to it, because there is so much to absorb and understand. Coming to grips with Latin plant names, discovering the best plants to choose for different types of soil and situation, and learning the seasonal maintenance requirements of the garden can seem too much like hard work—but it doesn't have to be. This book aims to make these tasks both pleasurable and inspirational, as well as simple to master. It explains the basic principles of planting and maintaining a garden, while at the same time offering a range of straightforward projects that can be completed in a relatively short time and with no previous experience.

The first section, "Starting to Garden," looks at the preliminary stages of making a garden and outlines the issues you need to address before you even think about picking up a tool. What kind of garden would best suit your needs, how much time do you have—or indeed want—to spend maintaining it, and what kind of garden appeals to you aesthetically? These are all questions you must answer if you are to create a garden you will be happy with and enjoy working in. This section provides easy-to-follow advice on how to analyze your requirements and choose an appropriate style of garden—one that will be of interest throughout the year and require a level of maintenance that suits your lifestyle. Do not be

Planning your space
(right) *When planning your garden, think about building centerpieces and seating into your scheme.*

Gardening in containers
(opposite) *However small your garden, containers offer the opportunity to grow a range of plants successfully, provided that you feed and water them regularly.*

tempted to rush through this preliminary stage in your eagerness to start planting—the effort you put into it will pay dividends when you start on the practical tasks of gardening.

The next section, "How Plants Grow," provides a brief explanation of just that, and of why there is such a variety of plants from which to choose. Without a grasp of basic botany and an understanding of how different climates have encouraged different types of plants to develop, it is difficult to make informed choices about which plants to buy and to make sense of general gardening instructions—this section provides the answer to "why," while later sections provide the answer to "how."

The section on "Soil" focuses on the growing medium. Soil may look inert but it is actually the powerhouse upon which any successful garden is based, and you ignore it at your peril. Here, you will find out how to test the soil you have, add the necessary nutrients for plant growth that it may not naturally contain, and improve it by recycling household and plant waste.

The "Tools and Equipment" section describes the range of equipment that you can buy to manage your workload in the garden more efficiently— from forks, rakes, and spades to watering and spraying equipment. It also explains how to use the tools correctly and successfully, from the right way to dig to how to move heavy equipment without damaging your back.

The next section, "Planning your Garden," explains how to create a planting scheme that answers a range of different needs: to give the garden both horizontal and vertical structure, to ensure it looks good throughout the year, and to provide privacy and shelter. Useful projects include planting and training climbing plants for vertical interest and how to make a gravel garden for horizontal appeal.

In "Planting Techniques" you will learn how to raise your own plants, from planting out nursery-grown specimens and germinating seeds to taking cuttings and dividing up existing clumps of perennials. There is even a project on how to graft one plant onto another.

The next section, "Garden Maintenance," provides essential basic information on the most important tasks in the garden to keep the plants growing strongly and maintain plant health—how to feed, water, and generally nurture your plants so that they perform at their peak. It also explains how to keep weeds at bay, and how to trim and shape plants

Planning your garden (left) *The planning section of this book will enable you to use plants to maximum effect. For example, this fountain bamboo is ideal for creating vertical structure and providing privacy in a garden.*

Planting techniques (opposite) *Use the planting techniques section to learn how to raise your own plants, such as these African daisies— you can sow seeds in spring or take semi-ripe cuttings in late summer to overwinter indoors.*

KEY TO SYMBOLS

SUN/SHADE

These symbols indicate which position the plants prefer.

- sun all day
- sun part of the day
- no sun

ZONE

The zones show the minimum winter temperature that plants can withstand.

- **1** below –50°F
- **2** –50°F to –40°F
- **3** –40°F to –30°F
- **4** –30°F to –20°F
- **5** –20°F to –10°F
- **6** –10°F to 0°F
- **7** 0°F to 10°F
- **8** 10°F to 20°F
- **9** 20°F to 30°F
- **10** 30°F to 40°F

MOISTURE

These symbols indicate how much water plants need to survive.

- dry
- moderately moist
- moist

SEASON OF SPECIAL INTEREST

These symbols will enable you to plan for year-round color in the garden.

- spring
- summer
- fall
- winter
- all year

TYPE OF SOIL

These symbols indicate the plant's preferred soil type.

- tolerates acidic soil
- tolerates alkaline soil
- tolerates any soil

so that they flower more abundantly. A short section on identifying and treating common pests and diseases is also included, plus practical tips on maintaining a water feature.

"Growing in Containers" discusses the special needs and attributes of container gardening—for many people living in cities, container gardening is their only opportunity to grow plants. In addition to discussing the wide range of containers available, it explains how to pot plants and provide for their special feeding and watering needs so that you get the best from them. It also includes interesting ideas for growing edible plants in containers and making attractive displays, such as a wigwam of sweet peas and a hanging basket.

The next section, "The Kitchen Garden," explains how to create a productive garden so that you can grow a wide range of fruits, vegetables, and herbs with the maximum chance of success. There is also advice on harvesting and storing your produce.

In "Lawns and Groundcover," the many different ways of covering garden surfaces with grasses and spreading plants is explained, from inspirational ideas on how to use ornamental grasses to the best ways to lay and maintain a close-cut lawn. It includes a project for making a wonderfully aromatic chamomile lawn, with its springy, grasslike surface that needs no mowing.

The last section is a "Plant Directory" containing a comprehensive listing, in A–Z Latin name order, of over 150 plants of every category: trees, shrubs, climbers, perennials, annuals, bulbs, bamboos, grasses, ferns, herbs, fruits, and vegetables. The informative but succinct descriptions of the hardiness, size, flowering time, color, watering requirements, and propagating needs of each plant are accompanied by "at-a-glance" symbols for quick reference on key information (refer to the box on the left for an explanation of the symbols).

Plant directory (right) *Plants such as this star magnolia are featured in the comprehensive directory at the back of the book. Use this section to select the plants best suited to your garden's growing conditions and design.*

Starting to garden

Analyzing your needs

When contemplating designing or redesigning your garden, you first need to work out your personal priorities. Consider what you want from the garden and how much time you have to spare, then plan for these needs in the overall design.

Sheltered garden (below)

Tall fences or walls provide shelter, enabling you to grow plants that might not otherwise survive in your region. Siting plants close together helps to reduce the amount of staking and makes weeding easier.

If you are gardening for the first time, you will be faced with a number of choices. You can, of course, enlist the help of a professional garden designer who will, for a price, makeover your entire garden or, less expensively, offer advice on which areas you might change or improve. Whether or not you opt for the services of a professional, you will have to ask yourself some key questions: what do you want from your garden, and how do you propose to use it? How much time can you spend on its upkeep? How important is it to you that your garden is maintained on ecological principles?

Garden styles

First of all, you need to recognize that certain garden styles are more labor-intensive than others. The traditional garden, with a central rectangle of lawn surrounded by flower beds, is fairly hard work, as is a large, productive garden of edible plants (perhaps the most time consuming of all at certain times of the year).

In terms of maintenance, the garden calendar is at its heaviest in spring and autumn, when most soil cultivation, planting, and pruning take place, but summer can also be labor-intensive if the climate is dry and your plants are not drought-tolerant. Winter is a time of relative quiet.

From an average-sized garden, most people require an area in which to relax and entertain, ideally with a hard surface; a variety of flowering plants, hopefully blooming at different times of the year; and, for some, the opportunity to grow at least a few edible plants such as strawberries, raspberries, and tomatoes, plus some salad crops.

Those with larger country plots will be concerned with managing the garden and may opt to convert a large area to grass; areas farther from the house may well be turned into small woodlands, or even rough meadow. Larger plants—mainly trees and shrubs—will be needed for scale, and borders will be composed of flowering shrubs and perennials.

If you want a garden that more or less looks after itself, you will probably need to convert existing areas to a suitable hard surface such as paving, gravel, or decking. You may also need to replan any planting to include ground-cover, shrubs, and trees, rather than more laborious borders of perennials that require staking, dividing and weeding.

Planting choices

The plants and how they are planted will inevitably be governed by the climate, soil, and conditions in the garden. Gardens in full sun, for example, require very different plants from those that are in shade for much of the day. If you pay attention to the conditions when choosing the plants, you will find that they survive much more easily, and

involve less work for you, as they are less likely to fall prey to pests and diseases if they are healthy.

If your garden is exposed, your planting choices will be more limited than if it is sheltered, the microclimate of the latter situation enabling you to grow a more inter-

esting range of plants. Where space is limited, clothe vertical surfaces with climbing plants or use container plants, which can take center stage when they are looking their best and can be moved to a less prominent position at other times.

Patio garden (left) *In an urban setting, where hard surfaces usually predominate, containers provide the obvious solution. Trees, climbers, shrubs, and perennials can be planted in this way to provide variety of height, form, and seasonal color.*

Color themes (below) *Informal perennial borders are becoming increasingly popular. Unity of color, as with these yellows and oranges, creates a harmonious look to a mixed planting scheme.*

PLANNING CHECKLIST

When planning and designing your garden, you will need to take a wide range of factors into consideration.

- ☐ *Which direction does it face?*
- ☐ *Has it been tilled recently?*
- ☐ *How much time can you spare to work in the garden?*
- ☐ *Will you use it to sit in?*
- ☐ *Will children use it?*
- ☐ *Will you want to entertain outside?*
- ☐ *Do you want flowers?*
- ☐ *Do you want a lawn?*
- ☐ *Do you want any trees?*
- ☐ *Do you want a water feature?*
- ☐ *Do you want to grow vegetables and fruit?*

Finding a style

Garden designs range from the minimalist, in which the chief concentration is on form and architecture (such as the formal shrub garden), to those with an exuberant character that concentrate more on color and variety (like the informal cottage garden composed mainly of herbaceous perennials and a few edible plants).

In minimalist-style gardens, hard materials or water cover much of the horizontal surface, leaving relatively little for the gardener to do. This style of garden can be very low maintenance but lacks variety and offers relatively little in the way of seasonal change. As a style, it is ideally suited to formal buildings and it makes an excellent choice for a shady city garden, for example, where many plants will struggle to survive in the relatively low light conditions. To achieve a harmonious look, the design requires careful planning. The relation-ship between the horizontal and vertical planes is important, and generally this style is executed using straight lines rather than soft curves (although garden designers like the late Charles Jenks experimented with a minimalist style using curves rather than straight lines).

The cottage garden style, exemplified by Margery Fish's garden at East Lambrook Manor in England, relies more on herbaceous perennials, grown together in glorious profusion. To succeed with this style of garden, you will have to develop your gardening skills—but remember that even the greatest gardeners had to start somewhere! The nature of the plantings will be determined by the local climate, the aspect of the garden, and the type of soil. Most herbaceous perennials do best on alkaline or neutral soil. Different plants can be grown on acid soils—large shrubs like azaleas (*Rhododendron*), rhodo-

Formal style (left) *This combination of hard surfaces, an area of lawn, and mixed shrub and perennial plantings has been used to create interest here, instead of the more usual emphasis on flower power.*

dendrons (*Rhododendron*), and photinias (*Photinia*) do well, along with smaller, tougher plants such as heathers (*Calluna*) and blueberries (*Vacciniums*).

Clay soils and very sandy soils also impose limits on the plantings unless steps are taken to improve them (see pages 44–45). Deep-rooted perennials and shrubs do well in clay soils, and roses, for example, are well known for preferring these conditions. Free-draining dry, sandy soils can cause problems in times of drought. They are best planted with Mediterranean-type plants with small, fibrous roots. Mulching the soil surface with gravel or bark chips improves water retention and allows a wider range of plants to be grown.

Modern minimalism (left)
This drought-tolerant, ultra-modern garden uses inanimate materials to powerful effect, with the help of a few well-placed plants in containers.

Cottage garden (below)
Edible plants and flowers can be grown together for great impact, especially when contained by formal hedges. Clipped boxwood provides the ideal frame for mixed beds of herbs, vegetables, and flowers, which create an attractive as well as practical display.

PLANNING YOUR GARDEN

Gardening is about much more than getting your hands dirty. An interest in horticulture can grow into a pastime that gives you pleasure both in and out of the garden. Reading and learning about gardening can provide you with invaluable information on how to build your ideal garden as well as giving you hours of enjoyment.

Part of the fun of gardening lies in the planning, both of the design and of the tasks for the year ahead. Early autumn, as the nights become shorter, is the ideal time to surround yourself with gardening books and magazines. Draw inspiration from articles on individual gardens that catch your eye; tear pages out of magazines that show planting schemes

and color choices that particularly appeal to you. It is also a good idea to look through the advertisements featured in gardening magazines for specialty suppliers of seeds, bulbs, plants, and garden furniture. If you are able to make a trip to a gardening or flower show, this is a great opportunity to indulge your new hobby and gain lots of inspiration.

One of the joys of "armchair gardening" is that the weather does not spoil your fun. With a sketch book and paints, you can create different color schemes for the garden you wish to create. By gathering together the elements you may want to use in your design, you can see how they complement one another prior to creating the real thing in the spring.

Keeping your own garden journal is always a good idea: not only does it provide you with a record of what you planted where (extremely important in winter with herbaceous perennials and bulbs, when nothing is left to mark the spot), but you also have a useful diary of the development of your garden. It is fascinating, for example, to record the dates on which different plants bloom, and to see how much this changes from year to year as climatic differences come into play. A mild winter can bring many plants out early, only to have them fall prey to late frosts.

Gardening is an adventure, and both delightful surprises and rude shocks are the inevitable lot of any gardener.

Gardening throughout the year

Plants' lifecycles determine the look and character of your garden.
One of the greatest delights in gardening is the impact of seasonal change
on plants, because colors, forms, and textures play a different role in
various parts of the garden at different times of year.

Autumn and winter (below)
At this time of year, the
skeleton of the garden
becomes more visible, and the
eye concentrates on form.
Berries and hips provide color
while frosts emphasize seed-
heads and evergreen leaves.

The gardener's calendar begins just at the point at which nature is winding down. Autumn is the time of year to plot, plan, and dig over the garden so that everything is ready for growth the following spring. If you have recently acquired a garden, take note in late summer of what is growing where, and which plants you enjoy and will want to keep.

By late autumn, any herbaceous perennials will have disappeared, and you may inadvertently dig them up if you fail to mark them.

The fall is a good time not only to dig over the soil and remove any weeds, but also to add fertilizer, ideally in the bulky form of compost or manure, which will enrich the soil and improve its structure.

If the garden lacks vertical features, use this time to plant trees, shrubs, and climbers (see pages 112–115) to give them a chance to settle in before the new growth starts in spring. In a small garden, choose plants that offer more than one season of interest—spring flowers and autumn color, for example, or scented flowers, aromatic foliage,

and attractive fruit. Evergreens are useful for providing the garden with a permanent structure throughout the year, but even the naked skeletons of deciduous trees will help to give the garden shape in the winter months. It is worth including one or two winter-flowering shrubs or trees, such as the delicately scented witch-hazel (*Hamamelis*), with its golden flowers, or the winter-flowering Higan cherry (*Prunus subhirtella* 'Autumnalis').

Spring-flowering bulbs are also planted in the fall, mostly around four to six months before flowering time. For convenience, you can order your bulbs from one of the many specialty mail-order companies. Catalogs are sent out by seed companies in late summer, so that you can choose your flowers in plenty of time.

The growing season

At the tail end of winter, you can start sowing edible plants and summer-flowering annuals indoors to be transferred outside when the frosts have passed. Once spring is fully underway and the soil warms, you can plant summer-flowering bulbs. Prune summer-flowering climbers and shrubs in early spring. New lawns can be sown now if this was not done the previous autumn.

Once the weather begins to warm up in spring, the grass will start to grow and you will need to establish a regular mowing routine for any lawns (generally once a week). Weeds will also begin to generate themselves at an alarming rate and will need to be removed. (You can suppress their growth by surrounding shrubs and other plants with a mulch, such as chipped bark.)

Soft-stemmed perennials and vigorous climbers will need support, and climbers that are not self-clinging will need to be tied in to their supports. As the flowers bloom and die, you will improve the appearance of the plants, and encourage more flowers if you regularly remove the dead or dying blooms.

Any spring-flowering shrubs should be pruned after flowering, but if the garden is new to you, wait one season and observe what flowers when, and then organize the pruning the following year.

Spring and summer (above) *In spring and summer, the garden blossoms into a rich tapestry of flower colors and shapes, from the brilliant hues of early spring bulbs to almost decadent displays of softly petaled roses in midsummer.*

(inset boxes, opposite left to right) Dryopteris filix-mas; Castanea sativa; Cotoneaster; Rosa rugosa; Buxus sempervirens; Dicksonia antarctica; Narcissus; Lychnis chalcedonica; Acanthus mollis; Iris; Tulipa '*Striped Bellona*'; lavender.

Time management

Maintaining a garden well and in minimal time requires organization: You need to assess the tasks that must be done and then plan a schedule of work. If the work is too much for you to handle, you will need to redesign specific areas (or even the whole garden), so that you can look after it in the time you have available.

It is important that you understand the nature and extent of any maintenance work you will have to do in the garden, and that you keep this in mind when planning the garden. Nothing is more depressing than planning a visually stunning garden that fails to perform because you do not have the time to look after it. Opt for quality over quantity and keep the plants you choose in full health and vigor.

The flower-and-lawn gardens, so popular in the 1940s and 1950s, which still form the basis of what most people regard as a garden, were usually tended by the women of the house, whose largely home-based lifestyle allowed them time to garden. These days, with both partners often working full-time and raising a family as well, there is little time to spare and leisure

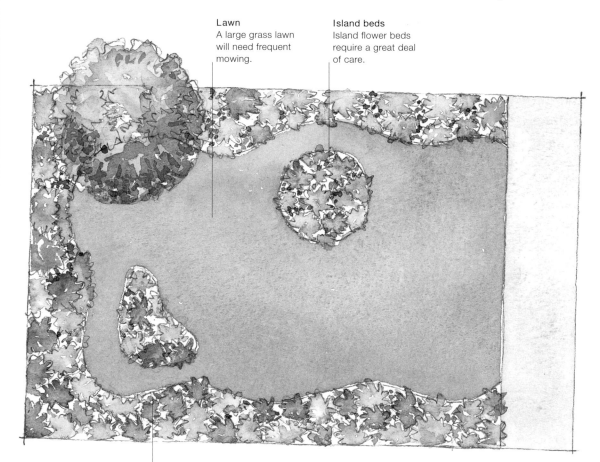

Lawn
A large grass lawn will need frequent mowing.

Island beds
Island flower beds require a great deal of care.

Perennial borders
Large perennial borders require a lot of time and effort to maintain.

HIGH-MAINTENANCE GARDEN

Shrubs
Planting shrubs will
ease the workload.

Water feature
A pond can be
maintenance-free for
most of the year.

Decking
Once laid, a hard
surface requires
little work.

Seating area
Less gardening allows
for more leisure time.

Low maintenance (above)
With hard materials such as decking and paving replacing lawn, the gardener creates more free time.

LOWER-MAINTENANCE FEATURES

Listed below are some of the garden features that require less maintenance than average.

Long-grass areas
Naturalized bulbs
Pond
Bog garden
Planting in gravel
Mixed shrub borders
Hard surfacing—decking, paving, gravel, etc.
Evergreen groundcover
Grasses and bamboos
Natural perennial plantings in drifts
Mulched borders (plastic and bark chips)
Mixed informal hedges
Drought-resistant plants
Raised beds

---

hours are very precious. However, the idea of having a garden as an oasis of calm in an otherwise over-pressurized world is more appealing than ever.

You can achieve this with intelligent planning and some outlay of time and money at the beginning, but you must start with a plan that can be looked after in, at most, an hour or two per week. In a smaller garden, this means devoting at least one-third of the space to hard surfacing and ensuring that the remaining plantings are more or less maintenance-free. Evergreen shrubs that have a strong architectural outline and require little pruning are ideal for creating the "bones" of the design, and bulbs and small perennials provide spot color in different seasons.

Better planning

Keep the higher-maintenance areas close to the house—at least you won't have to walk as far when maintaining them. Make sure that all paths are wide enough for wheelbarrows and are even, well constructed, and easy to walk on (wheeling heavy barrows over gravel is difficult). Try to make sure that deciduous trees do not overhang parts of the garden, such as ponds, where leaf drop is a problem. If you have a paved patio, make sure no berrying shrubs and trees hang over it or unsightly splashes of fruit will spoil the look.

Remove complex areas of plantings, simplify the planting scheme to include more shrubs and fewer perennials, and keep the shapes of borders simple. Ideally, ensure that there is a narrow path at the back of each border to make tending it easier. Make sure that all hard surfacing areas are properly laid on a level bed of hardcore so that paving stones do not move. Gravel must be laid thickly on top of landscape fabric to prevent weeds from growing up through it.

How plants grow

Origins of plants

The range of plants available to the everyday gardener includes many species from around the world, some of which are now so familiar that we regard them as indigenous.

However, we owe a great debt to the plant hunters who, several hundred years ago, traveled the world seeking out new plants in far-flung habitats, often at great personal risk.

In Europe, the use of plants for medicinal purposes spawned a great study of the habit, nature, and properties of plants, but as the New World and the East opened up to travel in the 16th century, so too did reports of fascinating plants from other countries. From Sir Walter Raleigh's potato onward, the excitement of the new has been a source of fascination. The first serious plant hunters in Europe were the Tradescants: John Tradescant the Elder, gardener to King Charles I of England, brought back plants from Russia and Spain. But it was not until the 19th century and the invention of the Wardian case (which enabled plants to cope with long sea journeys) that major importation of plants began with exotic collections arriving from far-flung corners of the globe.

Much of what will grow is determined by climate and habitat; plants have evolved different characteristics over millions of years to help them cope with their growing conditions, as this world map emphasizes.

CACTUS
(*Cactaceae*)
North America

DAHLIA
(*Dahlia*)
Mexico

NORTH AMERICA

ATLANTIC OCEAN

PACIFIC OCEAN

SOUTH AMERICA

N
W E
S

SWEET POTATO
(*Ipomoea*)
South America

FUCHSIA
(*Fuchsia*)
Chile and Argentina

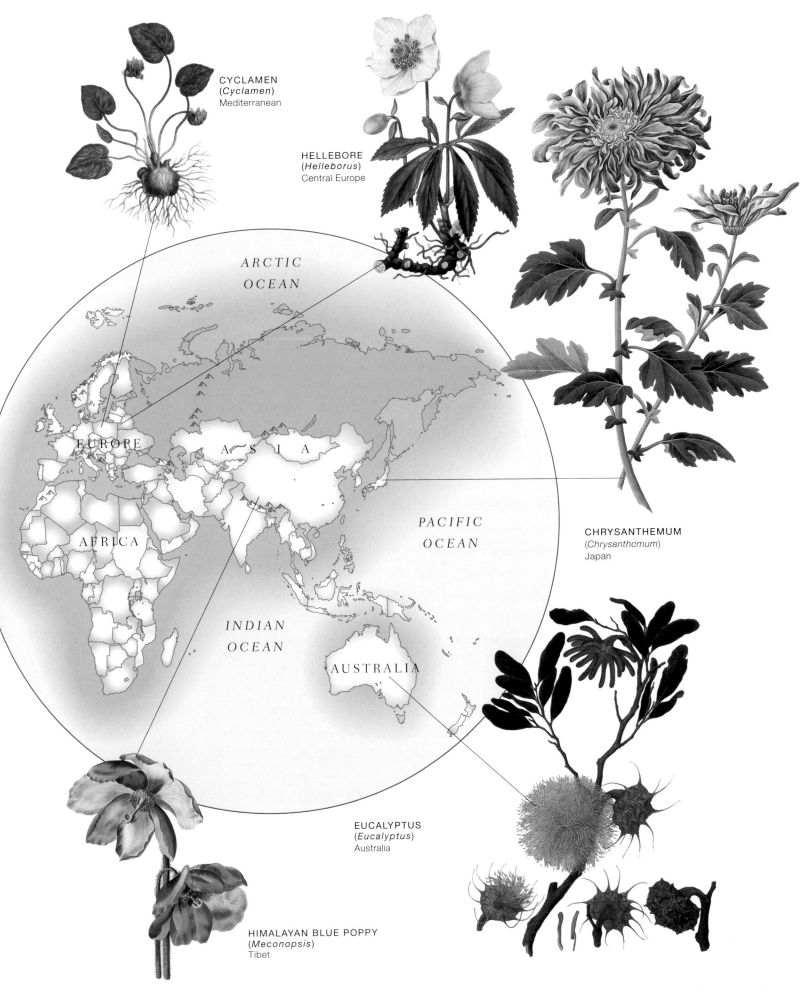

CYCLAMEN
(*Cyclamen*)
Mediterranean

HELLEBORE
(*Helleborus*)
Central Europe

CHRYSANTHEMUM
(*Chrysanthemum*)
Japan

ARCTIC
OCEAN

EUROPE

ASIA

AFRICA

PACIFIC
OCEAN

INDIAN
OCEAN

AUSTRALIA

EUCALYPTUS
(*Eucalyptus*)
Australia

HIMALAYAN BLUE POPPY
(*Meconopsis*)
Tibet

Plant families

Plants have various individual characteristics to distinguish themselves from one another. Botanists have used these features to classify them into different groups. As new knowledge comes to light, these groups change, so scientific plant naming is never static. New developments and changes occur all the time.

Plant names, particularly Latin names, cause many gardeners anguish and irritation. In the first place, the Latin names are difficult to pronounce—one person's *CotONeaster* is another's *CotoneASTer*—making discussion fraught with pitfalls. Another problem is that botanists frequently change these Latin names; just as you have gotten used to calling a plant a "datura," someone comes along and says it is now a "brugmansia." At least lily of the valley (*Convallaria Majalis*) keeps its name for good. However, common names are often regional and now that gardening has become more international (with plants shipped in from nurseries around the world), the confusion can be overwhelming.

The man responsible for the Latin name system was Linnaeus, the Swedish naturalist whose *Species Plantarum* (1753) applied a binomial (two word) system to all the plants in his vast collection. The first of these names, the genus, described the broad group to which the plant belonged and the second name, the species, the more closely linked group. Later, Pierre Magnol, a botanist from Montpellier, introduced the concept of plant "families"—a broader group than the genus in which a variety of similar characteristics might be found.

Botanical sketch by Linnaeus (right) *Detailed studies of plant families by Linnaeus some 250 years ago gave us the internationally recognized botanical structure by which all plants are broadly identified today. Here we see some of the detailed sketches he used to support his theories.*

Carolus Linnaeus, 1707–1778 (above) *Linnaeus established the modern-day binomial system of nomenclature (genus name plus species name) for both the plant and animal worlds.*

The link between the groups was found by Charles Darwin, who worked out that if plants were alike it was because they had common ancestors, and that true classification stemmed from genealogy. Plants therefore have a family tree.

If you delve a little deeper, you will discover that Latin names can be quite helpful, since many of them describe the plant's characteristics (albeit in what is, initially, an unfamiliar language). For example, if you see the word *fragrans* in the Latin name, the plant is scented; if you see *variegata*, it means that it has striped or blotched leaf markings; *glauca* means waxy; *nigrescens* is black and *alba* is white. Once these become more familiar, you can start to make sense of the elements of the plants' names. Equally, plants are often named after the person who discovered them or bred them, so that *Primula forrestii* is named after George Forrest who cultivated it.

The search for variety

Exactly how plants adapt and change is still a mystery. Various mutations are thrown up from time to time; when these occur, a new "variety" of a species appears that may or may not take hold and produce progeny in its own likeness. The endless search after novelty has led mankind to try to create new varieties by selective breeding from naturally occurring varieties or "sports." There is, therefore, great excitement at the discovery of any new departure. This was seen at its height among the tulip breeders in Holland in the 17th century.

Cultivars (left) *These Astrantia 'Roma,' are cultivars of great masterwort (Astrantia Major), which occurs naturally. Cultivars have been bred to emphasize or alter certain characteristics of the species plant.*

Old variety of tulip (above) *Some groups of plants, such as tulips, have attracted the attention of plant breeders over the centuries, each eager to develop their own particular strain. At the height of tulipmania in Holland in the 17th century, new cultivars changed hands for huge sums of money.*

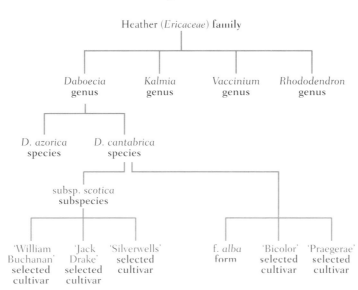

PLANT'S FAMILY TREE

Plant species have a recognized two-part scientific name written in italics. The plants are grouped together into families (e.g., heathers are matched with rhododendrons), which will share similar features.

Heather (*Ericaceae*) family

| *Daboecia* genus | *Kalmia* genus | *Vaccinium* genus | *Rhododendron* genus |

D. azorica species | *D. cantabrica* species

subsp. *scotica* subspecies

'William Buchanan' selected cultivar | 'Jack Drake' selected cultivar | 'Silverwells' selected cultivar | f. *alba* form | 'Bicolor' selected cultivar | 'Praegerae' selected cultivar

How plants grow

All plants need a regular supply of light, oxygen, moisture, and nutrients to thrive. It helps us to become better gardeners if we understand how this process takes place and how we can help to provide the right conditions in our gardens for the plants that we grow.

Once you reach that stage in life where the idea of cultivating a garden is more interesting than shouting over loud music in a bar, however, botany ceases to be quite so boring and actually becomes relevant. In fact, as the third clematis you have bought in as many summers fails to thrive and dies, you begin to wish you had paid more attention in school!

Learning the techniques of gardening while steadfastly refusing to inquire about how the plants themselves function leaves you at a considerable disadvantage. You may know how to carry out the necessary tasks, but you have no clear idea at all about why you are doing them. The instructions are much easier to remember if you have some idea as to the reasons behind them. It is

usually extremely tempting to ignore what appears to be a lot of fuss over nothing, disregard the fine print, and do what comes naturally. Only when you lose a large number of plants, or realize that those you have planted have failed to grow properly, do you then consider re-reading the instruction manual and, maybe, move on to read the bits about botany.

Most of us can manage to recognize the primary elements of a plant: roots, stem, leaves, flowers, and fruit or seed (although plants are quite good at disguising themselves; what we think of as a root—the bit that is underground—may well turn out to be a swollen stem, as in the case of a crocus). What we are less clear about is how the plant nourishes itself and grows, and why it does so only at certain times of the year.

The one common feature of all plants is that they survive by a process known as photosynthesis. Here, energy from sunlight is absorbed by the green pigment in a plant's leaves (chlorophyll), and water from the soil and carbon dioxide from the air are changed into sugars and oxygen. Water, along with certain minerals, is

The parts of a plant

(right) *The plant depends on a two-tier system to survive. The roots delve into the soil in search of water and nutrients, which are then fed via the stem to the shoots, leaves, flowers, and fruit. The leaves in turn manufacture chlorophyll (see opposite).*

absorbed by the plant's roots and then carries these sugars to the cells of the plant. The oxygen is released into the air.

The neglected part of any plant is often the root system. The state of the leaves will focus the gardener on the welfare of the plant, but the trouble often starts farther down, out of sight. Contrary to what you might expect, roots need oxygen. Soil that is too dense, without any air in its makeup, will eventually cause the plant to suffocate. It is of vital importance to ensure that the plant's root system is well cared for and that the soil around it is nutritious and uncompacted. For this reason, it is a good idea to create a planting hole several times the diameter of the root ball. The fine roots will reach out in an expanding circle to draw water and nutrients from the soil, and they can only do so if they encounter favorable conditions. Only the toughest plants can barge through solid clay (see pages 44–45).

Once you realize that roots are not all alike, you will also understand that you have to provide the right conditions. Plants with fine roots spread out close to the soil surface; those with tap roots can search deep for water.

While trees, climbers, shrubs, and perennials survive from year to year—provided they receive adequate light, nourishment, and moisture—a small number of plants (known as annuals) will need to be started afresh each year from seed, because they die after flowering; biennial plants will grow from seed one year and flower the next before they die.

Sunlight

Water loss

Carbon dioxide

water

Water drawn up through roots and stems

Carbon dioxide and oxygen diffuse in and out of leaves

Water lost through leaf pores

LEAVES AND SUNLIGHT

The leaves are the plant's powerhouse. They work rather like solar panels, harvesting energy from the sun to turn sugars and starches into chlorophyll—the green pigment in leaves that extracts carbon dioxide and water from the atmosphere and turns into energy.

(left) In the process known as photosynthesis hydrogen from the water and carbon dioxide combine to form a simple sugar—glucose. Oxygen is given off as a by-product of the process. The sugars are transported through the plants cells, providing them with food.

TYPES OF ROOTS

Plants have developed different root systems in their need to adapt to different kinds of environments. Some have deep single roots, known as tap roots, while others have much more fibrous roots that spread sidewise, absorbing water close to the soil's surface. Tap roots are strong and tough, and can delve deep into the hardest soils to penetrate, such as heavy clay. Fine roots are many-branched in order to gather as much in the way of nutrients and moisture from very thin soils.

(left) A fibrous rooted plant, with a many-branched rooting system.

Plant adaptations

Water is the key component for both plants and people. We can survive long periods without food, but only a relatively short time without water. Our body weight, and that of plants, is made up principally of water. Seventy percent of your body weight is water, but a cabbage is made up of over ninety percent water. Small wonder then that rainfall plays such an important part in determining what grows where.

Climate changes (below)

The climate changes the farther north or south you move from the equator. Some plants are very hardy and can tolerate extreme northern and southern temperatures; some will only thrive in the hot temperatures of equatorial regions; and others have a wide range of temperature tolerance. The map and key below show the different climates in the various regions of the world.

Polar
☐ Ice cap
☐ Tundra

Cooler Humid
☐ Subarctic
☐ Continental cool summer
☐ Continental warm summer

Warmer Humid
☐ Temperate
☐ Humid subtropical
☐ Mediterranean

Dry
☐ Steppe
☐ Desert

Tropical Humid
☐ Savanna
☐ Rain forest

While we watch the rain fall on our gardens, we need to remember that the water will, eventually, return upward again through a process known as transpiration. Only one-third of rainfall drains away; the other two-thirds is taken up by the plants. A big tree can draw 300–400 gallons of water a day from the soil, releasing it back into the atmosphere through its leaves.

In various parts of the world, the rainfall is very high or very low at certain times of the year, and the plants in these areas have adapted to survive in these conditions.

One thing quickly becomes clear to you when you neglect to water your garden: some plants quickly wither and die while others survive apparently untroubled. Why should this be so? And what can you learn from this?

Plants from great extremes of climate have evolved to cope with different quantities and timings of water delivery, and their cell structure has adapted to cope with these fluctuations. The most obvious manifestation of this is in leaf shape. If you look around a garden, you will see a wide variety of leaf shapes. Since the leaves are the main means by which a plant captures sunlight through

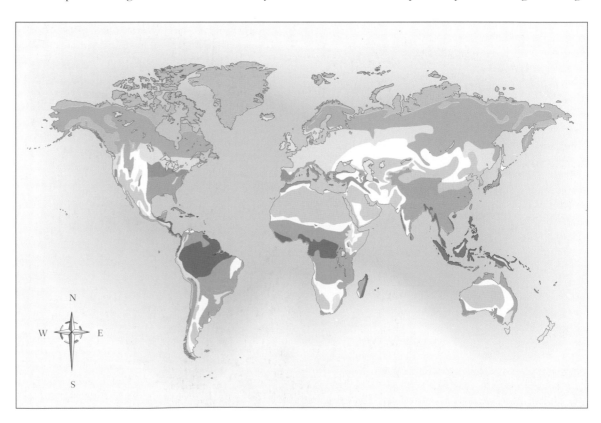

the pigment chlorophyll (see box, page 31), a plant in low sunlight needs larger leaves with more pigment to produce food. The leaves of good shade plants, therefore, tend to be large and green.

Since reduced sunlight lowers the possibility of leaf scorch, these leaves need less surface protection than those in strong sunshine, where the leaves may be coated with wax, felt, or hair to prevent moisture loss. In low light areas, the way the leaves are held may be significant. The leaves of ivy are held flat and face the light to absorb the maximum amount.

In desert regions, the characteristics of the plants are rosettes of leaves that catch the water in their base, a waxy or glaucous coating to the leaves, and fierce spines to deter predators.

On the sunny slopes of the Mediterranean, plants have evolved with fine, divided, felted, or waxy leaves in order to reduce moisture loss. In the prostrate form of rosemary, the grayish leaves help to reflect light and keep the leaves cool, which prevents water loss.

In areas where water loss may jeopardize the plant, leaves are often fine and needle-like. This is true of hot regions and also of very cold ones, where the wind dries the moisture and where, in frozen ground, the plant needs to prevent transpiration.

Quirks of nature

Nature also produces oddities. In some plants albino forms develop, with leaves that have no or patchy coloring. These quirks have become sought-after variations, in the form of variegated leaves, which are exploited by plant breeders to produce an even wider range of characteristics.

Canna 'Phaison'

Cornus alba 'Spaethii'

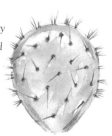

Euonymus 'Emerald Gaiety'

Acer palmatum f. atropurpureum

LEAF SHAPE AND CLIMATE

Leaf shape has evolved to cope with different conditions. Leaves from hot, dry parts of the world are often waxy or hairy to help prevent water loss; those from tropical areas growing low on the forest floor are large to maximize their ability to absorb light and soft because of the plentiful moisture.

Large, soft leaves
These are usually found in plants originating in shady, moist parts of the world, such as the rainforests.

Succulents
Plants that grow in very dry areas have adapted to the conditions by storing water in their cells. Spines help to deter predators.

Small, glossy leaves
These are often found in plants originating from hotter regions, such as the Mediterranean. The waxy coating helps reduce moisture loss.

Divided leaves
These are often found in temperate regions of the world and are the norm for many plants.

Needle-like leaves
Conifers grow in very cold areas with leaves made up of needle-like leaflets that are heavily coated to provide protection from freezing conditions.

Linear, waxy leaves
Long, sword-like leaves tend to be found in hot, sunny climates where there is less need for the leaves to act as solar panels. The waxy coating helps to reduce moisture loss.

GROWING FROM SEED

From the magic beans that grew into the giant beanstalk in the children's fairytale to planting your first seeds in the garden and watching them grow, the miracle of a seed becoming a plant has an endless fascination.

Children are often encouraged to grow a few seeds of mustard and alfalfa on blotting paper. The speed with which these sprout into life is almost magical. Growing your own plants from seed is a fulfilling and absorbing process, and one that involves relatively little expense. Simply provide your seeds with the right amount of moisture and warmth, and

sometimes darkness, and wait. The plant that grows from the seed forms both shoots that push up toward the light and roots that push down into the soil. Once the seed casing that surrounds the powerhouse of the plant falls away, germination is well under way.

However, the length of time that this process takes and the ease with which

seeds germinate varies hugely from plant to plant. Some are easier to raise from seed than others, those plants that mature in one season—known as annuals—being the obvious candidates (see pages 270–289). Plants with woody stems, such as shrubs and trees, take much longer and are often best raised from sections of the parent plant—stems, leaves or even roots—which are planted and tended until they, too, turn into miniature clones of the parent. This process involves a variety of techniques that you will need to master (see pages 126–131).

Seeds require specific conditions of soil, water, and temperature in order to germinate successfully, and you should always check these prior to either sowing or storing. The length of time for which seeds remain viable varies from species to species. Some can only be stored for a year, while others can be left to hibernate for several years until you wish to sow them. If you are buying seeds, always check the sell-by date to ensure that you are not buying old stock that may not germinate well, or at all.

Plant breeding

The aim of all plant breeding is to "improve" upon nature in some way. Unsatisfied by a dwarf habit or single flowers, for example, the plant breeder tries to alter the gene pool to create a structural difference that will enable the plant to meet the desired criteria more exactly.

This science is not new: the Chinese were practicing it more than one thousand years ago. However, modern advances in the understanding of genetics have enabled plant breeders to become increasingly sophisticated in their work, while the recent controversy over genetically modified (GM) plants has brought the subject into the arena of public debate.

How plants reproduce

To understand the plant breeding process, you need to know how plants reproduce using the process of pollination, in which the male anthers in a flower shed pollen that is transferred via the stigma to the female ovule in a flower. Once the ovule is fertilized, a seed develops and, given the right conditions, this seed will later germinate to produce the next generation of the plant, bearing the characteristics of both its parents. In a garden setting, it is never completely clear which plant's pollen has fertilized another plant's ovule, and the offspring can, therefore, be something of a surprise. Plant breeders who wish to control the characteristics of the progeny take great care to ensure the parentage of the new generation of plants, and those who wish to experiment will actually carry out the pollination process themselves (see below).

The seed of a plant is capable of independent life from the moment it is shed, provided the conditions are right, and these vary from plant to plant. Heat, moisture and oxygen all play a part in this development, and

HAND POLLINATION

Hand pollination is one way of ensuring that seed is set. The aim is to brush the pollen from the anthers (male parts) of the flower onto the stigma (female parts) of the other flower.

1 *Start by carefully removing the anthers of the flower that is intended to produce seed. Using a soft-haired brush, collect pollen from the anthers.*

2 *Using the same soft-haired brush, carefully dust the pollen you have collected onto the stigma of the flower that is intended to produce seed.*

3 *Once this process is complete, cover the pollinated flowerhead with a paper bag to prevent it from being pollinated accidentally by any visiting insects.*

many seeds are able to remain viable but dormant for a number of years, until exactly the right conditions act as a catalyst for germination.

While we normally expect plants to carry on reproducing themselves in this way, mankind has, for a whole host of reasons, decided to give nature a helping hand at various points. The aim of the plant breeder is to manipulate the processes of nature, in which cells from the parent plant combine to create various possible genetic combinations, leading to different traits or characteristics. In this way, some hybrid varieties will grow tall, for example, others small. Some traits in plants (just as in people) are recessive and some are dominant, thereby assuring that certain characteristics are more likely to be retained over generations of breeding.

Selective plant breeding attempts to gather attractive traits into a particular category. While this used to be, to some extent, a game of trial and error, new research into DNA is making it increasingly likely that plant breeders can conjure characteristics to order.

Pollination

There are two principal methods of pollination: wind pollination and insect pollination. Plants have adapted their pollen to suit one or another of these methods.

Wind pollination demands copious quantities of pollen grains, all of which must be light and easily blown around. For example, a hazel bush of average

size with 300 male catkins, would yield over 600 million pollen grains. In wind-pollinated plants, fragrance and nectar are usually absent.

In insect-pollinated plants, various helpful devices have been developed that enable the insect to do the job of pollination more efficiently. "Flight-path" markings on the petals indicate the route to the pollen grains, and the pollen grains are heavier and stickier, ensuring that they cling to the insect's legs. Some other flowers have characteristics that make them particularly attractive to certain insects—a long spur, for example, may mean that the flower attracts only butterflies that have a particularly long proboscis, which reaches down to collect the nectar.

When buying plants, you will often find that they have been categorized according to the way in which they have been bred. Plants described as open-pollinated have

been allowed to breed naturally, with no specialty hybridization. Progeny of these plants will breed more or less true to type.

F1 hybrids have been bred by deliberately crossing two pure-bred parents. The resulting plants will tend to display increased vigor and uniformity of appearance, but they will not necessarily breed true to type.

Insect pollination (above)
The bumblebee is the workhorse of the garden, helping to transport pollen over a wide area as it goes about its task of collecting nectar.

Wind pollination (left)
Floating on the wind: this dramatic shot highlights the huge amount of pollen that is carried on the wind.

Climate and its effects

All forms of gardening are a balancing act between the forces of nature on the one hand and the desire of the gardener on the other to coerce or cajole nature to perform to his or her command. From the earliest times people learned to grow plants for food and, if we were not to starve, we learned to offer nature a helping hand: providing irrigation in times of drought or shelter in particularly hard winters.

Any gardener who fails to pay attention to the demands of climate will ultimately pay the price of reduced performance in their plants. Gardeners must be aware of the climate conditions in which they live, as well as the climate conditions demanded by the plants they wish to grow. Nevertheless, there are margins for error and, nature being what it is, surprises in store: The plant labeled "tender" survives a really hard winter, while another cited as drought-resistant fails to cope with even a week without rain.

However, these are exceptions to a generally applied rule. Plants evolved over thousands of years to cope with specific climatic conditions. We now import many of these plants from all over the world; we therefore need to be able to work out whether they will grow as well for us as they do in their native habitats. A great many of the plants we regard as indigenous are, in fact, imports brought back by plant hunters several centuries ago; they have survived and adapted so well that they are now, to all intents and purposes, indigenous.

Climate zones

To aid our understanding of plant hardiness, botanists have created maps showing zonal bands that chart the climates around the world (see page 32). Plants are then given zonal ratings that indicate their ability to withstand different degrees of cold. However, even these 'hardiness' zones are not foolproof. A plant that is subjected to a long period of wet weather before the temperature drops to freezing will cope less well with the cold than a plant that was dry, since it is the

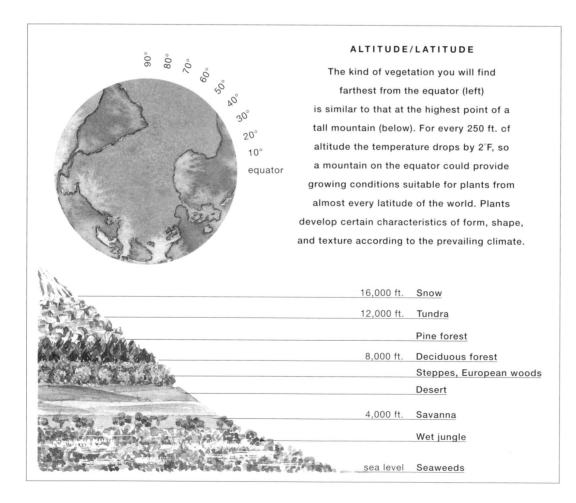

ALTITUDE/LATITUDE

The kind of vegetation you will find farthest from the equator (left) is similar to that at the highest point of a tall mountain (below). For every 250 ft. of altitude the temperature drops by 2°F, so a mountain on the equator could provide growing conditions suitable for plants from almost every latitude of the world. Plants develop certain characteristics of form, shape, and texture according to the prevailing climate.

90° 80° 70° 60° 50° 40° 30° 20° 10° equator

16,000 ft.	Snow
12,000 ft.	Tundra
	Pine forest
8,000 ft.	Deciduous forest
	Steppes, European woods
	Desert
4,000 ft.	Savanna
	Wet jungle
sea level	Seaweeds

combination of both cold and wet that is likely to cause a plant to fail. Equally, wind-chill can have a very adverse effect on plants, even when the ground temperature is perhaps within the "safe" band; therefore, where you plant—on a sheltered site or an exposed one—will play a part in the ability of the plant to survive.

Plant hardiness ratings indicate the lowest temperature at which any given plant will survive. The United States Department of Agriculture has mapped the country into zones of consistent annual average minimum temperature. A similar map has been developed for Europe. These temperature bands, defined by a zone number from coldest to hottest (1–10), are then used to describe the performance of the plants. For example, if a plant is allocated a zone 9 rating, this indicates that it will survive the annual average minimum temperature of that band, but it will not survive the colder winter temperatures of zone 8.

The maps that accompany this zoning information are rough guides only, as individual factors will affect the temperatures: south-facing slopes will be warmer than north-facing ones (and vice versa in the southern hemisphere), cities will be warmer than open countryside. The greatest factor in changing the zone bands locally is altitude: a 330 ft. rise will mean a consequent 2°F loss of temperature.

It is unfortunate for the gardener that zoning information is little more than an indication of hardiness. Unseasonal weather will quickly render it useless, as

late spring frosts can kill off plants that, all things being equal, should have survived; therefore, you may need to be careful about growing plants that are only just within the band of tolerance in your area.

Levels of sunlight (left)
In summer (red line), the sun is higher in the sky and more of the garden is exposed to sunlight. In winter (blue line), the light levels are much lower and only particular parts of the garden will receive full sunlight.

MICROCLIMATES

Even in the smallest garden there will be a range of conditions. Some areas will be sunny, others shaded. Some will offer protection from prevailing winds, while buildings and trees may funnel the wind through certain areas. One answer is to build semi-solid windbreaks. Choose tough plants so that they can shelter more tender ones.

Solid windbreak *A windbreak can only redirect the force of the wind. When the wind hits a solid object (a wall or solid fence, for example), areas of turbulence are created on both sides of the object.*

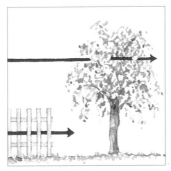

Semi-solid windbreak
A slatted fence, shrubs, or deciduous trees will form only a partial barrier to the wind, reducing its speed without causing it to change its direction.

Large buildings *These deflect the wind, causing it to build up speed; it will then create havoc once it leaves the area of the wall. This is a common problem in cities, where tall buildings create wind tunnels.*

Addition of shrubs (or trees)
The shrubs are planted about 5 ft. away from the house as a shelter belt. They act as a secondary filter to the wind that is bouncing off the building.

Choosing the right plant for your site

A primary consideration in gardening is to ensure that the plants you choose will flourish in the environment you are offering them. It is not enough to want to grow a particular plant: each species has preferences, and your garden may include only some of a plant's preferred conditions.

Fortunately, even the most modest garden has some naturally varying conditions: spots in full sun, areas in shade, and maybe parts that are drier or more moist than others. However, the soil in your garden has certain characteristics that will determine to some degree which plants you can grow.

Acid or alkaline?

Plants have preferences as to the level of acidity or alkalinity of the soil, and although some plants are not too fussy, others have strong likes or dislikes and will simply refuse to flourish if planted in the wrong conditions. Plants that originate from coniferous areas of the world have learned to adapt to

---

PLANTS FOR VARIOUS SOIL TYPES

Soil types vary according to the underlying geology. You can do a certain amount to improve the soil—widening your choice of plants—but you will still be limited to some degree by the conditions in which you garden. The main soil types are chalk (alkaline), peat (acid), clay (generally acid), and sandy (generally acid).

Plants for clay soil	Plants for sandy soil	Plants for peaty/ acid soil	Plants for alkaline soil
Escallonia	Anthemis	Acer	Allium
Geranium	Calluna	Camellia	Alyssum
Hemerocallis	Centranthus	Cornus	Anchusa
Ligularia	Cistus	Daboecia	Aquilegia
Ligustrum	Cytisus	Epimedium	Bellis
Mahonia	Echinops	Eucryphia	Brunnera
Phlox	Fuchsia	Fothergilla	Buddleja
Pyracantha	Genista	Kalmia	Clematis
Rosa	Helianthemum	Magnolia	Erysimum
Rudbeckia	Kniphofia	Phyllodoce	Gypsophila
Solidago	Lupinus	Pieris	Lonicera
Spiraea	Monarda	Rhododendron	Phlomis
Thalictrum	Papaver	Vaccinium	Syringa
Viburnum	Potentilla		Verbascum

high levels of acidity; if they are not given similarly conditions in your garden, they will eventually curl up and die. Notable examples are the rhododendrons and azaleas that naturally grow in the shade of coniferous trees, relishing the acid soil and damp conditions. Other plants, having learned to cope with the thin limestone-based soils of their native countries, will not flourish in soils with a high level of acidity.

One of your first tasks as a gardener is to determine the acid balance in your soil (see pages 46–47) and ensure you grow plants that enjoy these conditions. To some degree, you can improve or alter the soil conditions yourself, but it is a slow process and you are generally better off limiting your choice of plants to what will naturally grow there before taking on more demanding plants.

Damp conditions

Very few gardens have natural boggy areas, but if you want to grow moisture-loving plants, it is not particularly difficult to create a pool or bog garden. Damp-loving plants vary from those that prefer deep water through to those that prefer moist conditions. In a pool, it pays to have more than one level so that you can accommodate both deep-water and shallow-water plants. Water lilies, for example, generally need about 3 ft. of water, while marsh marigolds prefer shallow water about 6 in. deep.

If you create a small bog garden using a rubber liner to act as a water-retaining membrane (just as you would for a pond), you can grow a wide range of moisture lovers. Plants to try include the ornamental rhubarb (*Rheum palmatum* 'Atrosanguineum'), hostas (*Hosta*), and astilbes (*Astilbe*), to name just a few. A bog garden not

only varies the character of the plants in your garden, but also makes the pond area appear more natural, as you are mimicking nature's own provision where the surrounds to a pond or stream are inhabited by these natural moisture lovers.

Dry conditions

Your garden will almost certainly have areas where the conditions are drier than elsewhere. This is nearly always the case at the foot of walls and on the sheltered side of any tall building. Failing to choose appropriate plants for the conditions will mean you have to pay a great deal more attention to watering than might otherwise have been the case. Plants that enjoy dry conditions tend to have smaller leaves, which are waxy or hairy (to prevent water loss). Species that grow on hillsides in the Mediterranean region— herbs such as rosemary (*Rosmarinus*)—fall into this category, as do the more extreme desert plants such as sedums (*Sedum*) and agaves (*Agave*).

Dry conditions (above and below) *Many herbs originate from Mediterranean areas and are adapted to dry conditions, with either needle-like, leathery leaves such as those of lavender (above) or tough, coated leaves like those of sea holly (Eryngium maritmum) (below).*

Soil

Types of soil

Healthy soil is essential for successful gardening, particularly if you garden according to organic principles. To the uninitiated, one lump of soil looks pretty much like another, but it is in fact made up of varying quantities of rock, organic matter, water, air, and microorganisms.

The basic mineral composition of the soil will determine its fundamental character, but the quantity of organic matter it contains will influence its fertility —soil with no organic matter would be incapable of supporting plant life. Equally important to plant health are moisture and oxygen: soil that has been compacted (for example, by heavy machinery) loses its oxygen content, and the plants' roots will suffocate.

The gardener's aim is to create a soil that has a good, crumbly texture, with plenty of organic matter, and to ensure that there is an adequate amount of water. Be careful not to compact the soil by tramping over beds you have dug.

Mineral content

Whether your soil is made up primarily of sand, silt, or clay (the principal mineral ingredients) is determined by local geology. You can do nothing to influence this characteristic, but you can affect the soil's ability to retain moisture or to drain by adding the right material. Adding organic matter to sandy soil will enable it to hold moisture better; grit and organic matter added to clay will improve its oxygen-retaining qualities— without these additions, the particles stick together in a gluey mass.

To discover your soil's type, you can conduct some simple tests.

Soil types

There are five main types of soil that gardeners will find in their gardens and will have to plan for as they decide what to plant and grow. These soils can either be the predominant constituent of the garden, or there may be a mixture of two, usually with organic matter thrown in as well, so it is best to check with a soil testing kit to be sure. In this way you can get to know what you have to work with and will be able to judge what additions may be required in order to achieve your goals.

Loam

Chalk

Silt

Peat

Clay

Do I have clay soil?

After a couple of days of rain, gather a loose ball of soil in your hand and squeeze it. What does the soil feel like? Sandy soil feels gritty, and it will only form a ball with difficulty. Predominantly silty soil forms a ball quite easily and feels moist but powdery, while clay soil feels sticky to the touch. Drop the ball onto the ground. If it crumbles, the soil has a balanced texture. If it stays in a ball shape, it has a clay-based texture.

Does my soil drain easily?

Dig a hole roughly 2 ft. deep and fill it with water. As soon as the water drains away, fill it again; this time, measure how long it takes for the water to drain away. If it has not all drained away several hours later, you have a drainage problem.

Is my soil too dry?

Water a small area of bed and then two days later dig a small hole roughly 6 in. deep. If the base of the hole is dry, your soil does not retain adequate water.

Improving clay soil

If your soil is very heavy, the best solution is to add grit or sand and organic matter to it. You will need to do this in fairly large quantities, so you will have to settle for improving one area of the garden at a time. If you are growing edible crops it makes sense to tackle these areas of the garden first, as soil health and texture have a direct bearing on productivity. For areas in your garden where you cannot improve the soil, consider planting those

species that thrive in heavy soil, such as primroses, astilbes, ferns, and hostas.

Adding bulk to the soil

The best forms of bulk to add to a heavy or very light soil are composted chopped leaves and straw, or compost. Compost is rich in nutrients, and you will need to add less of it as a result. Straw should be spread quite thickly (around 4 in. deep) over the surface of the soil. Do this in autumn so that the winter frosts and the activities of earthworms in the soil will help to incorporate the organic bulk matter into the soil structure by the following spring. Alternatively, you can collect fallen leaves in black plastic bags in autumn, and then spread them over the ground six months later.

Improving soil texture (right)
Incorporating farmyard manure and bedding, such as straw, adds nitrogen to the soil and improves texture.

POOR DRAINAGE

If your garden does not drain well and the soil remains boggy and wet, there are a number of options you can try to improve (or make the best of) your situation. Some of these are suggested below.

- *If the area with poor drainage is not under deciduous trees, consider whether a pond would look appropriate in the context of your garden. Dig out the area and line it first with a thin layer of sand, and then with a flexible pond liner.*
- *If an investigation pit about 2 ft. deep reveals a thin layer of hard compacted soil, consider growing groundcover such as comfrey and then digging it into the soil, ideally by double digging the area (see pages 204–205) to break up the hard layer.*
- *In a vegetable garden, a raised bed system (see pages 202–203) can be used. The additional height means that the water drains into the channels around the beds.*
- *A large-scale drainage problem will have to be dealt with by incorporating a drainage system leading to a soakaway pit. Professional help should be sought for this.*
- *If the problem area is a small part of the garden, make the best of the situation and use it to grow moisture-loving plants in a natural bog garden.*

Soil balance

To grow plants successfully you need to ensure that the soil has the appropriate chemical balance. Some plants prefer acidic soil; others prefer alkaline. You can determine the acidity/alkalinity levels of your soil with a simple test. If necessary, you can also correct overly acidic soil by adding lime.

In addition to understanding the structure of the soil, you need to know its level of acidity or alkalinity. This is determined by the lime (officially calcium) content of the soil, and is known as the pH. It not only affects the type of plants that you can grow in your garden, but also has an effect on the structure of the soil itself. Lime improves the structure of clay soils by causing the soil particles to stick together in clumps, so that the soil becomes lighter and easier to work. If you have heavy clay soil, which tends to be acidic, it is a good idea to add lime to it to improve its composition, as well as to increase the range of edible plants that will grow well in your garden.

Look around your area to see what plants are growing in neighboring gardens, as they will help you to work out the likely chemical balance of the soil in your garden. Heathers (*Calluna* and *Erica*) and rhododendrons need an acidic environment in order to thrive, and if they are growing in or near to your garden this indicates that the soil is acidic. Poppies and trees such as ash (*Fraxinus*) and beech (*Fagus*) prefer soil that has a more alkaline pH, as do most members of the pea (*Lathyrus*) family.

The proliferation of certain weeds is often an indicator of the nutrient content, too, so check what is growing before removing them. Nettles enjoy living in a soil that is high in phosphorus, while clover prefers soil that is low in nitrogen.

TESTING THE SOIL

Standard soil-test kits are accurate and readily available from garden centers. This will tell you level of acidity of your soil and help you to choose the right plants or take appropriate action.

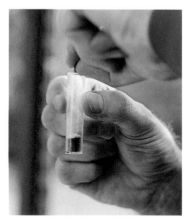

1 *Remove a small handful of soil from the area to be tested and add it to the test tube provided. Then add the soil-test powder included in the kit.*

2 *Next, add distilled water to the soil and test powder, filling up to the level marked on the side of the test tube.*

3 *Secure the lid and shake the test tube. Wait a few seconds for the liquid to change color, and then compare it with the chart supplied.*

4 *A yellow or orange liquid indicates an acidic soil. A bright green liquid indicates a neutral soil. Dark green indicates an alkaline soil.*

Assessing your soil

To achieve a more accurate assessment of the chemical balance, you need to test your soil. There are special test kits available that contain a chemical solution which changes color when soil is added, according to the level of acidity or alkalinity. A neutral (or average soil) has a pH value of 7. Soils with a higher pH (on a scale measuring up to 14) are alkaline. Those with a pH below 7 are acidic. The easiest growing conditions are those in which the pH of the soil falls somewhere between 5.5 and 7.5.

Balancing your soil

To reduce the acidity of the soil, you can add lime to it. Although this may possibly be worth doing if you are attempting to grow certain vegetables that will only perform well in a more alkaline soil, for ornamental plants it is probably easier to live with the limitations of the soil you have and grow acid-loving plants. For the vegetable garden, you can apply ordinary lime (calcium carbonate). Ideally, it should be added to the soil well in advance of planting (therefore, fall is the best time for the vegetable garden, as most planting is done in spring), and according to the manufacturer's instructions. At least six months should be left clear between liming and manuring, as the lime will react with the manure. Sandy soils will need lighter applications, and clay soils will need the heaviest applications. The quantity depends on the degree of alkalinity you are aiming to achieve: 5 lb. of lime spread over 100 ft². will increase the pH value by around 75 percent.

RANGE OF pH SOIL VALUES SUPPORTING PLANT GROWTH		
pH value	**level of acidity**	**typical plant growth**
3.5–4	extremely acidic	none
4–4.5	very acidic, peaty soil	coniferous trees
4.5–5	very acidic	blueberries, cranberries, rhododendrons
5–5.5	moderately acidic	potatoes, tomatoes, raspberries
5.5–6	moderately acidic	grasses
6–6.5	slightly acidic	most garden crops, most ornamental plants
7.0–7.5	neutral to slightly alkaline	most garden crops, most ornamental plants

ADDING LIME

Do this on a windless day and wear gloves, as lime is caustic.

Apply at the manufacturer's recommended rates.

1 *Wearing suitable protective clothing, shake the lime over the area to be covered, spreading it well to ensure even coverage.*

2 *Lightly fork the lime into the soil and cover. Do not add manure to the soil for at least six months after applying the lime.*

Alkaline-friendly plants (above) *Many plants require alkaline soil. For example, Jupiter's beard (Centranthus), much loved by bees, thrives in very alkaline conditions, often growing in the mortar of old stone walls. It self-seeds with abandon.*

RIGHT PLANTS FOR THE SOIL

When you have decided on the type of garden you want, you must find out what types of plants your soil will support. Understanding the basics will save you time and money in the long run, so it is best to test the soil and then plan and plant the garden accordingly.

Although soil appears inert and lifeless, it is actually a hive of frenzied activity—or rather, it should be. In addition to earthworms and other soil-burrowing creatures who literally process and regurgitate the soil, bacteria and various enzymes are constantly at work breaking down the components and improving the life-sustaining capacity of the soil.

Good soil is a balanced mixture of mineral particles, decomposed vegetable matter (humus), water, and oxygen. Humus provides the nutrients on which the plants depend; without oxygen and moisture, the plants' roots cannot do their jobs. Your job as gardener is to ensure that the soil is in its optimum condition for supporting healthy plant life.

There are myriad plants you can select for a particular soil—dogwoods (*Cornus*) for clay soil; laurels (*Aucuba*) for alkaline; fothergillas for acid soil; and elaeagnus (*Elaeagnus*) for sandy soil. All these plants require a specific level of nutrients, drainage and water. There are some plants that will flower on a variety of soils, but generally those that grow in acid soils—

such as heathers (*Calluna* and *Erica*) and tupelos (*Nyssa*)—will not tolerate other types. By preparing your soil well, whether by first eradicating weeds and debris, or by introducing fertilizers and composts, you can increase the chances of growing your plants successfully. However, the pH of your soil will not change dramatically in the long term, so it is best to grow plants

that will be best suited to the soil you have in your garden.

Whatever plants you decide to purchase, you must ensure they are healthy, otherwise their chances of flowering fully will be reduced. Make notes of plants that will match your design and then look for the best examples in your local garden center.

Soil nutrients

Whatever its type, soil contains a great many nutrients that plants use to manufacture food and therefore grow and reproduce. The major nutrients are the big three: nitrogen (represented by the symbol N), phosphorus (P), and potassium (K).

Each of these three major nutrients plays a significant role in plant health and also in promoting particular elements of growth. Nitrogen facilitates general leaf growth, phosphorus helps to create strong roots and potassium promotes flowering and fruiting.

In addition to these nutrients, which are needed in fairly large quantities, there are a number of trace elements that are needed in lesser amounts but are still impor-tant to plant health. The principal ones are magnesium (Mg), zinc (Zn), sulfur (S), manganese (Mn), molybdenum (Mo), and boron (B).

It is possible to make a detailed study of the nutrient requirements of your chosen plant, since plants vary in their needs. However, for most amateur gardeners with a mixture of orna-mental and edible plants, general-purpose fertilizers (in which the different nutrients have been combined in particular formula-tions) will be quite sufficient. The exact quantities of different nutri-ents are obviously of far greater importance if you are growing plants to show, or if you run a farmer's market and your liveli-hood depends on the size and quality of your crops. If you are growing crops for the table, you may need to concentrate slightly harder on the condition of the soil than if you are growing plants that are purely decorative. You may well discover that your soil is

---

NUTRIENT DEFICIENCIES

Leaves are often good indicators of any nutritional deficiencies in your soil.

Look out for these common symptoms of a lack of nutrients.

■ Older leaves turn yellow and main stems stay green.

Indicates magnesium deficiency

■ Unnatural shortening of stems. Leaf tips turn brown and look as if they have been scorched.

Indicates potassium deficiency

■ Leaves appear too pale or yellowish. Older leaves turn yellow at the tips.

Indicates nitrogen deficiency

■ Leaves are very dark and the whole plant becomes stunted. Older leaves turn purplish.

Indicates phosphorus deficiency

For fruit and vegetable gardeners, the following are worth noting:

■ In apple trees (*Malus*), yellowish markings appear on the leaves, which eventually turns into holes.

Indicates manganese deficiency

■ Cabbage plants develop inward curling of the leaves, producing a cupping effect, and the leaves often become narrowed.

Indicates molybdenum deficiency

■ Root crops, such as turnips (*Brassica rapa*) and rutabagas (*B. napus* var. *napobrassica*), turn gray and soft at the center.

Indicates boron deficiency

Fertilizer types

Fertilizers come in both organic and inorganic forms and are packaged as either "compounds" or "straights." Straights will provide one of the three key elements your plants require (potassium, nitrogen, or phosphorus), whereas compound fertilizers contain all three. Read the listings on the packaging and/or ask the supplier to give you details of the makeup of the compound so that you can gauge what you need.

Controlled-release fertilizer

Compound fertilizer

Dried chicken manure

Fish blood and bone

Dried blood

lacking in certain nutrients or trace elements when common symptoms appear on your plants (see box, opposite).

The application of fertilizers is discussed on pages 146–148.

Replacing soil nutrients

There is a range of organic products available that contain varying amounts of the major nutrients: nitrogen, potassium, and phosphorus (see table, right, for common sources of these nutrients and the percentages found in them). Nitrogen is the most important and is best applied in the form of bulky manure. The more concentrated the nitrogen, the less of that substance you need to apply. For example, generally 1 lb. 2 oz. of cow manure will supply enough nitrogen for 1 ft². of soil; however, with dried poultry manure, which is far richer in nitrogen, you would only need one-fifth of this amount. Hoof and horn, dried blood, fishmeal, and soot all include generous quantities of nitrogen in their makeup.

Ready-mixed fertilizers in various forms can be bought from garden centers and applied according to the manufacturer's instructions. If you are mixing your own general-purpose fertilizer, then a good formula for a once-a-season application might include 1 part dried blood, 2 parts bonemeal, 3 parts wood ash, and 4 parts leaf mold. To increase the nitrogen content of this mix, increase the blood and bonemeal component. You can dilute the mix with garden compost or sand for topping up throughout the season.

ELEMENTS IN ORGANIC FERTILIZERS BY PERCENTAGE			
material	nitrogen	phosphorus	potassium
bonemeal	4.0	21	0.0
fishmeal	4.0	3	4.0
leaf mold	7–8	0.6	
dried blood	14		2.0
fresh seaweed	1.7	0.8	3.0
hoof and horn	12–13		
cocoa shells	13–14	2.5	2.0
hay	1.5		0.6
straw	0.4	0.2	0.8
mushroom compost	0.8	0.6	0.7
wood ash	1.5	0.5	1
soot	5–11	1.1	0.4
farmyard manure (dried)	2.0	1.8	2.2
horse manure	0.7	0.3	0.6
chicken manure	1.5	1.2	0.6

Making a raised planter bed

A raised bed provides a neat, clearly defined growing area where it is possible to work without having to stoop or bend too much. It can also provide extra growing "space," because by using plants with a creeping growth habit you can cover both the horizontal and vertical surfaces of the bed. This helps to soften the lines and disguise the material used for the retaining wall, if you wish.

Acid-friendly bed (right)

Acid-loving plants have been chosen for this triangular raised bed, which has been filled with acidic compost.

Raised beds bring an extra dimension to the garden. Growing vegetables, which requires close attention in the form of feeding, watering, and weeding, involves a considerable amount of bending. If you use raised beds for growing your crops, you can cut down on a lot of hard work. Because of this, raised beds are also practical for disabled or elderly gardeners to use, and, if high enough, they can be tended from a wheelchair.

One big advantage is that the soil (or compost) within the bed can be of a different type from that of the garden, allowing acid-loving plants to be grown there, even though the surrounding soil is quite alkaline. It is possible to grow these plants within the main garden, but it will always be a battle to keep the soil or compost around the roots acidic where one soil overlies another. One of the best ways to counteract this is to keep the raised bed isolated from the soil below by building it on a hard surface. Discarded railroad ties are popular for this, but there are attractive (and cheaper) alternatives.

TIP

Raised beds are an ideal way to plant herbs and create a mini kitchen garden, because you can supply them with plenty of drainage beneath the soil.

MAKING A RAISED BED FOR ACID-LOVING PLANTS

Tools and materials

- log-roll fencing
- angle plates
- wood screws
- heavy-gauge polyethylene plastic
- sharp general-purpose knife
- compost

1 *Use three sections of log-roll fencing 5 ft. long and 1½ in. deep to form a triangular bed. Fasten the corners together (top and bottom) with angle plates and wood screws.*

2 *Using wood screws, fasten a section of fencing over the apex of each corner to hide the joints and strengthen the corners.*

3 *Line the inside of the triangular bed with a sheet of heavy-gauge polyethylene plastic, pressing it firmly into the sides of the bed. Make several small drainage slits in the base with a knife to allow excess moisture to drain away.*

4 *Fill the bed with acidic compost specifically suited to plants such as azaleas, camellias, and rhododendrons. Pack the compost into all of the angles in the bed (this will reduce settling later).*

5 *Remove the plants from their pots and plant them into the raised bed, making sure that the compost is firmly packed around the rootball of each plant.*

6 *Once the raised bed has been planted, use a sharp knife to trim away any surplus plastic just above the level of the compost.*

Composting

Composting—encouraging plant matter to rot down—is an important gardening technique, because when plant material decays it produces nitrogen, the most important nutrient for the soil. Although you can buy compost ready-made, a homemade compost heap is always of superior quality.

You can buy concentrated manures to add to the soil, but they lack the organic bulk of homemade compost and do not benefit the soil structure to the same degree.

You could, of course, simply till the dying remains of your garden plants into the soil, but the bacteria that rot the matter use nitrogen from the soil to do so, thus temporarily depleting it of this nutrient. The nitrogen will return to the soil when this process is complete, but it will take a while and in the meantime your plants will be starved of the nitrogen they need. The simplest solution is to make your own compost pile and add the fully decayed matter to the soil a couple of times a year, normally in spring and autumn.

The easiest organic method of getting nitrogen into the soil is to use well-rotted manure from farmyard animals—cows, horses, and chickens—combined with straw from their bedding. Applying farmyard waste to the soil is still a valuable method of fertilizing it, and you can easily get a hold of supplies from farms and stables.

The decaying process

The compost heap decomposes through the action of heat and moisture which, if kept in balance, cause the bacteria in the organic matter to do their work more quickly than if the material were just sitting on the soil surface. The aim then is to ensure that the compost heap has optimum conditions to rot. Do not add anything to the pile that is too large: shred material down to roughly 2 in. in diameter at most. Anything very woody or tough may need to be shredded into even smaller pieces.

In addition to organic garden waste, raw vegetable household waste can be used on the compost heap, along with small quantities of shredded paper, coffee grounds, teabags, and eggshells.

Rapid results (above) *For rapid results, chop, crush, or shred any thick stalks or large leaves into smaller pieces —this will speed up decomposition.*

Making compost

If you make your own compost, you will discover that it is something of an art, and exponents have their own favorite methods. The basic principle, however, is to encourage the material you are composting to rot down reasonably quickly and efficiently, so that in roughly six months' time you achieve a good, crumbly, well-rotted mixture that you can add to your soil.

A good size for a compost heap for an average-sized garden is about 5 ft. square and 3 ft. deep. Position the heap in a convenient spot in the garden to which you can transport the material easily.

Tip a layer of vegetable matter straight onto the soil to a depth of around 9 in. Then sprinkle on a thin layer (around 1 in.) of animal manure or other activating agent, such as sulphate of ammonia or nettles. Keep building the layers in this way until you reach the final height. Ideally, mix the materials in each layer: for example, do not build layers of grass clippings, because they will heat up considerably. Mix up prunings, grass clippings, and vegetable waste as much as possible. Water the heap if the material is very dry when it is added. Include a few spadefuls of soil from time to time. Finally, cover the heap with a piece of old carpet or a plastic sheet. This will prevent heat loss, which can slow down the composting process.

Soil fertility

Perhaps the most beneficial effect of composted organic waste is the improvement in soil fertility. After the organic matter has been applied to the soil, it decomposes further and organic acids are released. These acids help to release plant nutrients that may be locked in the soil. Soil-borne organisms like bacteria, beetles, and worms help with decomposition. Added to a clay soil, compost will help to open it up (allowing in more air), improve the texture, and make it more workable. In a poor, free-draining sandy soil, extra organic matter will increase the water-holding capacity and fertility.

MAKING COMPOST

Organic waste contains some nutrients that are not only valuable to plants, but are also ideal for improving the overall fertility of a soil—and compost is very cheap and easy to make.

1 *Spread the first layer of material over the floor of the bin, covering it evenly. Do not press down; allow it to settle naturally.*

2 *Add a second layer of different materials (such as grass clippings and vegetable waste) to the heap, scattering it evenly.*

3 *Add an activator, such as a layer of animal manure or a sprinkling of nitrogenous fertilizer, for every 9 in. depth of the heap.*

4 *When you have finished layering the compost, cover it with a piece of old carpet or plastic sheet and allow it to rot down.*

Making a compost bin

Before you begin enthusiastically collecting your household and garden waste for composting, think about where and how you intend to store your compost in the garden. If you are gardening on environmental and/or organic principles, it is a good idea to make a homemade compost bin from reclaimed or spare pieces of wood.

Making your own compost bin is good for your garden and environmentally friendly. However, rotting waste piled up in the garden is a not a desirable feature, and it is a good idea to keep your compost out of the reach of small children and any passing pets—cat waste is not a good addition to garden compost.

To keep your compost heap tidy, it is best to contain it. You can do this in a variety of ways, ranging from smart ready-made units of varying sizes to weird and wonderful homemade constructions created from recycled materials—oil drums, old floorboards, leftover bricks, or chicken wire. Probably the most efficient is any structure with a simple front opening made of slats of wood that you can add or remove at will to raise or lower the height of your bin. Truly dedicated gardeners will have as many as three compost heaps, in varying stages of decomposition, so that there is always one pile ready for use when required.

A good use of everyday waste (right) *You can use garden waste, straw, sawdust, hay, leaves, grass clippings, shredded prunings, hedge trimmings, household waste, shredded newspaper, vegetable and fruit (peel, rotted, or waste), tea leaves and coffee grounds, and eggshells.*

TIP

Use stable or poultry manure, dried blood, or bonemeal to add nutrients to your compost heap.

BUILDING A COMPOST BIN

Tools and materials

- tape measure
- mallet
- 4 posts, at least 4 in. thick
- level
- nails
- 1 in. mesh-wire panels
- stapler and staples
- 2 x 2 in. wood
- heavy-duty plastic sheeting
- chicken wire
- wooden boards

1 Mark out an area of up to 5 ft². At each corner, knock in a 5 ft. post, leaving about 3 ft. above ground level. Use a level to check that the posts are upright.

2 On three sides of the square, nail on a 3 ft. length of 4 x ¾ in. wooden board (leaving the front open).

3 Erect a 3-ft. high fence of 1-in. mesh-wire panels, and staple it to the outside of the four posts to form a three-sided bay. On the two front posts, nail on two 3 ft. lengths of 2 x 2 in. wood to hold the front boards.

4 Line the inside of three walls with heavy-duty plastic sheeting, and nail this to the inside of the posts. This will keep the bin's contents warm toward the outside, as the plastic absorbs the sun's heat, and will prevent the compost from getting too dry close to the bin edges.

5 Make a floor for the bay using a layer of chicken wire. Fold the surplus up the sides so there is an overlap of at least 6 in.

6 Cut the wooden boards to length. These slot just inside the two front corner posts to make the final (front) wall of the bay. The boards are added as the compost bin is filled, and the growing heap of waste will hold them in place against the front posts.

Tools and equipment

Forks, spades, rakes, and hoes

You will need at least some of the equipment shown here. The size and style of the tools you buy will depend on the size and nature of your garden and on your own size and strength. While larger spades and forks will do the work more quickly, if you are small it is better not to opt for the largest or heaviest in any category. Buy the best-quality tools you can afford, because they will be lighter and much more durable than cheaper models. Test the feel of the tool before purchasing, as balance is also an important element.

FORKS

There are two principal sizes: the standard fork and the border fork, which is narrower with smaller tines. Use forks for turning over the soil, forking in fertilizers, and lifting vegetables. Those with stainless steel tines are expensive but light and easy to use. The handle can be in the shape of a D or a Y. Choose whichever you find most comfortable.

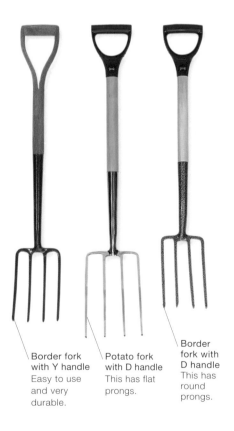

Border fork with Y handle
Easy to use and very durable.

Potato fork with D handle
This has flat prongs.

Border fork with D handle
This has round prongs.

Border spade
Suitable for the smaller gardener, enabling you to dig without causing too much strain.

Border spade
A coated blade makes this type easy to clean and keep free from rust.

Standard spade
The tread on the top of the blade relieves pressure on the instep.

Shovel
An ideal tool for mixing compost.

Post spade
Very heavy duty, used for installing fence posts.

Cornish shovel
An unusual tool that can be used for heavy tasks such as digging a trench.

SPADES AND SHOVELS

Again, there are two principal spade sizes: the standard spade and the border spade. Spades are for digging; the border size is best for smaller people and for more restricted situations. A well-made, well-balanced spade is essential, as it takes a lot of punishment and you will find it much harder work if it is not well-balanced. Again, the handle type will be either a D or a Y. Shovels are useful for shifting bulky organic manures; Cornish shovels are used in Europe in place of spades to dig the soil.

RAKES

These are useful both for creating finely tilled soil for a seed bed and for gathering up leaves. Some rakes have retractable handles, making them easy to store. For creating a planting bed, a steel rake with short, closely spaced tines is valuable. For gathering up leaves, the spring-tine rake with more widely spaced tines is useful. It is also good for removing dead moss from lawns.

Steel rake
The lighter the rake the better, but make sure you purchase one with fairly closely spaced teeth and a flat, forged head.

Lawn rake
Used to clear moss and dead grass from the lawn.

Debris rake
Rubber-toothed version that is good for raking up stones and other debris.

Broom rake
Made with lighter wooden materials, this version is ideal for raking up dead leaves.

Dutch hoe
Ideal for weeding and marking out for sowing.

Border hoe
Again, very good for weeding and getting into tighter areas.

Swan-necked hoe (also known as an Arrow hoe)
Used to hoe out large weeds with a chopping action.

HOES

These are useful for removing annual weeds from vegetable patches and borders. There are two principal styles: the Dutch hoe, with a rectangular, flat blade, and the swan-necked hoe, which has a blade mounted at a right angle to the shaft. Choose whichever type you prefer. Hoes with retractable handles can be stored easily.

Using forks, spades, rakes, and hoes

It is important that you handle the tools you purchase efficiently and well. When digging or lifting heavy weights in the garden, try to keep your back as straight as possible and bend at the knees, to avoid putting extra strain on your spine.

All gardens need to be tilled at some stage. Soil that has not been cultivated for some time will need to be double dug—that is, dug to two depths of the spade. You will also need to incorporate some bulky organic matter into the soil—it is best to use a fork for this. Lighter digging—known as single digging—is usually done each autumn. This allows the gardener to turn over the soil and add more organic matter. Borders that are filled with herbaceous perennials may need to be partially tilled as old plants are removed or divided and new ones are added. Small border spades and forks are the best tools for completing this task.

When you are digging, make sure that you always work systematically in rows. The first row of removed soil will need to be moved to the end of the plot to fill in the last row. You may find this task easier if you mark out the area that you plan to dig with garden twine. If you are digging over a reasonably large plot, you will be left with a lot of soil and it may be easier to use a wheelbarrow to transport the newly dug soil to its destination.

DIGGING

Digging creates better growing conditions for your plants and is the easiest and quickest method of creating a weed-free, fine layer of soil. Digging not only improves drainage, but it also opens up the soil to the air, allowing organic matter to break down more easily to release nutrients.

1 *Insert the spade vertically into the soil, with one foot pressing onto the blade of the spade. Ensure that the handle is sloping slightly away from you.*

2 *Should the topsoil be compacted due to heavy use, making it difficult to proceed, work the spade backward and forward to gain the depth required.*

3 *Pulling the handle toward you, slide your right hand down the shaft of the spade, bend your knees slightly (for correct balance), and lever out the soil.*

4 *Lift the soil onto the spade, slowly straightening your legs so that they, rather than your lower back, take the weight. Work in a rhythm, and take easy loads.*

With better cultivated soil, you can get away with just forking it over. Use the fork to remove weeds, stones, and other objects from tilled soil.

Weeding

You will need to remove weeds (see pages 148–149). A lightweight hoe is ideal for removing annual weeds. Push or pull the hoe across the surface, chopping weeds off at the base.

Smaller forks with either long and short handles are also useful for weeding, and for small planting jobs.

Using a rake (right) *By raking over the whole of your proposed plot for a bed or border, you will produce a finely tilled bed for sowing or planting.*

ADDING MANURE WHILE DIGGING

The lifeblood of a healthy soil is animal manure or garden compost. The method for incorporating this conditioner into the soil with a fork is a simple technique to master.

1 *During digging, put a 2–3-in. layer of well-rotted manure into the first trench and mix it with the soil in the bottom, before the trench is refilled.*

2 *Once you have opened the second trench and refilled the first trench with soil, place a 2–3-in. layer of well-rotted manure in the bottom of the second trench.*

> **TIP**
>
> If the drainage is poor, the soil in the bottom of each trench can be broken up with a fork before the manure is added to the trench and then covered over.

Hand tools

There is a wide range of hand tools available for specific gardening tasks. The two essential items are a small fork and a trowel. For general maintenance tasks, a hammer and mallet are necessary; if you have a deck, you will need a wire brush and a scrubbing brush to remove deposits of algae. A dibble (a pointed tool for making holes), string, and knife are also needed. Less important, but useful, is a bulb planter, particularly if you are planting bulbs in large numbers (see pages 110–111).

TROWELS

As with spades, these come in several sizes and shapes. The most commonly used is the short-handled trowel, but a long-handled version can be handy for awkward spaces, as is a trowel with a slender blade. Those with stainless steel blades are more expensive, but they are lightweight and easy to use.

HAND FORKS

The hand fork is another indispensable gardening tool with both short- and long-handled versions available. Again, those with stainless steel tines are the best choice. Make sure that the shank of the fork is firmly fixed to the tines, because in cheaper versions the shank rapidly separates from the tines.

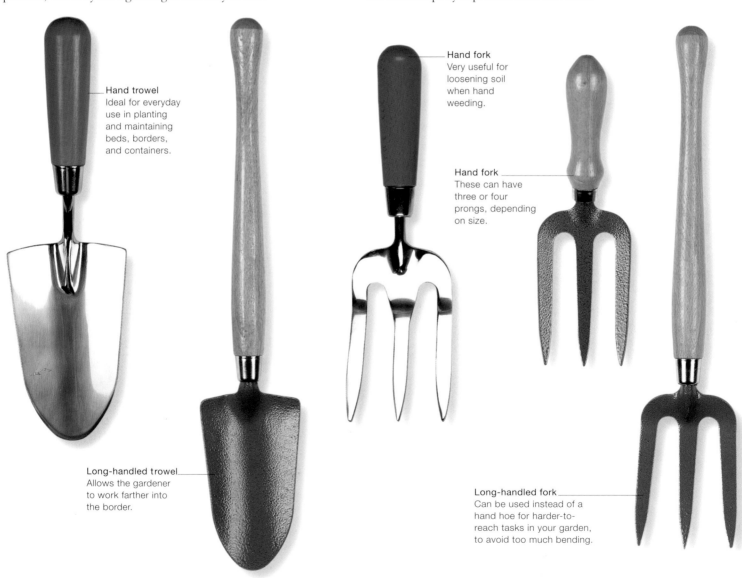

Hand trowel
Ideal for everyday use in planting and maintaining beds, borders, and containers.

Long-handled trowel
Allows the gardener to work farther into the border.

Hand fork
Very useful for loosening soil when hand weeding.

Hand fork
These can have three or four prongs, depending on size.

Long-handled fork
Can be used instead of a hand hoe for harder-to-reach tasks in your garden, to avoid too much bending.

HAND HOE

When weeding small beds and borders where space is limited, a hand-held hoe is the best choice. This works in precisely the same way as the normal garden hoe.

Onion hoe
Enables the gardener to hoe at close range and thus with more accuracy.

HAMMER AND MALLET

For all sorts of maintenance jobs, from repairing fences and sheds to hammering in nails for supporting wires, you will need a hammer and a mallet.

Claw hammer
Always handy for everyday do-It-yourself tasks you may have to tackle in the garden.

Sledge hammer
Ideal for hammering in tree stakes and fence posts.

Wooden mallet
Handy for knocking in stakes and canes that might break under heavier implements.

WEEDING

Weeds are not just a problem in beds and borders—they can also spread to paving and gravel paths.

Pavement weeder
Allows you to weed right into the cracks.

WIRE BRUSH

If you have wooden surfaces in the garden, you will need to scrub them regularly to remove algae deposits. Choose a heavy-duty brush with a stout handle.

Wire brush
This is the perfect type for the multitude of jobs that involve cleaning algae deposits.

STRING

String is a multipurpose accessory that can be used for everything from tying up plants to marking out new beds.

Garden line and marker
This is the basic tool you need to lay out perfectly straight borders, paving, and rows in vegetable plots.

LABELS

Vital accessories for gardeners who wants to know what they planted and when, labels come in a range of shapes, materials, and colors.

Using hand tools

Gradually, you will build up a collection of hand tools that will serve you well for years. As with all tools, it is important to choose hand tools that suit you and your garden and to maintain them well. Take time to plan what tools you will need at the beginning and give some thought to storage, as your little collection of essential items will soon grow.

Hand tools are the most frequently used of all garden equipment and, in many ways, are the gardener's best friend. With time, you will become very attached to certain tools and will look for a particular manufacturer's version if it is light, comfortable, and efficient for you to use.

Unfortunately, small hand forks and trowels with brown handles blend beautifully into piles of leaves, and it is not uncommon for you to find them again months later when the tines have rusted and the handles have partially rotted. To avoid this, you can paint the handles or bind them with brightly colored tape, which will be much more visible amid the natural tones of the garden.

Hand forks and trowels

These should be robust and well-made, with a good feeling of balance when held in the hand. The quality of the tool lies not only in the materials from which it is made, but also the manner in which the handle and the blade are joined. Poorly made tools will often split or come apart at the shank, so it is always worth investing in good-quality equipment. The best-quality tools have a stainless steel blade or tines.

Maintaining hand tools

Like all gardening equipment, hand tools must be looked after. It is worth giving them a special place in the garden shed or tool cupboard so that you can find them quickly and they will not become damaged by other equipment. Remember to clean your tools after use, and oil any non-stainless steel blades regularly.

Using a hand fork (right) *Hand forks are essential tools for light weeding. A good-quality fork should last you for some years, so take time to choose one that is comfortable to use.*

Using a hand trowel (far right) *Trowels are invaluable for planting containers or transplanting small plants. Always clean well after use.*

Using a hand hoe (above)
*Draw the hoe across the soil by pulling
the blade toward you, thereby removing
weeds from the soil.*

Dibble (above) *A dibble is ideal
for making holes for transplanting,
particularly vegetables that have
been raised in a seed bed.*

Wire brush (above) *Excellent tool
for cleaning your gardening equipment
or, as shown here, the stonework of a
pond or water feature.*

Other garden equipment

In addition to the battery of hand tools required, you will need an array of equipment, which is best kept
stored in an accessible, handy storage box. Nothing is more irritating than to plan to spend time in the
garden, only to find that the string, labels, indelible marker, or whatever you wanted is not in its right place.

String or twine

You will need at least one ball of
string or twine, either green or in its
natural color. If you buy string in
a cellophane wrapper, do not
remove the wrapper: simply cut a
hole and pull out the end of the
string. If you unwrap the ball it will
eventually unravel, become
tangled, and you will never find the
end. Store the string in a dry place
to prevent rotting.

Garden wire

In medium or heavy gauge, garden
wire is invaluable for training
climbers on walls, by fastening it to
vine eyes hammered into the wall.

Masonry nails and vine eyes

These are used when creating
supports for wall-trained plants. You
will need a hammer with which to
knock them in. Masonry nails and

vine eyes should be inserted into the
mortar joints between bricks.

Ties and supports

All sorts of ties are readily
available, from thick, specially made
rubber ties for trees to the little
plastic and wire strips that are used
to close garbage bags. Supports
come in many forms.

Plastic gallon jug

This is very useful when diluting
fertilizer or insecticidal sprays.
Be careful to mark the jug and keep
it separated from your everyday
kitchenware!

Labels and marker pens

These are essential. Labels come in
many forms, from very fancy metal
labels based on old country-house
designs to straightforward white
plastic labels on which you write the

plant names using an indelible
marker pen. The marker is essential: pencil disappears and ink is
washed off by the rain.

Baskets

These are useful when deadheading and for harvesting cut
flowers and vegetables. Traditional
cane or wooden baskets look
much nicer than the cheaper
plastic ones and are well worth the
extra expense.

Plastic sheet

This is useful for transporting large
quantities of leaves or other
garden waste.

Lawn bags

Essential if you live in a city and
have to dispose of garden waste in
the city dump, these are stronger
than normal garbage bags.

Cutting and sawing equipment

There are many tasks in the garden that demand the use of special cutting equipment. Pruning trees and shrubs is a common task; for cutting grass, there is a wide range of specialized mowing machines for close cuts, as well as trimmers for dealing with longer grass. Safety is paramount. Any electrically powered equipment needs to be used carefully. Never use it in wet weather and make sure a circuit breaker is installed (this will cut the power instantly in case of an accident).

SAWS AND TRIMMERS

There are large saws for heavy tree branches and smaller folding saws that are invaluable for dealing with branches that are too large to cut with shears. Saws must have very sharp blades.

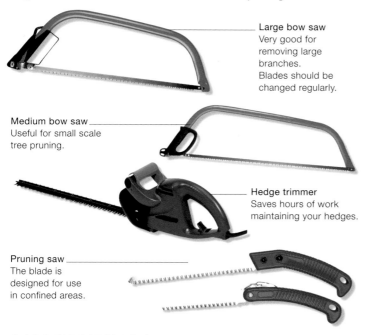

Large bow saw
Very good for removing large branches. Blades should be changed regularly.

Medium bow saw
Useful for small scale tree pruning.

Hedge trimmer
Saves hours of work maintaining your hedges.

Pruning saw
The blade is designed for use in confined areas.

GARDEN SHEARS AND KNIVES

Apart from a stout garden knife and garden scissors for general cutting, you will need garden shears for small pruning jobs. There are several types of garden shears tailored to specific cutting jobs.

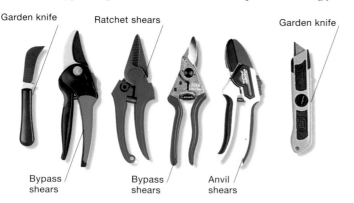

Garden knife

Ratchet shears

Garden knife

Bypass shears

Bypass shears

Anvil shears

AX

For chopping wood, you will need an ax, which should be of good quality with a very sharp blade. This can be professionally sharpened for you, as needed.

Ax
Used for heavy-duty tasks in the garden.

PRUNING SHEARS

You can trim hedges with a pair of shears. There are various kinds available. Make sure that the blades are made from high-quality steel.

Long-handled shears
Try to buy shears with notched blades, as they will hold the branch or stem better when cutting.

Pruning shears
An essential tool for cutting larger branches.

Shears
Available in various sizes, so buy a pair that is comfortable to use for a number of hours' work.

GRASS AND LAWN CARE

Long grass requires different equipment from the traditional mown lawn. Scythes (either short- or long-handled) and gas-powered or electric nylon-line trimmers are very useful. Trimmers come in a range of types, from lightweight to heavy-duty, depending on the nature of the task they have to perform.

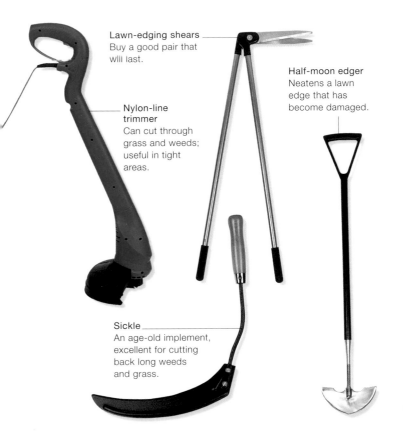

Lawn-edging shears
Buy a good pair that will last.

Nylon-line trimmer
Can cut through grass and weeds; useful in tight areas.

Sickle
An age-old implement, excellent for cutting back long weeds and grass.

Half-moon edger
Neatens a lawn edge that has become damaged.

Electric hover mower
Allows you to get into most areas of the lawn and cut across paving.

Electric cylinder mower
Provides an excellent close-cut finish.

Gas-powered rotary mower
Clippings collected in the bag are perfect for compost.

SAFETY EQUIPMENT

Many accidents in the garden can be avoided if the correct protective clothing is worn. Goggles will protect your eyes from chips of wood, stout gloves prevent your hands from getting scratched, ear protection is essential when operating noisy equipment, and a helmet and steel-toed boots are essential when pruning heavy branches.

Hard hat
Essential when cutting heavy branches.

Ear muffs
Make sure that they fit correctly and are comfortable.

Gloves
A wide range are available, depending on the type of job you are doing.

Goggles
Necessary for all tasks that involve flying debris.

Steel-toed boots
Strength and protection are paramount.

Knee pads
To protect your knees when kneeling for long periods.

Using cutting and sawing equipment

Woody plants can be quite tough, so sharp blades are essential. Remember that you are cutting into a living organism, so, like a surgeon, you must make clean cuts to avoid damaging the plant. This also ensures that pruning wounds heal more quickly and efficiently.

Good-quality cutting tools will make short work of tough jobs, so choosing the right equipment is vital.

Cutting equipment

The first essential piece of equipment is a pair of pruning shears. It is worth having one really good pair that you take special care of and a couple of pairs of lesser rank for snipping the odd shoot here and there. Shears come with various kinds of blades and different closing mechanisms.

There are many opinions on what type you should buy, but much depends on the kinds of jobs you are doing and what you personally prefer. If you have only one pair, choose one with a bypass action.

In addition, you will probably need a pair of garden shears for clipping hedges. Balance is important, as is the right weight, or you will find that your arms and shoulders tire quickly on any large-scale job (for which an electric hedge trimmer might be the better option—see page 72).

Garden knife

A good garden knife is essential for a wide variety of small jobs that you will encounter in the course of maintaining your garden. Tasks such as taking cuttings, picking flowers and vegetables to bring indoors, and pruning can all be carried out with a sharp general-purpose folding knife. Keep the blade oiled, and sharpen it at regular intervals: a blunt-edged blade that does not cut properly is likely to damage the plant and will encourage disease to penetrate through the ragged wound.

Garden shears

Garden shears are used for trimming hedges and for cutting down dying perennials in fall. You can also use them for smaller jobs, such as maintaining a small area of lawn. To achieve a good, even cut, keep the blades parallel to the line of the lawn or hedge, following a previously laid line of twine or string, if need be.

Pruning shears

Pruning shears are used for more heavy-duty tasks such as cutting back branches. Purchase a good pair with really sharp blades to make the job that little bit easier.

Using garden shears (above) *For branches less than ½ in. in diameter, garden shears are ideal. Do not attempt to cut thicker branches as it will damage the blade.*

Using pruning shears (above) *Shears can be used for clipping hedges and topiary. Make sure the blades are kept sharp and oiled to produce the cleanest, fastest cuts.*

Lawn edgers

If you have a mown lawn, you will need lawn-edging tools with long handles to keep the edges tidy. You will need a half-moon blade, which cuts through the turf to make a perpendicular edge, and lawn shears, which are much like ordinary shears but are mounted vertically onto long handles so that you can clip away long grass.

Pruning saw

A small pruning saw is very useful. The best ones fold up, protecting you from the serrated teeth, which are exceptionally sharp. Despite being small, they will make short work of a stoutish branch and are especially valuable for minor pruning jobs or in awkward places.

Long-handled shears (above) *These are ideal for cutting back thick shoots that garden shears cannot tackle.*

Lawn edgers (above) *Mounted at an angle to the long handles, lawn-edging shears will produce a neat edge to your lawn without your having to bend down.*

USING A SAW

Saws are often used for cutting larger branches when pruning trees and shrubs. Because the wood of live plants is often wet and relatively soft, these saws usually have large teeth to prevent them from clogging. For tasks such as removing branches even with a suitable saw, it is safer to follow a set procedure rather than risk injuries to the plant or to the person doing the cutting.

1 *Make an undercut about 6–8 in. away from the trunk, cutting up to one-fourth of the branch's diameter.*

2 *Make a cut 2–3 in. farther along on the top of the branch, allowing it to split to the first cut without injury to the trunk.*

3 *The next stage is to remove the remaining stub of the branch close to the trunk of the tree as carefully as possible.*

4 *Cut back to the branch collar, the swollen area where a branch joins the main trunk. Leaving the collar intact promotes rapid healing.*

Power tools

Electrically operated tools provide the gardener with the opportunity to cut down on much of the hard slog of garden maintenance. However, they need to be handled with great care and safety regulations must be observed to the letter, since the combination of water (ever present in the garden) and electricity is always dangerous. Heavy-duty power tools can be rented for short or longer periods, and unless you are likely to use them very frequently you are probably better off renting, thereby avoiding the need for maintenance. Make sure you rent the equipment from a reputable company and that they explain exactly how to use it and that they supply the appropriate safety equipment.

Powered hover mower (right)
Excellent for cutting across a variety of surfaces in the garden, and with a bag attachment, this is ideal for adding grass clippings to the compost heap.

Hedge trimmers

The powered hedge trimmer you choose will be determined by the height and length of the hedge and its distance from the house. For front yards, an electrically operated hedge trimmer with a blade approximately 16 in. long is probably the best choice. Those with longer blades are uncomfortably heavy for general amateur use. For large gardens, where it would be difficult to reach the power supply, a gas-powered trimmer would be best. Gloves and goggles are always recommended for your safety.

Lawn mowers

Your choice of lawn mower will depend on the size of the lawn and whether or not you want it to have a traditional striped appearance. If you want a finish without loose grass, you will need to buy a lawn mower with a grass-collecting bag. For small lawns, a manual lawn mower is perfectly adequate, but for larger ones a

Hedge trimmer (above)
Power tools are ideal for tackling large jobs. Here, a Leyland cypress (Cupressocyparis leylandii) is being cut using an electric hedge trimmer.

Powered lawn mower (right)
For large gardens, tractor-type lawn mowers are the best solution. They come in a wide range of styles and sizes and are gas-powered.

powered lawn mower will save a great deal of effort. There are both push, or "walk behind," power lawn mowers, with either a cylinder action or a rotary action, and "ride on" or tractor-hauled gas-powered mowers for much larger areas. Cylinder-action lawn mowers usually have a back roller that produces the "striped" effect of the traditional lawn. Rotary and hover mowers cut the grass with a scythe-like action and are particularly good for rough or long grass.

Great care must be taken when using an electric mower, and a circuit-breaking device must be used to prevent accidents in the event that the cord is cut. Never use an electrical mower (or any other electrical appliance) in the garden in wet weather.

Trimmer (left) A trimmer is the best tool for cutting long grass or grassy banks. Protective goggles and heavy-duty boots are an essential safety precaution.

Trimmers and brushwood cutters

These are ideal for cutting grass and light brush in awkward areas (on slopes, for example). The trimmers operate with a whirling, flexible nylon cutting line and are useful for light grass cutting. The brushwood cutters have a rotating head with a metal blade and are useful for cutting heavier plant material. Both can be gas-powered or electrically operated. Some trimmers are battery operated, allowing greater freedom of movement. However, the battery will need to be recharged frequently.

Rotary cultivators

These make light work of digging over a large area and are ideal for bringing a new piece of ground into use. However, the rotary cultivator can also cut up perennial weeds and scatter them widely, thus propagating them. Ideally, fork out any deep-rooted perennial weeds before you start.

USING A ROTARY CULTIVATOR

There are many different kinds of powered cultivator available, and they all operate on the same basic principle: rotating steel blades turn over the soil. Most machines are equipped with a depth adjuster, which works by limiting the depth to which the rotating blades can penetrate into the soil. The traveling speed of the machine and the rotating speed of the blades will determine how finely cultivated the soil will become.

1 *Start by setting the depth gauge. If the ground is hard, cultivate to a shallow depth before repeating, cultivating to the desired depth.*

2 *If a finely tilled bed is required, set the forward speed on slow and the rotor speed on fast. Allow the machine to travel at an even pace.*

3 *Allow the rear flap to trail out over the freshly cultivated soil just behind the rotor to help level the soil and leave an even surface.*

4 *Switch off the motor and disconnect the power cord. Remove any soil with a scraper, such as a piece of wood. Clean the blades with a hose.*

Watering and moving equipment

Watering is essential for plants' growth. Unless you are able to install a watering system in your garden, the basic watering can provide one way to maintain plant health. However, there are also a multitude of modern devices available that make the process a great deal easier than relying solely on a watering can. In contrast, when moving tools and materials around the garden, the age-old wheelbarrow is still by far the most efficient piece of equipment you can use.

WATERING CANS

Watering cans are primarily used for containers and for watering individual plants such as seedlings and cuttings. There is a variety of types and sizes available at all garden centers and some do-it-yourself stores.

Plastic watering can
A long-spouted plastic watering can is perfect for the container gardener.

Metal watering can
The larger type of watering can is particularly useful for the gardener whose area may suffer a garden hose ban due to drought.

Rose
This is detachable and provides a coarse or fine spray, depending on the size of the holes.

Watering (above) *The rose on this watering can has been turned upward, providing a fine spray.*

Garden hose
Store your hose neatly coiled; otherwise, it will become inoperable over a period of time.

GARDEN HOSES

In large gardens a hose is essential; it will be cheaper in the long term to pay a bit extra for a better-quality hose that will give years of service. Hoses come in a range of lengths, so look for one that is long enough to reach all areas of your garden. Try to maintain your hose in good condition by preventing kinks from developing. Modern hoses come with a wide variety of snap-on attachments that allow the gardener to implement a strong jet of water, spray, sprinkle, shower, or feed.

Transportable hoses
These allow you to transport water to the farthest reaches of the garden without straining your back.

NOZZLES AND SPRAYS

Nowadays there is a wide variety of appliances that enable the gardener to reach every area of the garden that requires water. Whether you are watering on a daily basis or at set times of the day, directing the spray to a specific area or covering as large a mass of lawn and borders as possible, manufacturers have come up with something to help you win the battle against drought in the summer.

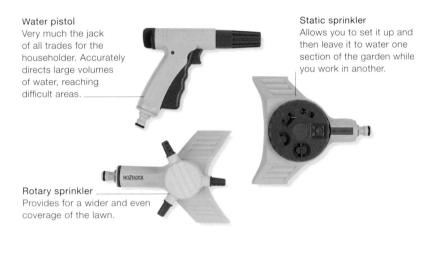

Water pistol
Very much the jack of all trades for the householder. Accurately directs large volumes of water, reaching difficult areas.

Rotary sprinkler
Provides for a wider and even coverage of the lawn.

Static sprinkler
Allows you to set it up and then leave it to water one section of the garden while you work in another.

Watering wand
Perfect for watering hanging baskets and plants that are difficult to reach, such as greenhouse pot plants.

Oscillating sprinkler
Provides a concentrated watering of one area before being moved on to another. Ideal for the gardener with a high-maintenance or large lawn.

WHEELBARROWS

When you have heavy materials such as compost to move from one part of the garden to another, a wheelbarrow will save time and energy. The "navvy-barrer" is the classic design, but try to purchase a galvanized wheelbarrow rather than a plastic one, as it will last much longer, thereby giving you more for your money.

Wheels
Make sure that the wheelbarrow has a pneumatic wheel, as it will be easier to push.

Bin
A galvanized metal bin is preferable, because it will be stronger and resistant to rust. It is deeper at the front, thereby allowing more weight to be moved.

Handles
Make sure that the handles have a good grip and will not come loose over time.

Supports
A strut at the front point of the wheelbarrow helps to make unloading much easier.

Using watering and spraying equipment

You will inevitably spend a large portion of your gardening time making sure that your plants have an adequate supply of water. Before purchasing any watering equipment, consider your requirements carefully, and always remember that water is a precious resource that should never be wasted.

There is a very wide range of watering equipment and systems available to the gardener. The equipment you will need depends on the style of your garden and the local climate.

Watering cans

You will almost certainly need a hand-held watering can for plants requiring individual attention, and for watering seed trays and young seedlings. Traditional watering cans are made of galvanized metal; although they look more attractive, they are heavier than plastic. The best watering cans are well balanced, with a carrying handle on top and a steadying handle at the back of the can. The can should have a long spout. You can buy watering cans in a range of sizes, holding anything from ¾ pint to 3 gallons. The largest will probably be uncomfortably heavy for most people when full, so choose a size that is comfortable for you. A can should pour easily, as soon as it is tilted. Watering cans usually come with a rose (a perforated nozzle) for spraying water evenly and lightly.

Garden hoses

For more distant parts of the garden, or to supply water over a large area, you will need a garden hose, with some kind of spray nozzle. Make sure you buy one that is long enough to reach the farthest corners of the garden (although hoses can be joined together with suitable couplings).

These days, most garden hoses are made from PVC, with various finishes to prevent the pipe from kinking. Double-walled, reinforced hoses are the most resistant to kinking, but they are expensive. It is a good idea to buy a reel, so that the hose runs out easily and does not tangle.

Various nozzles are available, including lances and pistols, which direct a fine or coarse jet of water over a distance. Sprinklers can be attached to create a fine "shower" over a wide area: you can buy oscillating, rotary, or static types that direct the water in different ways.

Automatic watering systems

For easier watering, you can install a soaker hose or irrigation system. There are many different kinds on the market, ranging from the simplest "leaky hose" version, in which irregularly spaced holes deliver water randomly along the length of the hose, to more sophisticated versions with valves, automatic moisture sensors, and timing devices. These will do your watering for you when you are not at home.

Soaker hose system (below) *This is the perfect way to create a cheap and easy watering system that waters all parts of your vegetable plot, beds, and borders evenly.*

The fine nozzles of some automatic watering systems may clog with soil, however. To avoid wasting such a precious resource, position the system carefully as you need the water delivered close to the base of the plant.

Spraying equipment

Keep a separate set of spraying equipment for handling chemicals. You can buy everything from small hand-held sprayers with a trigger mechanism, holding as little as ¾ pint, to knapsack sprayers with a compression pump that hold large quantities.

Using a sprayer

You must only spray chemicals on windless days and ideally after all beneficial insects have retired for the night. Wear protective clothing, and if your skin comes into contact with any of the chemicals, wash it thoroughly.

Watering containers and pots (above) *Seedlings and plants growing in containers require frequent watering, especially during the warm summer months.*

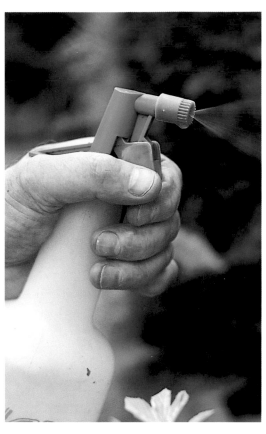

Selective spraying (above) *A small hand-held sprayer is ideal for small plants, or for spraying a small area of a larger specimen.*

USING A SPRAYER

Spraying is one of those mainstay operations that have been an essential part of gardening for generations. Even with the shift in emphasis back toward organic gardening, many of the materials used to help control pests and diseases are still applied as foliar sprays. It is important to clean the sprayer before use by flushing it through with clean water, and after use by flushing it through with a detergent solution, followed by clean water.

1 *Start by measuring out the correct amount of chemical concentrate. Wear protective clothing, including goggles and disposable gloves.*

2 *Next, half-fill the sprayer tank with clean water before adding the measured amount of chemical concentrate to the tank.*

3 *Add the rest of the water until the water/chemical level is up to the required mark on the tank. Using a clean stirrer, stir the contents to ensure they are mixed thoroughly.*

4 *Finally, seal the spray tank and pump it up to the correct pressure, before spraying the plants. Never spray plants in windy conditions.*

Lifting and moving techniques

Gardening generally involves some heavy work, so it pays to equip your-self with adequate carting and carrying equipment. You also need to learn how to lift heavy loads and how to move specific large objects, such as a heavy container, without injuring yourself.

Your choice of lifting and moving equipment depends to some degree on the size and nature of your garden. Whatever load you are attempting to lift, remember to bend at the knees to pick it up, rather than bending your back. If you keep your back straight, your legs rather than your spine will take the strain of the load, with much less chance of damage.

In small gardens, instead of a wheelbarrow it may be more practical to opt for a small but sturdy dolly, which can be used to move heavy objects such as compost bags or containers. Slide the load onto the lip and then tilt the dolly to move it. Ideally, you need a second person to help you steady the load as you maneuver the dolly to its destination.

**Moving heavy materials
(right)** *To avoid back injury, always maintain an upright posture when moving a heavily laden wheelbarrow. Provided that you do not overload the wheelbarrow, it should move perfectly smoothly over the majority of garden surfaces.*

Wheelbarrows

If you have an average-sized or large plot, you will almost certainly need a wheelbarrow of some kind. There are two principal types: the traditional wheelbarrow with a fairly narrow, single, solid wheel or a wheel with a pneumatic tire, and the ball-wheeled barrow, which has a round ball-like single wheel. The former is best for transporting heavy loads on solid ground, and the latter if you are wheeling across newly dug land. Remember that if you invest in a good-quality metal wheelbarrow, although it will generally last longer than a cheaper plastic one, it will rust eventually (although storing the wheelbarrow upside down when not in use will delay the process).

Carrying sheets or bags

These are usually made from woven plastic and have carrying handles (at each corner for sheets). They are ideal for transporting pruning waste or large quantities of leaves.

Baskets

Traditional shallow baskets made of wood can be used for a variety of garden tasks, from hand weeding to collecting flowers and vegetables from the garden. Plastic baskets are available, and although they are more durable, they are a great deal less pleasing aesthetically.

Moving heavy containers

When you have to move heavy containers around, you must plan ahead. You need a helper, and you will also need a heavy-duty board and several dowels—lengths of narrow-gauge piping are ideal. With the aid of your helper, slide the container onto the piece of board, the front end of which has been raised using a length of piping or doweling. Then slide a second piece of piping under the front end of the board, and roll the board with the container on it forward, placing a

third piece of piping under the front end. Pick up the first piece of piping as it emerges from the tail end of the board, and insert it at the front. In this way, you can roll the board with the container on it over level surfaces.

Alternative method

All you need for this is a helper and a large piece of strong plastic. Rock the container slightly until it rests on top of a large piece of plastic. You and your helper then grasp one corner of the plastic each and slowly pull the plastic along, complete with its load, to the new site. This is a very straightforward method, but you should try still to adopt a safe posture so as not to cause yourself serious injury.

Alternative method

(above) *Containers can also be moved by placing them on heavy plastic sheeting and then dragging them to their new position. Always have a helper, keep a low center of gravity, and do not overexert yourself.*

MOVING HEAVY CONTAINERS

If you do not have a wheelbarrow or dolly on hand but you do have a helper nearby, you can utilize other materials to move heavy containers around the garden.

1 *Begin by using a strong plank of wood that is wide enough to carry your container. Place a dowel beneath it for leverage, then drag the container onto the plank.*

2 *Immediately place another dowel beneath the plank and begin to push the improvised wheelbarrow along. As each dowel drops out at the back, place it at the front.*

3 *You now have sufficient momentum to push the container to its new location. Obviously, this will only work on flat, hard surfaces, not grass or gravel.*

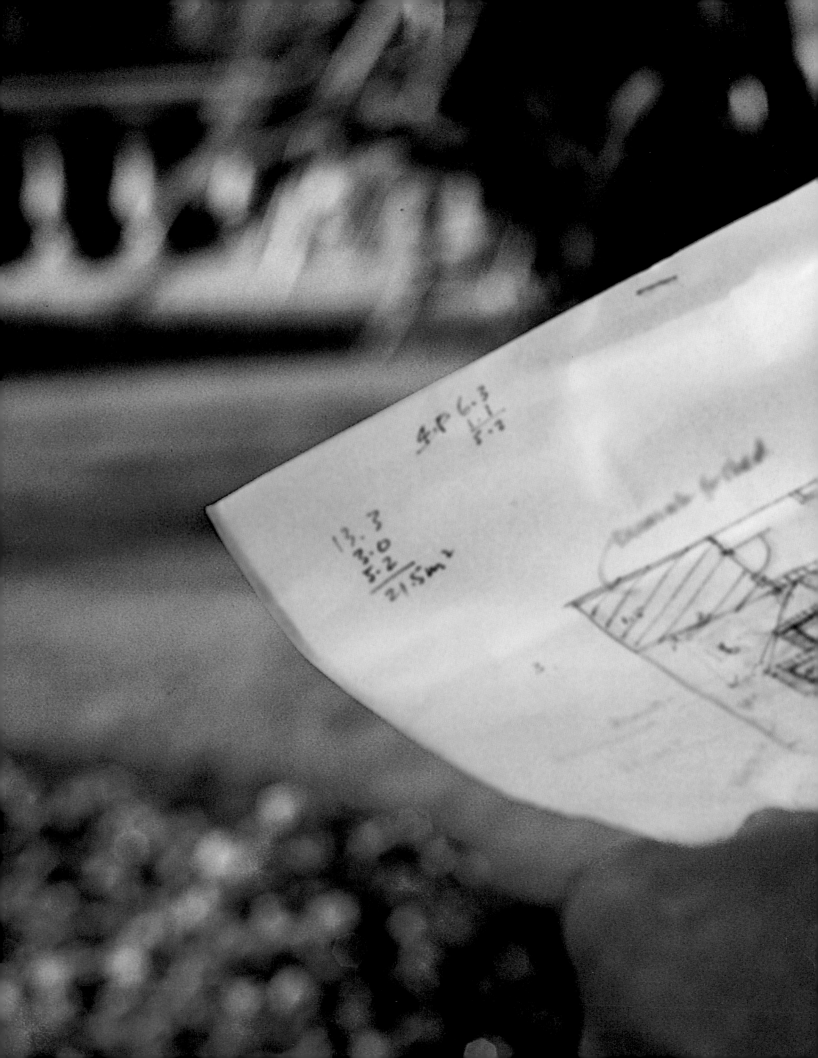

Planning
your garden

Planning the planting scheme

To create a good planting scheme, you have to consider not only the 3D effects, but also scale, color, and changes over time. Orchestrating these different elements takes careful planning, but a border need not necessarily be elaborate or particularly time-consuming in order to be effective.

Any planting scheme needs a variety of material in order to look good. Ideally, you should grow plants with a range of heights, forms, and foliage types. Trees, with their single stems and canopies of foliage above, will help to create areas of shade and add privacy; they also provide a much-needed habitat for wildlife, but remember that the roots run to the extent of the canopy and large trees should never be planted close to house walls. Some shrubs grow as high as 20 ft., while low-growing, spreading varieties act like groundcover. Choosing a mixture of evergreen and deciduous shrubs will help to ensure that the garden has all-season appeal, and it is always worth checking any preferred plants to see if they look good out of season—for example, do they have attractively colored bark, fall foliage, or perhaps scented winter flowers?

Planting style

The style of planting you choose will be determined not only by the space available, but also by the time you have to tend the garden. Good, low-maintenance plants include shrub borders, groundcover, and foliage perennials such

Traditional herbaceous border (above) *Here, tall verticals (mulleins) add interest to a border and act as a focal point, drawing the eye to this part of the bed.*

Drifts of color (left) *In this large garden, perennials in tonal colors provide groundcover that is relatively easy to care for. Large blocks of color give the garden a feeling of unity.*

as ferns, bamboos, and grasses that require minimal attention.

Perennial borders

For those with more time to spare, a traditional herbaceous perennial border is a great delight and will stretch your talents as a designer as you strive to orchestrate a display of appropriately sized plants in your chosen colors as the seasons unfold. Not only do you need an artist's eye to plan the color scheme, you also need to be able to work out the eventual height and spread of each plant, so that the border rises in height toward the back, ensuring that each plant is seen in all its glory. More recent developments in design have embraced the use of grasses in herbaceous borders. Proponents of these mixed plantings, like Beth Chatto and Piet Oudolf, have fostered an interest in a much more relaxed style, which involves less or no staking and allows nature a freer hand. This kind of planting tends to concentrate on large blocks of color in tonal shades, and the plants are chosen for their similarity in height and form, creating a gentle sweep of color across the garden.

No planting scheme will work well unless you have chosen the right plants. Separate areas of the garden have different soil conditions and varying levels of light. A dry, sunny border would require a very different mixture of plants from a damp, shady area; similarly, a border on alkaline soil needs a completely different type of plants to one on acidic soil.

Ferns, bamboos, and grasses (above) *Not all planting schemes rely on color to create a stunning visual effect in a border. Texture and form are just as important color, as this all-green assemblage of grasses and bamboos demonstrates.*

	COMMON BORDER PLANTS		
	cool colors (pale pastels) pale blue, cream, lemon, pale pink, pale mauve	hot colors (vibrant) yellow, orange, red, bright pink, bright blue	contrast colors (light and dark) white, black, dark purple
Spring	*Anemone blanda, Clematis montana, Crocus, Narcissus 'Ice Follies'*	*Muscari armeniacum, Primula, Scilla, Tulipa 'Golden Age'*	*Galanthus, Geranium phaeum, Hyacinthus* (white), *Narcissus 'Thalia', Purpurea group, Viburnum opulus, Viola riviniana, Tulipa 'Queen of Night', Wisteria sinensis 'Alba', Zantedeschia aethiopica*
Summer	*Dicentra spectabilis, Geranium × oxonianum, Phlox stolonifera, Verbascum chaixii*	*Brachyglottis 'Sunshine', Crocosmia 'Lucifer', Delphinium, Geranium psilostemon, Geum rivale, Hemerocallis, Lychnis chalcedonica, Papaver orientale, Pelargonium* (various), *Salvia, Tagetes, Verbena*	*Clematis 'Etoile Violette', Crambe cordifolia, Heliotropium, Hosta, Leucanthemum, Lilium regale, Nicotiana sylvestris, Paeonia, Petunia* (white), *Pelargonium* (white), *Rosa 'Iceberg', Viola 'Molly Sanderson'*
Fall	*Aster novi-belgii, Chrysanthemum* (pale shades), *Dahlia* (lemon and pink), *Osteospermum 'Buttermilk'*	*Nerine bowdenii, Pyracantha 'Mohave', Spartium junceum, Tropaeolum*	*Aster, Galtonia candicans*
Winter	*Daphne mezereum, Hamamelis mollis*		*Ophiopogon planiscapus 'Nigrescens'*

Plants throughout the year

In addition to choosing the right plants for the place, you need to think about how the planting scheme will look at different times of the year. In most gardens, the greatest display occurs in high summer, when most of the perennials and annuals are in flower. However, in spring, fall, and winter, you can still choose from a good range of flowers and other attractive plants, from bulbs to climbers to ornamental trees.

It is easy to be seduced by the abundance of color available from spring- and summer-flowering plants, but remember that the garden needs to look good all year. The right planting scheme will ensure that your garden will be a pleasant place to be in every season.

Spring

This is the major season for bulbs (although there are many that flower in summer, and some in fall and winter, too). The new shoots unfurl in delicate shades of apple-green, and the color palette of the flowers is predominantly pastel, including whites, pale yellows, blues, and pale pinks.

In the earliest months of the year, you can enjoy a display of snowdrops (*Galanthus*), which will naturalize and spread if grown in suitable conditions. Crocuses (*Crocus*) and daffodils follow, with anemones (*Anemone*), hyacinths (*Hyacinthus*), grape hyacinths (*Muscari*), and tulips in swift succession. Flowering shrubs include winter jasmine (*Jasminum nudiflorum*), ideal for growing against a wall, with slender, bright green stems and starry yellow flowers; the little flowering quince (*Chaenomeles*); scented daphnes such as *Daphne bholua*; bright yellow forsythia (the arching, more delicate *F. suspensa* is more attractive than the more commonly grown *F. × intermedia*); viburnums (several, such as *V. × burkwoodii*, are deliciously scented); and flowering currants like *Ribes sanguineum* 'Tydeman's White.' A small flowering tree, like the ornamental cherry (*Prunus*), will complete the picture.

Mid- to late spring (above) *As spring advances, bulbs such as tulips take the place of earlier-flowering species like snowdrops and narcissi.*

Late spring (above) *In late spring, plants such as the white Dame's violet (Hesperis matronalis var. albiflora) start to flower. These are seen against a backdrop of browns and greens as the garden begins to come to life again.*

Summer (above) *As the weather gradually becomes milder, the color palette warms up considerably, with the glorious pinks, mauves, and blues of ornamental onions and columbines.*

Autumn (above) *By fall, the flower color has all but disappeared, with only the russet, red, and gold hues of the leaves remaining. The bones of the garden become much more obvious at this time.*

By late spring the bare earth will have disappeared under a carpeting layer of foliage. Perennials grown for their leaves, such as the magnificent hostas, look their best at this time of year, the newly unfurled leaves having an almost translucent quality.

Early and midsummer

The color palette warms up as summer progresses, starting off with pinks, blues, apricots, and yellows, then moving toward hot reds, oranges, shocking pinks, and purples in the hottest months. In gardens with a large expanse of grass, keep the color palette subdued: too many strong reds and greens can be jarring. However, in city gardens or those with paved surfaces, big pots of hot-colored perennials and annuals look terrific.

For softer colors, perennials such as bleeding hearts (*Dicentra*), Solomon's seal (*Polygonatum*), columbines, lupines, marguerites, and delphiniums (*Delphinium*) look particularly good. At the hotter end of the spectrum, geraniums (*Pelargonium*), mulleins, lobelias (*Lobelia*), and hot zinnias (*Zinnia*) are ideal for the front of the border or small containers.

This is the best time of year for many climbers, including a great range of roses and clematis—both the hybrids with large flowers and the more delicate *Clematis macropetala* cultivars.

Later summer and early fall

As the days shorten, plants that prefer a shorter day length take center stage. Among them are chrysanthemums, dahlias, and asters in a truly magnificent range of colors. Some of the clematis, such as the yellow-flowered *C. tangutica*, flower in autumn. Many plants that flowered in early summer, particularly modern roses, will have a "remontant" phase at this time of year, producing a smaller flush of blooms.

As the fruits start to swell, the garden takes on a more mellow hue. Rose hips, mountain ash, and pyracantha berries add to the visual and actual feast in the garden. It is always worth growing some berrying plants in order to feed the local bird population.

Winter

Once the frosts begin, most of the soft foliage will die down and the garden takes on a different character, the forms and shapes of trees and shrubs becoming more prominent. This is when the evergreen plants comes into their own. A few neatly clipped box or privet bushes, a mahonia with its glossy leaves and whorls of bright yellow flowers, the neat, dark leaves of *Skimmia japonica* with its white, pink or red fragrant flowerheads, and the scented flowers of witch hazel (*Hamamelis mollis*) all help to give the garden interest in winter. At ground level, the little Algerian iris (*I. unguicularis*) and the Christmas rose (*Helleborus niger*) are among the few winter-flowering plants.

Creating a planting scheme

If you are planning to plant a new garden, or replant an existing one, you will need to draw up a plan. This can embrace the whole garden, or just a portion of it. If you plant one part, make sure that the scheme blends well with the remainder of the garden. Too abrupt a change in character between sections without a screen can make the garden feel uncomfortably restless.

You need to consider key practical elements at the outset. Where will you sit? How will you get to the garden shed? Or, if you do not have one, do you need one? How will you move from one part of the garden to the other? It is best to avoid winding paths—inevitably, no one will take the longest route unless you make it impossible for them to do otherwise. However, straight runs right through the garden are not inviting either, so the secret is to make small barriers of boxwood (*Buxus*) or lavender cotton (*Santolina*)—or perhaps to create a bed running two-thirds of the way across the garden—so that the view from the house to the far end is interrupted. This also makes the garden appear larger.

Adding height

It is important to consider the vertical elements as well as the horizontal ones. The addition of a couple of small trees or very large shrubs creates a feeling of enclosure, privacy, and security in the garden. If you have no features in the garden taller than the average person, the garden can feel rather exposed! By including the occasional larger feature, you create an area of shade underneath it. This allows you to vary the style of plantings, since the form and character of shade-loving plants (large leaves and smaller flowers) is very different to that of sun-loving ones (often brighter colors and smaller leaves).

Starting to plan

If you have never undertaken a planting scheme before, then the key is to keep it simple. On a scale sketch of your garden, map out the structural plantings first: the large trees and shrubs, and any hedges or vertical elements (pergolas, arches, etc). Once you think you have the position of these key elements as you want them, you can start to consider the infill plants.

Most people find it hard to make the mental transition from a flat plan to the 3D reality of a garden. One solution is to take photographs of the garden and get them enlarged. Then, using a felt pen, sketch the proportions of the

Using a photograph (right) *A photograph enables you to envisage your existing garden in three dimensions, which makes the planning process much easier.*

outlines and shapes of the new plantings on the photograph.

It is important that you plan your plantings carefully in order to do the plants justice. You need to make a note not only of the color of the flowers, but also of the form of the leaves, the flowering season, and the likely height and spread of the plants. The best planting plans are those in which you make a rough sketch of the forms and shapes of the plants you intend to grow.

Write the flowering time on the drawing and color it appropriately. If the plant is grown predominantly for foliage, use the foliage color as the main guide.

When working out how many plants to include, take note of their eventual height and spread and leave sufficient space for them to grow. Not all plants perform exactly as stated on the label, but if you allow roughly two-thirds of the space indicated, you will get it more or less right.

While you are waiting for gaps to fill in during the first couple of years, plant fast-growing large annuals or perennials that you can remove easily. Flowering tobacco or plume poppy (*Macleaya cordata*) are good, large infill plants. Larger plants are, on the whole, better than smaller ones for this purpose, as their character, size, and color often suit the overall look of the scheme better than those of smaller plants, which can become lost in a complex planting scheme. And nothing looks more out of place than tiny, brightly colored bedding plants dotted at the front of a large shrub border. The sudden change of color and scale is simply too startling.

Tobacco plant (right) *This tall, elegant summer annual, flowering tobacco, is ideal for filling in at the back of the border. It has a striking architectural shape and contributes a heady evening scent to the garden.*

Using a scale drawing
(left) *When using a scale drawing to plan your scheme, begin with the basic structure, including any permanent features such as walls or arches, and any large plants like trees and large shrubs. You can then fill in the details.*

Vertical features

A garden that exists only on the horizontal plane, with all the plants well below eye level, can be monotonous. Try to include vertical features— man-made or natural—at appropriate intervals. They will help to anchor the rest of the plants and make the garden feel less exposed.

Any planting scheme needs to have a vertical as well as a horizontal dimension. Ideally, you need to create these changes of level at several points, so that the eye does not travel automatically to the farthest distance. One trick is to create "compartments" within the garden, so that it is made up of smaller gardens within the whole. These can be screened off completely or partially as you wish.

Among the vertical elements at your disposal are the tallest plants—primarily trees and shrubs—as well as man-made structures such as screens, arbors, tunnels, and arches over which climbing plants can be encouraged to grow. Try to match the style of any structure to the garden. There are various materials and forms you can choose. Natural materials, such as willow or hazel, have become increasingly popular; they are ideal materials for rustic-style obelisks, screens, or trellises, which suit cottage-style plants such as clematis, roses, and sweet peas (*Lathyrus odoratus*).

If you create trellis screens, either to increase the height of boundary fences or walls or to create compartments within the garden, opt for stout branches rather than flimsy, commercially produced trellis. Paint the wood a soft sage-green or blue-gray, to match the plants and act as a preservative. Any trellis will need stout posts at intervals to secure it. These should be sunken into the soil and fitted with lead caps to prevent rot. Consult a fencing specialist for detailed information.

Hedge divider (above) *These box hedges create divisions while adding shape to the ground plan.*

Trellis divider (above) *In this Japanese-themed garden, reed and bamboo have been used to give a vertical dimension that is in keeping with the minimalist style of Japanese gardens.*

Vertical planting

If you enjoy roses, it is worth creating an arbor or rope trellis on which to display them. Old-fashioned climbing roses are among the most spectacular examples, with softly quartered petals and a fine scent.

Foliage can also be used to clothe vertical features. The crimson glory vine (*Vitis coignetiae*) has huge heart-shaped leaves that turn a rich, ruby-red in autumn. The golden-leaved common hop (*Humulus lupulus* 'Aureus') creates a splash of pure gold in a sunny area.

Plants will cascade downward as well as grow upward. You can use the tops of walls for tumbling plants such as rockcress (*Aubrietias*), twinspur (*Diascias*), or nasturtiums. Pots can be mounted on otherwise plain walls and then filled with plants. For unity, color-theme the plants to shades of one color, or perhaps to a color that is warm-toned (hot reds, yellows, oranges, purples, and pinks) or cool-toned (whites, pale blues, pale pinks, and pale lemons). Good plants for settings like these are verbenas, pansies (*Viola*), and petunias, combined with foliage plants such as licorice plant (*Helichrysum petiolare*).

You can plant large shrubs or trees at strategic points to create a "stop" or focal point. Large containers of tall plants, such as yuccas (*Yucca*) or cordylines (*Cordyline*), can also be used and, being portable, enable you to make changes at different times of the year, depending on which features you wish to highlight.

Clothing walls with climbing plants produces an enormous area of flower power for a relatively small investment of horizontal space. In small gardens particularly this is a great bonus.

Post-and-rope rose boundary (above) *Swags of roses grown over ropes divide the space without concealing it. They can be used equally well in formal and informal settings and in small or large spaces.*

MAKING AN ARBOR

An elegant arbor decked with gorgeous climbing and trailing plants creates a stunning focal point and can distract attention from less-favored areas. It is an ideal site for growing fragrant plants, such as roses and honeysuckle, so you can enjoy a perfumed stroll through the garden.

1 *After calculating the amount of timber required, cut the sections of wood to length before you begin to assemble the arbor.*

2 *To assemble the framework of the arbor, drill the holes and screw each panel into position as the assembly progresses.*

3 *Once all the parts are in position, move the completed arbor into position and check that the framework is square and level (use a level if necessary).*

4 *Paint the whole structure with a suitable wood preservative to prolong the life of the arbor. Paint any sawn ends of the wood with at least two coats of preservative.*

Planting a border

Whether you are planning a very small border or something much more elaborate, think carefully about the color, eventual height, and spread of your plants. Consider also their suitability for the aspect and soil type: sun or shade, damp or dry, acidic or alkaline, sand or clay.

If you want to create a herbaceous border, you will need to work out the positions of the plants and their likely spread, as well as their eventual height. You need to think in terms of planting in groups, not single plants. Most experienced designers plant in groups of odd numbers—three, five or seven—which give a relaxed, flowing feeling to the plants. You will be much better off opting for larger groups of fewer plants than a scheme that is too busy. Inserting the occasional key plant into this grouped border will give the whole scheme greater

impact. A neatly clipped boxwood pyramid might be sited in the center of a border, or perhaps at one end to make a punctuation point where the border joins the rest of the garden design. Two or three flowering standards could be planted to give additional height to the border.

In a traditional backed border, the tallest plants go at the back and then grade down in size to the front of the border, so that they can be seen properly when in bloom. Unfortunately, although reference books offer information on height and spread, these are

only approximate, as each plant performs differently in particular conditions. For example, if the plant in question likes moist, warm conditions and you plant it in dry shade, it will either fail to thrive at all or grow to a fraction of its anticipated height. The plant next to it, which happens to like the conditions, will perform according to specifications, and your carefully planned border will fail to materialize as intended.

Even the best gardeners make mistakes, and one of the tricks of gardening experts is to move those plants that fail to flourish to

PLANT HEIGHTS

Bear in mind that shrubs grow both in height and width; perennials grow in width. Leave sufficient space around the plants to accommodate their anticipated growth in two to three years' time. After that, you may have to divide perennials and prune back shrubs to keep them in check.

2nd year

1st year

3

2

1

ft.

3

2

1

ft.

a place where they do. If a plant
is not putting on the expected
growth over a couple of seasons,
then try it in a site that is markedly
different from the one you origi-
nally planted it in.

When planting a small border,
it makes sense to lay the plants
out in their intended positions
before planting them permanently. You may well find
elements in your plan that do not
work as well in reality—for
example, the foliage colors may
not look good together—so be
prepared to make some changes.

Preparation

Once a border is planted, it will
be hard to get into it to dig, so
make all the major preparations
before planting begins. You must
be meticulous about removing
perennial weeds, like couch grass
(*Elytrigia repens*) and bishop's
weed (*Aegopodium podagraria*);
every scrap should be dug out and

burned. It is all too easy to
be impatient or lazy, but you will
pay a heavy price later for taking
the easy route as the rampant
weeds start to choke your prized
plants and the roots run under,
through, and around your carefully chosen specimens.

Ideally, prepare the ground
for the border in autumn, digging
it over , weeding it thoroughly, and
incorporating plenty of bulky
organic matter. The following
spring, as soon as the soil warms
up a little, you can carry out
the planting scheme.

**A successful border
arrangement** (left)
*A good border should ideally
incorporate a mixture of plant
shapes, leaf textures, and
harmonizing or contrasting
colors. Tall plants are
positioned toward the back
of the border, with low-growing
varieties grown against the
paving in front.*

Hedges and screens

Hedges can serve all sorts of purposes within the garden. They make excellent screens and barriers, especially where walls and fences are not practical. They also provide a useful habitat for birds and other wildlife, as well as a natural backdrop for the other plants in the garden.

Privacy and shelter are important factors in any garden. A plot that is wholly exposed to the elements makes the work of the gardener much harder, and many cherished plants will be lost in bad weather. Equally, a garden that has no feeling of enclosure is not particularly relaxing. It is the wonderful sense of privacy that creates the greatest feeling of calm in the garden. It is well worth visiting some of the great gardens simply to observe the many different ways in which they have been enclosed or screened from neighbors, and parts of the garden from other areas.

Choosing a hedge plant

Yew hedges (*Taxus*) are a traditional, much-loved form of enclosure in gardens, but they take some time to develop to a useful height. They are not, however, quite as slow-growing as is often thought, growing about 7 in. a year. A primary reason for planting yew

---

GOOD HEDGING PLANTS

Evergreens	Deciduous
Buxus to 4 ft.	*Berberis thunbergii* to 4 ft.
Taxus baccata to 20 ft.	*Carpinus betulus* to 20 ft.
Elaeagnus × ebbingei to 10 ft.	*Crataegus monogyna* to 10 ft.
Escallonia to 8 ft.	*Fagus sylvatica* Atropurpurea Group to 20 ft.
Ilex aquifolium to 13 ft.	
Ligustrum to 6 ft.	*Fuchsia magellanica* to 5 ft.
Prunus laurocerasus to 10 ft.	*Rosa rugosa* to 5 ft.
Viburnus tinus to 8 ft.	

Several different hedging plants, including a mixture of deciduous and evergreen varieties, are combined in this tapestry hedge.

Creating patterns (above) *In this 21st-century version of a knot garden, hedging plants crisscross to form an interesting pattern that divides the space geometrically.*

is that it needs less frequent pruning than fast-growing privet, for example, which will need pruning three times as often. In less formal gardens, tapestry hedges of mixed plants make fairly rapid and attractive screens, and they have the bonus of being a popular haven for local wildlife.

Screening

Among the alternatives for screening a garden is the use of man-made structures over which climbing plants are grown. Stout trellis is often used for this purpose; on average, it will last for around eight years. Other possibilities include screens made of bamboo or willow. Living willow screens have become increasingly popular with gardeners in recent years and are often woven into attractive patterns.

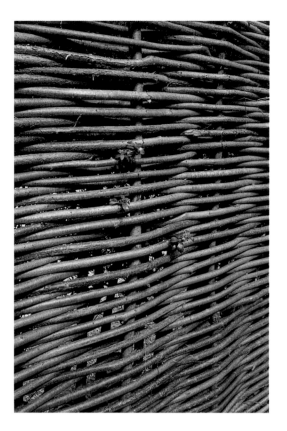

Hazel screen (above) *This tall, tightly woven screen of coppiced hazel makes an effective yet natural barrier. It provides privacy but allows the wind to permeate it— the best possible screen for plants.*

Willow screen (above) *Willow is equally effective as a screening material, but slightly less durable than hazel. Because it is more pliable, a range of interesting patterns can be woven successfully.*

BASIC WEAVING TO CREATE A SCREEN

A screen of hazel wood can make a perfect surround for a cut flower garden
or even a support for climbers such as sweet peas.

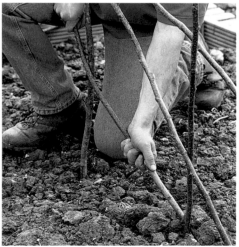

1 *Begin by pushing a series of uprights at least 8 in. into the soil, using the thickest and straightest rods as the vertical props.*

2 *Push the diagonals into the soil, putting the longest lengths into the central section and leaving a 1 ft. space between them.*

3 *Tie the diagonals to the uprights; where they cross, twist their tops around the horizontals and then tie them in.*

Planting hedges

The most effective hedges are evergreen, because they offer the greatest protection and privacy, but some deciduous plants also make attractive, if less dense, hedges in the winter. Thorny hedges, such as rugosa roses, can form effective obstacles against roaming animals as well as intruders.

Traditional garden hedges tend to be formal and closely clipped to a desired height and outline. They must be trimmed at least once a year (two or three times with some of the more vigorous plants) to grow well; also, replace the nutrients lost when the hedge clippings are taken away—these hedges tend to compete with nearby plants for nourishment. However, an informal hedge can be created quite easily by planting a row of flowering shrubs; this type of hedge has the advantage of needing pruning only once a year, after flowering.

The best time for planting depends on the type of plants. Deciduous plants are cheaper bought bare root in bundles for planting between late autumn and early spring, while broad-leaved evergreens and conifers are usually available as container-grown plants, which may be planted in early autumn or from late spring to early summer.

A hedge is a long-term planting, so the soil should be well prepared beforehand; the plants must be trimmed regularly for the first few years, to encourage the growth to become thick and bushy at the base. Spacing depends to some degree on the speed of growth of the chosen plant, as well as its habit. As a guide, tall, narrow plants such as privet are spaced at 2-ft. intervals, and spreading plants such as barberry (*Berberis*) or rugosa roses at 3 ft. You can plant in a straight line or in a diagonally spaced staggered row. The latter creates a thicker, denser hedge.

TIP

Prune a flowering hedge after the flowers have finished. Cut back old flowered shoots of deciduous shrubs to young, lower shoots.

The first year's growth (left)
Once planted, for the first season keep the soil weed-free and well watered during dry periods.

PLANTING A NEW HEDGE

Tools and materials

- garden line
- spade
- wheelbarrow
- hedging plants
- organic mulching material

1 *Start by marking out the course of the hedge with a garden line.*

2 *Using a spade, dig out the hole for the first plant, and place the soil in a wheelbarrow (this soil can be taken to the end of the hedge line and used to fill the final planting hole).*

3 *Remove the plant from its container and position it in the planting hole, making sure the rootball is at the correct depth.*

4 *Dig out the hole for the second plant, and place the soil from this second hole around the roots of the plant in the first planting hole.*

5 *Adjust the level of the plant's rootball (if necessary) and firm the soil in the planting hole with the heel of your boot or shoe. (Repeat steps 3, 4, and 5 until the hedge is completed).*

6 *Finally, remove the garden line and cover the soil with a layer of well-rotted organic mulching material to suppress weeds and retain moisture.*

Topiary

The art of clipping evergreen shrubs into geometric shapes dates back to the Romans, whose desire for order in all things extended to their plants. The popularity of topiary has waxed and waned, although it has never gone out of fashion in France, where the famous designer André le Nôtre made it a feature in many celebrated gardens.

Topiary sometimes involves training plants into low hedges to make elaborate patterns, known as *parterres*. On a smaller scale, intricately woven shapes in the form of knots create the framework for groups of flowers or herbs.

The art of topiary also includes making fantastic shapes from clipped evergreens, ranging from an entire chess set to a scene from a fox hunt. Splendid examples of creative topiary, not always on a grand scale, can be seen in many famous gardens.

Although the more complex topiary shapes may demand a considerable degree of artistry, the simpler shapes are well within the capability of any gardener. Patience is essential, however, as it will take several years for any slow-growing evergreen to reach the final desired shape and size.

Plants for topiary

The best plants for topiary are those with small evergreen leaves and a fairly slow habit of growth, so that only infrequent clipping is required. In colder climates the plants must be hardy. Some plants will be suitable for very basic shapes—simple spheres, cones, or balls—but more complex shapes require the smallest leaves and fairly pliable young shoots.

Garden sculptures (right)

A more unusual approach to topiary in a large garden demonstrates its sculptural qualities. Definitely not a project for the beginner!

Plant name	Eventual height; speed of growth	Description
Buxus sempervirens (many cultivars)	8 ft., very slow-growing	Very small leaves, according to cultivar
Chamaecyparis lawsoniana 'Green Hedger'	8 ft., slower-growing than species	Typical dense conifer foliage
Cupressus sempervirens	10 ft., medium growth	Slender, dark columnar conifer
Ilex aquifolium	13 ft., slow-growing	Spiny dark green leaves. In 'Golden Queen' leaves have a yellow margin
Laurus nobilis	10 ft., medium growth	Large glossy, oval, dark green aromatic leaves
Myrtus communis	10 ft., medium growth	Small, aromatic green leaves and small white flowers which will be lost during pruning

GOOD TOPIARY PLANTS

The plant most commonly used for topiary is boxwood, of which there are several suitable species and cultivars. It does, however, take about 10 years to reach 4 ft. so this is not a choice for large topiary shapes if you want fast results! Yew (*Taxus baccata*) is also slow-growing, but a little speedier than box, making 6 ft. in 10 years. Its dark foliage makes a good foil for brilliantly colored flowers. For the less fastidious topiarist, California privet (*Ligustrum ovalifolium*) is a good substitute, because it grows much faster; as a consequence, it will require more frequent clipping to keep its shape.

Cheating at topiary

If you do not wish to wait for slow-growing plants like boxwood to fill out, you can create topiary look-alikes using fast-growing ivies (*Hedera*). These are trained over wire frames in the same way as other topiary (using several plants to a 10-in. diameter pot). Station each plant at the base of the wire uprights and then feed and water regularly. Tuck in wayward shoots, and then clip the ivy once it has reached the required height. It will rapidly fill out to cover the frame and make an attractive dense shape. A secondary bonus of using ivy is that it will do well in quite deep shade, in which traditional topiary plants such as boxwood will fail to flourish (although it will do well in partial shade).

If you grow your topiary plants in containers you will be able to turn them around periodically, which will help them to grow straight. Be aware that topiary is sought after and not cheap, so chain any containers in the front yard to the wall for security.

Formal topiary (left)

Parterres, in which neatly cut low hedges create a pattern filled in with either gravel or plants, have been a major design feature in grand gardens for centuries. Miniature versions can be reproduced in tiny gardens.

MAKING A TOPIARY PYRAMID

The real secret to training topiary is pruning little and often, constantly checking the plants and trimming as necessary to form a dense, compact growth habit. Trim the shoots while they are short in order to keep them branching—pinching out the growing point between finger and thumb will help to keep young shoots in check and force them to branch from lower down.

1 *Shake out the branches. Make a template from bamboo canes and position it around the plant.*

2 *Clip over the plant, removing any excess growth; clip back to the level of the canes.*

3 *Make a ring that will fit around the widest part of the plant (old garden hose is ideal).*

4 *Start from the bottom and draw the hose into a tighter ring as you move up the plant. Clip as you go.*

Using climbers and wall shrubs

No garden should be without a good selection of climbing plants and wall shrubs. They add color and interest at various levels, creating attractive features out of otherwise unappealing walls and fences; they can also be encouraged to scramble over other plants to extend the flowering season.

Most climbers are fairly vigorous, and the problems tend to arise when their natural vigor requires some control. As the renowned garden writer Christopher Lloyd memorably remarked, nothing is more annoying than staring at the long, naked legs of a climber while the business end of your chosen plant has wandered into the neighboring garden. To prevent this kind of irritation, you need an appropriate pruning strategy (see pages 152–159).

Year-round color

It pays to have a good mix of foliage, flowering climbers, and wall shrubs, and to ensure that you have something in flower in most seasons. Starting in early spring, winter jasmine (*Jasminum nudiflorum*, not strictly a climber, but a useful wall shrub) does well on east-facing walls. Also good for clothing walls early in the year are flowering quince (*Chaenomeles speciosa*) with white or scarlet flowers, and many camellias (both used as wall shrubs). By early

spring, a couple of clematis may well be in flower, including the evergreen clematis (*Clematis armandii*), with anemone clematis (*C. montana*) and alpine virgins-bower (*C. alpina*) appearing not long afterward. Both the latter are a good choice for a cool wall. By early summer, Chilean potato tree (*Solanum crispum* 'Glasnevin') will be displaying a profusion of starry blue flowers and *Clematis macropetala* cultivars, with open bells of smallish flowers, will also be in bloom, but for a shorter time.

Clothing walls (right)

If you want good wall coverage, both wisteria (Wisteria) and the potato vine (Solanum jasminoides) will do the job. They provide good background color in this formal courtyard garden.

Roses come into their own from early to midsummer. The difficulty lies in knowing what to choose from such a wide range. The vigorous ramblers, such as *Rosa* 'Bobbie James' or *R. filipes* 'Kiftsgate', will make their way up to 30 ft. or more and are best allowed to grow over tall, free-standing structures, such as substantial trees. Next are the big performers like *Clematis* 'Jackmanii' with mauve flowers, and the flamboyant orange-red trumpet creeper (*Campsis* × *tagliabuana* 'Madame Galen').

Of the foliage climbers, the many different varieties of ivy do good service on shady walls. Choose from neat triangular leaf shapes, like English ivy (*Hedera helix* 'Sagittifolia'), or more dashing variegated cultivars like *H. helix* 'Buttercup' (the variegated forms will not do so well in shade). The ornamental vines and creepers have the bonus of wonderfully colored autumn foliage; the golden hop (*Humulus lupulus* 'Aureus') has large, ornamental leaves and will cope with partial shade.

For stunning effects, grow a couple of climbers against a wall or over an obelisk to give either mixed color in one season or a succession of color over more than one season, depending on the chosen species. Combinations worth trying are: *Rosa* 'Albertine' with *Clematis* 'Vyvyan Pennell' (summer—pink and mauve); Chilean potato tree with *Clematis alpina* 'Frances Rivis' (spring and summer—blue); golden hop with *Clematis tangutica* (summer and fall—golden foliage; autumn—yellow flowers); *Hydrangea anomala* subsp. *petiolaris* with *Rosa* 'Climbing Iceberg' (all-white summer combination).

Potted climbers (above) *A sweet pea "wigwam" provides a glorious scent and is an ideal way to use climbers in a limited space.*

Wisteria (above) *This is a popular favorite, with long racemes of scented flowers appearing in late spring. It will quickly cover any available surface, but it needs careful pruning to encourage plenty of flowers.*

Large-scale displays (above) *Large climbers such as this kiwi (Actinidia kolomikta) become heavy, so make sure your chosen support can take the weight.*

VIGOROUS CLIMBERS FOR PERGOLAS

Actinidia deliciosa

Anemone clematis

Campsis x *tagliabuana* 'Madame Galen'

Humulus lupulus 'Aureus'

Jasminum officinale

Lonicera x *brownii* 'Dropmore Scarlet'

Rosa 'Bobbie James'; *R. filipes* 'Kiftsgate'; *R.* 'Rambling Rector'

Vitis 'Brant'; *V. coignetiae*; *V. vinifera* 'Purpurea'

Wisteria floribunda; *W. sinensis*

Planting and training climbers

Climbing plants can be invaluable to the gardener in a number of different ways: to cover bare walls and fences; to hide unsightly structures and objects within the garden; and to act as groundcover—spreading over the soil as well as over other plants.

With the trend toward smaller gardens, vertical gardening has become increasingly popular in order to make sure that every available space within the garden is fully utilized.

As well as walls, fences, and other surfaces, poles, pergolas, and arches can also be used to support climbers and provide this added dimension to a garden.

However, even true climbers (those plants that have tendrils, sucker pads or twining stems), which are capable of supporting themselves, need some help to become established and start to make full use of any nearby support structure. Other plants, such as roses, will always need additional help from the gardener to keep them in place.

To reduce the amount of training required, always try to position any support structure between the plant it is holding and the source of light. The plant will grow toward the light, so this positioning forces it to make its way through its support structure to reach the light. A plant twining through its support will need much less tying and training than one that is merely resting against it.

Many climbing plants prefer their roots to be planted in a cool, moist, shaded position; however, as gardeners, we often plant them close to the base of a tree, wall, or fence, where the conditions are actually dry (and sometimes hot). Even young plants that have only been in their permanent position for two or three years will need at least 6 gallons of water each week in summer. So it is important that new introductions are planted well, to give them the best possible chance of survival over the first few years until they are established.

Training a young plant (left)
A simple grid structure will provide ideal support for a climbing plant. Here, slanting canes encourage the plant to grow toward the grid.

PLANTING CLEMATIS

Tools and materials

- clematis
- bucket of water
- spade
- wire mesh
- ties

1 *Before planting clematis, it is important to make sure that the compost it is grow ing in is well-watered. The best way to do this is to plunge the pot into a bucket of water and let it soak.*

2 *Lift the pot from the water and allow any surplus water to drain away before removing the plant from its pot.*

3 *Dig a hole at least twice the size of the plant's rootball in order to encourage the new roots to grow out into the surrounding soil after planting.*

4 *Refill the hole, firming the soil around the new plant as the hole is filled.*

5 *After planting, spread out the shoots to give them as much room as possible. For long, straggling shoots, position one tie about every 1 ft. along the stem to hold the plant close to the wire so that the new growth can become established.*

6 *Where possible, push the new growth into the space between the wires and the support structure—as the plant grows out toward the light, it will cling to the wires. After planting and tying are complete, water the plant with at least 2 gallons of water to settle the soil around the roots.*

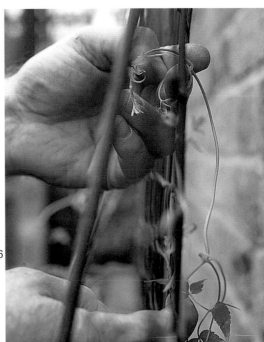

Planting for a quick fix

For any one of a number of reasons, you may need to find a short-term planting solution: to fill in a gap created by the loss of a permanent plant, to help cover bare soil in a new garden until the perennials and shrubs flesh out and take over, or to create color in summer during the famous early summer "gap," when the first flush of flower color has died down and the second has yet to begin.

Fast-growing annuals are ideal for this purpose and are available in sizes and colors ranging from towering sunflowers (*Helianthus*) to tiny jewels, such as sapphire-blue lobelia or multi-colored Livingstone daisies (*Dorotheanthus bellidiformis*), which are ideal for containers.

Annuals are normally grown from seed or bought in trays from the garden center as young plants. It is clearly less expensive to buy seed, but the seedlings will need care and attention in the form of frequent watering; it is easy to lose an entire sowing through neglect or, in colder climates, from planting out too early, when a late frost may strike. Young, tender plants are a great attraction for slugs and snails, so make sure you have taken care of the problem either by using slug pellets or, if you wish to garden organically, using slug traps containing beer.

Taller displays

Among the fast-growing plants that will offer you excellent gap-filling color in a summer border is the flowering tobacco plant, with its handsome large, soft apple-green leaves and heads of scented white flowers. It will grow to around 5 ft. tall and generally germinates easily from seed. Sander's tobacco (*Nicotiana × sanderae*) varieties in mixed colors, growing to about 24 in.

Using containers (below)
As long as the plants are relatively hardy year-round, you can introduce color closer to the house and patio by planting a range of containers.

Using height to good effect (above) *Fast-growing annual sweet peas will rapidly produce a good display of blooms and grow up to 6 ft. tall.*

Filling bare patches (above) *If you have a bare patch in your garden, then you might consider sowing cosmos seeds in spring. A great array of rich light and pink flowers will make a summer-long drift of color.*

tall, could be used in front of this species. The deep red and lime-green flowered forms look particularly good.

Grouped displays

An all-white display would look effective in most planting schemes; it can be used to fill a gap in a border, or it could even make a corner planting on its own. Grow the tallest plants of flowering tobacco and plume poppy at the back, with white snapdragons (*Antirrhinum* 'White Wonder'), white impatiens (*Impatiens*), and white candytuft (*Iberis amara*) at the front.

Smaller forms of the towering sunflower are also invaluable for summer borders, as are the brilliant flowers of the daisy-like cosmos (*Cosmos*). Plant the two species together for a dazzling display of clashing colors.

If you plant small annuals in containers, you can group the display to make it more eye-catching. To enliven a bare wall, put plants into wall containers and hang them on brackets.

Small displays

Infill plants for the front of a border include the bright orange French marigold (*Tagetes patula*); the poached egg plant (*Limnanthes douglasii*), with its mass of bright yellow, white-bordered flowers; scented stocks (*Matthiola incana*), with purple, pink, or white flowers in short spikes; and California poppies (*Eschscholzia californica*), with wonderful, bright orange flowers that last all summer.

Climbers

For additional height, grow the exquisitely scented and singularly beautiful sweet pea. Sweet peas come in a range of brilliant colors, but the very deep crimson—almost black—sweet peas have great appeal. Equally good are climbing nasturtiums, with their soft, rounded green leaves and brilliant orange, yellow, or scarlet flowers. Both of these climbers will need supports.

Making a gravel garden

Materials such as gravel, rocks, and different grades of pebbles have become widely used as an alternative to a lawn. More recently, gray or blue slate chips have become a popular alternative to pebbles, providing an attractive contrast to the plant foliage.

Low-maintenance groundcover (below)

Instead of using bark and mulch (which will eventually have to be replaced), the Welsh slate used here will last for many years.

Covering the soil with these types of materials will help to suppress weed growth (by preventing light from reaching the soil) and will reduce the amount of water being lost from the soil due to evaporation. This type of gardening lends itself particularly to hot, sunny sites, especially where the soil is light, sandy and very free-draining. However, in these situations, the plants to be grown must be carefully selected to cope with the warm, dry conditions, because the heat reflected from the stones can create a very hot microclimate. For this reason, the best plants to choose are those with silver or gray foliage and a covering of felt or hairs over the leaf surface.

Before the stones are laid, you will need to cover the soil with a water-permeable sheet or membrane, such as woven black plastic. This helps to control weeds, reduces the level of evaporation from the soil, and means you can use a shallower layer of stones. Covering the sheet with stones not only improves the overall appearance but it also helps extend the life of the sheeting, as most forms of plastic degrade when exposed to bright sunlight.

Alternative organic materials, such as wood chips or chipped or shredded bark, can be used to cover the membrane, but these materials will slowly decompose and need to be topped up every two or three years. They also tend to fade badly in sunlight, quickly becoming quite drab in appearance, and are inclined to blow around the garden if they dry out.

PROTECTING YOUR PLANTS

It is important to protect the smaller, younger plants in your bed before adding hard materials.

To avoid swamping smaller plants, cover them with an upturned plant pot before spreading the mulching material, then remove the pot. This is easier than having to pick gravel or chips out of the foliage and prevents the plants from being damaged by the gravel or stones you are using to cover the bed.

PLANTING IN A GRAVEL BED

Tools and materials

- heavy-gauge woven black plastic
- sharp knife
- trowel
- plants
- inorganic material (slate chips or gravel)

1 *Start by clearing and leveling the area before planting begins. Place a sheet of heavy-gauge woven black plastic over the bed and bury the edges at least 6 in. deep, stretching the plastic as tight as possible.*

2 *Using the heel of your boot or shoe, firmly close the groove in the soil that is holding the plastic sheeting.*

3 *Using a sharp knife, cut a cross in the plastic at the point where each plant is to be placed, and fold back the flaps of plastic to reveal the soil beneath.*

4 *Using a trowel, dig out a planting hole large enough to accommodate the rootball of the plant.*

5 *Holding the plant by its rootball, place it through the plastic into the hole, with the base of the rootball on the base of the hole. Using the trowel (or your hands, if you prefer), pull the soil back into the hole around the plant, and firm gently into place.*

6 *Immediately after planting, fold the plastic flaps back into position around the base of the plant. Pour piles of inorganic material like slate chips or gravel, onto the plastic around the base of the plants and spread out evenly. Finally, cover the whole area of plastic with a layer of the same material, spreading it evenly over the plastic until the plastic is completely hidden.*

Planting
techniques

What to buy

When you are deciding how to plant your garden, the first thing you need to do is work out a realistic budget for the plants. You also need to consider the timeframe in which the work can be undertaken. Both these aspects need to be covered before you purchase any plants for your new garden.

It is sensible to spread the actual planting out over several seasons, for reasons of both cost and time management. You also need to work out some kind of agenda of priorities for the planting. You can stage the work in a number of ways, depending to some extent on the size and type of your garden, and whether you are planting from scratch or simply redesigning sections of the existing garden.

Buying plants from a nursery or garden center

If you are stocking a garden from scratch, you need to plan for (and probably purchase) the largest elements first. Having decided what these key elements will be (see pages 82–87), you then need to go about selecting them. Your best source for large plants is a reputable nursery, where the stock has been raised by the owners. Garden centers operate by buying in stock from growers, but the quality may vary considerably, depending on the supplier. Having said that, a good garden center with a high turnover of stock is probably a safer option than a nursery which, for one reason or another, has begun to run down.

Any plant you buy must be in good condition; the bigger the plant, the more expensive, so it is important not to waste money on diseased or damaged trees or large shrubs. In addition to the health and vigor of the plant, it needs to have formed a good balanced shape, ideally with some formative training in its first seasons of growth. Strong, sturdy, and bushy are generally good; weak and spindly are generally bad! But the plant's natural habit will, to some extent, govern its form. Before you buy, check out the illustrated section of any good plant reference guide and establish what the plant you are planning to buy is supposed to look like. It is always

Seedlings (right) *When choosing young plants, make sure they are healthy; if not, they will fail to thrive.*

best to plant in the cooler seasons of the year, when there is less risk of the plant's drying out. If you plant in fall, it gives a full season for the plant to establish a good root system before the burst of active new growth in spring.

It is always a good idea to plant herbaceous perennials in groups, rather than in ones or twos, so although you may wish to purchase a wide range of different plants, it is far better to limit the choices and buy several of one kind. Not only will these then form a major feature, but the effect on the garden will be more harmonious and balanced. Opt for odd numbers of plants, as this makes it far easier to create an attractive group.

Buying plants by mail order

A number of nurseries will sell their stock by mail order or via the internet, offering you a choice of plants from a catalog that may or may not be illustrated; it will generally have a written description of each plant. The plants will then be sent out to you by mail or courier.

DEALING WITH
MAIL-ORDER TREES AND SHRUBS

Deciduous trees and shrubs purchased through mail order may be delivered to you in what is known as a "bare root" state while they are dormant.

The soil is removed from the roots prior to packing and mailing. As soon as the plant arrives, unwrap it carefully, taking care not to damage the roots. Then plunge the roots into a bucket of fresh water, and allow it to soak for at least 24 hours before planting in the usual way. Bulbs will arrive in packets and should be stored in a cool, dry place until you are ready to plant them.

POINTS TO CHECK WHEN BUYING PLANTS

It is probably easier to look out for things to avoid than to understand what constitutes a healthy plant. Here are a few of the major plant problems you may encounter. Choose a replacement if the plant you have chosen suffers from any of them.

Damaged leaves *This is most likely to be caused by pests such as mites, aphids, or slugs, but could also be due to poor soil, where nutrients are in short supply. If the plant is severely damaged, choose another.*

Yellow leaves *This can be the result of a number of problems, such as fusarium wilt, which results in the plant's wilting and dying. Also check for nutrient deficiency, and apply compost and nitrogen fertilizer.*

Checking for pests *The first thing to do when purchasing a plant is to scrutinize it closely for any signs of insect or larval activity. A number of pests can take hold and quickly overwhelm young plants.*

Planting perennials, annuals, and bulbs

These three plant types can be combined to form beautiful displays. Perennials add color and structure to the garden and should form the basis of your planting scheme. Annuals are one-year wonders that offer instant color and form. Bulbs require relatively little effort and produce a remarkably good display, mainly in spring and summer, and they vary from tiny jewels to show-stopping giants.

You will spend a great deal of time choosing your plants, and planting them correctly maximizes your chances of success.

Planting bulbs

A bulb is normally planted to at least twice its depth, so that bulbs measuring, say, 2 in. from top to bottom are planted at least 4–5 in. deep. Taller-growing bulbs such as gladioli (*Gladiolus*) will require fairly strong supports, such as bamboo canes, to keep them upright. Shorter bulbs with heavy flowerheads, such as hyacinths, will also need supporting, and an attractive cage can be made from flexible willow stems tied with raffia.

Heavy, poorly drained soil, which may cause the bulbs to rot, can be improved prior to planting by mixing in horticultural grit.

Ready for planting (above) *Narcissus 'Dutch Master' prior to planting out. The foremost bulb has an offset (smaller bulb) attached that will not usually flower in its first year.*

Glorious color (right) *Plant bulbous perennials, such as these highly scented hyacinths, in autumn with the tip of the bulb below the surface of the compost.*

Repeat flowering

If you want your bulbs to flower once again in their second year, you must feed and water them when their first flowering is over. This provides the necessary nutrients for the bulb (in effect a storage organ) to produce the following year's flowers. Do not remove the leaves until they are completely dead, as they are needed to manufacture food for the plant.

Planting perennials

It is usually best to plant out hardy perennials in either autumn or spring. Fall planting offers the best opportunity for the plants to establish themselves before the flowering season.

The planting hole must be of an adequate size—about 5 in. larger in diameter than the root-

ball. Before planting, fill the prepared hole with water if the soil is dry, and then mix a small quantity of bonemeal (or another similar fertilizer) into the base of the hole. Position the plant so that the crown is level with the surface of the surrounding soil, then fill in the hole. Finally, firm the soil around the plant carefully with the heel of your boot or shoe.

Planting annuals

Annuals raised in containers under cover are planted out in the same way as perennials, but this time you can dispense with the bonemeal at the base of the planting hole. Annuals that have been grown in biodegradable pots can be planted without removing the pots first, making handling a lot easier.

Annual favorite (above) *The sweet pea is a favorite garden annual, available as a tall-growing climber, which reaches a height of 6 ft.*

PLANTING BULBS

Bulbs, corms, and tubers are often grouped under the generic heading of "bulbs" when it comes to general care and planting. One thing they all have in common is that planting them to the correct depth in garden soil or compost can be critical to how well the plants will grow and whether or not they will flower. These gladiolus corms should be planted to three times their own height, to provide extra support.

1 *Check that the gladiolus corms are firm and solid when squeezed gently. Soft bulbs and corms are usually an indication that they have deteriorated.*

2 *Position the corms in random groups over freshly dug, weed-free soil, usually in groups of five or seven for border planting.*

3 *Using a trowel, dig a hole to a depth that is three times the height of the corm. Place the corm in the hole with the growing tip uppermost.*

4 *Press the base of the corm gently into the soil, then cover the corm with soil and gently firm the soil into place.*

Planting climbers and wall shrubs

Thanks to their vigorous growth, most climbers and wall shrubs need to be planted with care in positions where they will be able to extend themselves comfortably. You may have to supply the plants with an appropriate support, depending on their own climbing method.

Climbers are no different from trees in terms of the space demanded for the roots, but most need some help in the period after planting to encourage them to grow in the right direction, up the supports you have provided. Since climbers will be planted close to a support such as a wall, where the soil may well be dry and lacking in nutrients, more preparation than normal will probably be necessary in order to give the plants a good start and help them to establish.

Walls, pergolas, fences, trees, and old tree stumps will all provide a useful backdrop or support for a range of climbing plants. You can also grow climbers over shrubs, or over another climber, but in the latter case you need to take care that the more vigorous plant does not smother the weaker one.

Some climbers are exceptionally vigorous, and unless the support is strong the combined weight of foliage and flowers may break it. Included among these hefty giants are the large rambling roses, like 'Bobbie James' or 'Rambling Rector', which will easily reach 33 ft. and need a large tree over which to roam.

Clematis, with delicate stems and beautiful flowers, can be grown over shrubs, giving you flowers for a longer period than just those of the shrub (see pages 100–101). The suitable clematis have a short but exquisite flowering period. The small-flowered *Macropetala* and *Texensis* clematis are ideal for this setting, but the anemone clematis are probably too vigorous and need support.

VINE EYES AND WIRES FOR WALLS AND FENCES

First, you will want to check that the fence you are using is in good enough condition to hold the weight of the climber you propose to grow on the framework you will create. Extra supports (such as netting) can also be put in place once the climber is established.

1 *Screw in a vine eye using the shaft of a screwdriver as leverage. Attach these along the length of the fence at intervals.*

2 *Use galvanized wire, because it is resistant to rust and suitable for outdoor use. Take a length of wire, loop it through the eyes, and secure.*

3 *Using pliers, tighten the wire until it is taut; tighten the eyes along the length of the fence panel.*

HOW CLIMBERS PROGRESS

Climbers can be divided into three basic groups: clingers, twiners, and scrambling plants.

Clingers *Clingers, such as ivy, attach themselves with aerial roots or sucker pads and require no support.*

Twiners *Twiners, such as clematis, for example, will twist their long, flexible stems around a support.*

Scrambling plants *These climb by using hooked thorns along their stems—rambling roses fall into this category.*

Although most climbers prefer a wall in full sun, a few do well in shadier areas, including the golden hop (*Humulus lupulus* 'Aureus') and *Hydrangea anomala* subsp. *petiolaris*.

Planting climbers and wall shrubs

A planting hole for a new climber or wall shrub should be at least 5 in. larger than the diameter of the rootball and deep enough for the base of the stem to be level with the surrounding soil. Clematis should be planted slightly deeper, because it is susceptible to wilt. If this happens and the plant is deeply planted, it may grow again from the roots, so do not dig up an apparently dying clematis plant for at least one season.

Give the young plant a supporting framework and tie the leading shoot in to this to persuade it to grow in the direction you want.

Supporting sweet peas (far left) *As the plant begins to establish itself, it will grow through the framework to present a beautiful living boundary to the garden.*

A natural climber (left) *Bluecrown passionflower (Passiflora caerulea) is a grapevine with twining tendrils that allow it to gain a foothold along any physical barrier.*

Planting trees and shrubs

Whether you raise your own trees and shrubs or buy them from a garden center or nursery, at some point you will have to transfer them into their permanent positions. In order to give the young tree or shrub a good start, you first need to understand its specific requirements.

Tree roots

Trees and shrubs are quite an investment, both in terms of cost and their contribution to the garden. It pays to ensure that they get off to the best possible start by planting them carefully. Check first that the chosen shrub or tree is appropriate for the conditions in your garden: some have preference as to soil type and condition—for example, azaleas and rhododendrons will grow successfully only in acidic soils. Second, make sure that the chosen plant is not likely to cause problems, for example by being too close to house foundations.

Digging the hole

The planting hole for any tree should be dug wide enough and sufficiently deep to accommodate not only the existing rootball, but also the exploratory nature of the roots as they gradually push farther and wider in search of nutrients.

While it may be tempting on a cold autumn day to dig a hole for the tree as fast as possible and cram the young plant into it, the result will be a tree that appears to sit and sulk as a consequence. This is because you have effectively prevented the roots from searching out the necessary nutrients and moisture, so that the plant goes into a state of semi-dormancy. The result is less growth in the short term, although the tree may begin to make more progress as it grows older.

Providing support

Planting a tree requires a similar technique to planting a perennial, except that with a tree you will need to provide a support for the single stem; the support is not to prevent it from falling over, but to prevent it from moving around too much when there are high winds that cause it to rock, thereby

PLANTING A TREE

The planting hole must be wide and deep enough to take the rootball
and to allow for future root development.

1 *Mark out and dig the planting hole to about twice the diameter and depth of the tree's roots.*

2 *Break the sides of the hole with a fork, to allow the roots to grow into the soil around the planting hole.*

3 *Plant the tree and then fill the hole with soil, spreading it evenly around the roots and firming down each layer.*

SUPPORT FOR YOUNG TREES

It is essential that you provide young trees with adequate support so that they are
not rocked around during windy weather.

1 *Position the stake at 45 degrees to the plant's stem and about 10–12 in. above ground level.*

2 *Tie the tree to the stake, making sure there is a spacer between them to prevent rubbing.*

3 *Make sure the tie is about 1½ in. below the top of the stake to prevent the stem from hitting it.*

destabilizing the roots and preventing them from doing their work properly.

Planning ahead

A mixture of evergreen and deciduous trees provides the best framework for a garden. Even a small garden needs at least one small tree in order to provide some vertical interest (see pages 88–89). Knowing the ultimate size of the tree (height and branch spread) before choosing it will save you time, trouble and money later on. If you plant a young tree too close to other trees and shrubs, you will have to remove and replant it elsewhere within the first five to ten years of its life. To avoid this, visualizing the tree's height and spread in about 20 years' time will enable you to plan your planting accordingly.

Staking young trees (right) *This type of staking prevents root disturbance and encourages a strong stem to form.*

Planting in water

When it comes to creating interest in the garden, water is in a class by itself. Whether the water is moving or not is a matter of personal preference, but either way, it will attract wildlife in the form of animals, birds, and insects.

Ponds create a tranquil atmosphere in a garden that can be difficult to beat with any other feature. The sound of moving water is especially peaceful. At the same time, your pond can become a hive of activity, especially if you want to encourage wildlife to make use of your pond areas.

The pond year begins in spring as the water temperature begins to rise. Although it takes longer for the water to become as warm as the surrounding soil, slowly but surely the plants in the pond will start growing. Ideally, aquatic plants should be moved or transplanted while they are actively growing, as they actually reestablish better if moved during this time. Although many pond plants will produce large quantities of growth, they can be relatively slow to establish, so the best time to move them is in late spring. This will give them the maximum amount of time to grow and establish themselves in their new surroundings before the following winter.

You can grow most pond plants in submerged basket-like containers or cylinders such as clay drainage pipes. This makes the management of the pond and its plant population easier, because the plants can be lifted out of the water and tended to before being reintroduced to the pond. The main advantage of growing aquatic plants in containers is that it gives the gardener a greater degree of control over the plants' environment, because many of these species will put on large quantities of leafy growth if their roots are allowed to grow in an unrestricted area.

A "natural" pond (left) *The surroundings of a pond are important. Create a natural look with stones, pebbles, and plants.*

PLANTING IN A POND

Tools and materials

- suitable containers
- compost
- bricks
- water plants
- stones or pebbles

1 *If possible, fill (or at least half-fill) the pond with water several days before any new plants are introduced to allow any sediment to settle and the temperature stabilize. Where possible, position the planting containers, such as this drainage pipe, at this stage, leaving them part full of compost and ready for planting.*

2 *Position the plant into the drainage pipe so that the rootball sits on the layer of saturated compost and press the plant firmly into position. This is particularly important, because some plants may float if they are not firmly anchored.*

3 *It is important to ensure that plants are at their correct depth in the pond. If they are too deep, they will die due to lack of oxygen. House bricks can be placed in the water to stand containers on and keep the plant growing at its ideal depth. The bricks should be soaked in water for several days to wash out any chemical residues before being placed in the pond.*

4 *Once the bricks are in position in the water, place the container of your choice on top of them.*

5 *You can place a layer of stones or pebbles on the surface of the compost to stop soil and peat particles from floating to the water's surface.*

PROPAGATION

Propagation is the use of seeds or other parts of living plants to produce more of the same. This is not only economical, but it also gives you a real sense of achievement. You can propagate your own plants from seeds or cuttings, or by layering, division, or grafting. In these ways, you can take advantage of what you have already grown to create additions to your original stock.

Seeds Growing new plants from seeds is the most common method of propagating a large number of plants quickly. The timing for collecting seeds is critical. Too late and the seeds will have dispersed, too early and they will not germinate at all. If damp, leave them in the sun to dry thoroughly; if you are not sowing them immediately, store them in a cool, dry place until needed.

Cuttings Increasing your stock of plants by taking cuttings from their stems is a common way to propagate woody plants. Stem cuttings can be subdivided into three categories: *softwood*—which is taken from shoots of the current season's growth (spring and early summer); *semi-ripe*—taken from shoots of the current season's growth as soon as the base of a shoot has turned woody (late summer and

autumn); *hardwood*—prepared from the current season's growth once the leaves have fallen off (late autumn and early winter). Only take cuttings from a healthy plant, discarding any thin and weak shoots. For best results, choose non-flowering shoots as these will root more readily. However, if only flowering shoots are available, remove the flowers when preparing the cuttings.

Bulbs   Bulbs can be grown from seed successfully, although for some it can take up to seven years before the seedlings will flower. For this reason, it is preferable to use the propagation methods of scaling and scoring bulbs to get results quickly. Bulbs such as lilies can be scaled, which involves breaking their small, narrow scales away from the base of the parent bulb to plant as single new bulbs that will

grow the same year. Bulbs such as hyacinths should be scored, which involves taking the parent bulbs from their pots in early autumn, cutting grooves in the base with a knife, and then planting them in compost. Bulblets will form and be ready for planting out by the following fall. Both methods are carried out under glass or clear plastic and produce flowers that can be identical to the parent plant.

Propagating your own plants

Many plants can be reproduced (propagated) relatively easily to increase your stock. The simplest forms of propagation—raising plants from seeds, taking cuttings, layering shoots, or dividing clumps—are easy for even the amateur to master, providing an inexpensive supply of new plants, as well as offering a great sense of satisfaction for the gardener.

Choosing a plant for propagation by cuttings

This container-grown shrub has a well-developed root system and healthy stems and shoots. The compost surrounding the rootball is free from pests.

How you propagate your plants is determined by the nature of the plant and by the timescale at your disposal. Nature being what it is, some plants are incredibly simple to propagate, while others have to be coaxed into reproduction with exactly the right conditions—optimum warmth, light levels, and moisture. Some plants, such as annuals, grow very quickly from seed, creating a magnificent display of flowers within a few weeks of planting. Others, such as most trees, will take years to grow into a reasonable sized plant and you would be better advised to obtain these as bare-root plants via mail order or as container-grown specimens. Other plants will grow well but may not flower for many years.

Seeds or cuttings?

Plants naturally reproduce themselves from seeds, in a process known as sexual propagation; however, their cell structure is such that it is also possible to create a new plant just from a cut portion (a "cutting") of the leaf, stem, or root. Other methods include division, grafting, and layering. All these methods come under the heading of vegetative propagation and are covered in the remainder of this chapter.

The method of propagation you choose depends largely on which is the most successful and reliable. Although most plants will grow well from seeds, the process can be slow and occasionally the plants do not breed true to type, so that the seedlings differ substantially from the parent plant. If it is particularly important to you that the offspring closely resembles the parent, vegetative propagation is usually the best option.

Whichever method of propagation you choose, the first thing you must ensure is that the parent plant looks strong and vigorous, because its state of health will affect the quality of its offspring.

If you are collecting seeds yourself, make sure they are fully ripe. You will be able to tell when the seed is ready to be collected, because the pods or seed cases will begin to crack. You should collect seeds on a dry day. For cuttings, choose non-flowering shoots or, if that is not possible, remove any flowers from the cutting. This will ensure that all of the plant's energy is directed into the formation of new roots.

Propagation equipment

If you plan to propagate your own plants, you will need to know the appropriate conditions in which to raise them. The ideal place is a greenhouse (see pages 222–223), provided it has some form of heating in winter, and shading and ventilation in summer. If you cannot afford a greenhouse, then soil-warming cables in a garden frame provide a good alternative.

For small-scale propagation, a small table by a window or a wide window ledge will be adequate, although a heated propagating case (in effect, a mini greenhouse) will certainly improve your chances of success. Although not vital, it helps to control the two factors that most influence successful germination: warmth and moisture. A propagating case is also recommended for use in a greenhouse.

In addition to ready-made propagation units, you can construct your own in various ways. Covering trays with sheets of glass or clear plastic wrap is a simple option. You can cover pots of cuttings with cut-down clear plastic bottles, or you can make your own mini cloche from wire hoops and plastic sheeting.

Alternately, you could use a heated propagation unit, which can warm the compost to a temperature of 59°F in winter and early spring, which is ideal for most temperate region plants. Tropical plants require more heat, however.

Basic propagation equipment *The basic equipment you will need consists of seed trays and pots, a pressing board for firming compost, a pair of shears, and a sharp garden knife, as well as labels.*

Propagating unit *A propagating case helps to ensure successful germination of seeds and rooting of cuttings.*

Sowing seeds

Most of the plants that are grown from seeds are annuals (plants that grow from seed to flower in one growing season) or biennials (plants that do so over two growing seasons). Another group is plants that are frost-tender, but that are perennials in their native countries where the climate may be warmer. This group is grown as annuals in colder climates and can be propagated by sowing seeds or by taking cuttings.

When raising plants from seeds, it is important to realize that the seed itself is a tiny powerhouse containing all the genetic material for the plant. This has evolved over centuries, to result in the most successful method of reproduction. For germination to take place, most plants have very specific needs that are, in effect, a replica of their natural habitat. Seeds from plants from temperate regions, for example, will germinate at temperatures of 59–70°F, but those from tropical regions will need higher temperatures and therefore will probably require artificial heat.

For successful germination, you need to provide the seeds with a controlled environment, such as a greenhouse. Novice propagators usually fail because they are not consistent in caring for their seeds. Regular watering, well aerated and free-draining compost, stable temperatures and adequate light are all essential.

Storing seeds

Seeds are most likely to germinate if relatively fresh, so do not keep packets of seeds for more than a year, and make sure that they are stored in a cool, dry place.

PREPARING CONTAINERS

Successful sowing indoors requires careful preparation. Taking time to create the optimum conditions will give your seeds the best chance of success.

1 *Start by deliberately overfilling a suitable container with seed compost (the light, open compost will tend to settle slightly as the container is filled).*

2 *Using a piece of wood, remove any surplus compost above the rim of the container. Pass the straightedge over the container in a "sawing" motion to remove the compost.*

3 *Using a wooden presser, gently firm the compost evenly over the whole surface until it is about ½ in. lower than the rim of the container. This creates a firm, level seed bed.*

Preparing seeds

Some seeds have a particularly hard outer casing, and you will find germination takes place much more easily if this casing is scored lightly before the seeds are sown. Other seeds may benefit from being soaked in water for 24 hours to soften the outer casing.

Compost for seeds

The ideal medium for germinating seeds indoors is made up of two layers. The base layer is seed or multipurpose compost, and the upper layer is horticultural grit or vermiculite, which is free-draining. The advantage of this two-layer system is that the seeds are sown in the free-draining layer of grit, but the compost below provides the nutrients required once rooting begins. The alternative is to fill the container in which the seeds are to be sown with proprietary seed or multipurpose compost (as shown below). Soil-free compost is popular for this purpose.

How to sow

Having assembled the necessary pots, compost, and equipment, you need to establish a good light area in which to grow the seeds. The average temperature should be around 59°F and should not drop too far below this at night. Ideally, germinate seeds in a heated propagating case in a greenhouse. Once you have sown the seeds (see below), keep the containers well watered, ensuring that they do not dry out or become waterlogged. Even quantities of water at frequent intervals produce the most successful results. A fine rose fitted to the watering can will ensure that the seeds are not washed away.

PLANTS THAT ARE EASILY PROPAGATED FROM SEEDS

Annuals	Perennials	Ranunculus
All	Achillea	Rudbeckia
Shrubs	Agapanthus	Salvia
Abutilon	Aquilegia	Sisyrinchium
Buddleia	Campanula	Stachys
Callistemon	Cynara	Tellima
Chimonanthus	Delphinium	Tiarella
Deutzia	Dianthus	Verbascum
Eccremocarpus	Diascia	Veronica
Exochorda	Erysimum	Viola
Fatsia	Geranium	
Fremontodendron	Geum	**Bulbs**
Fuchsia	Helianthus	Crocosmia
Hydrangea	Heuchera	Galtonia
Lavatera	Iris	Gladiolus
Pittosporum	Libertia	Lilium
Rhododendron	Monarda	Nerine
Skimmia	Nepeta	
	Penstemon	
	Potentilla	

SOWING SEEDS IN TRAYS

Remember that many plants will not germinate without some extra warmth.

A large number of the plants used for summer bedding are half-hardy annuals, and their seeds will not germinate

in garden soil until early summer; therefore, sow them in spring under glass or clear plastic wrap.

1 Fill a seed tray to the rim with suitable compost. Firm gently until the compost is ½ in. below the rim. For very fine seeds, sieve another thin layer of fine compost over the surface and firm lightly.

2 Sow the seeds as evenly as possible over the surface. Sow half in one direction, then turn the tray and sow the remainder in the opposite direction to ensure even distribution.

3 Sieve a thin layer of fine compost over the seeds and firm gently. If you have very fine seeds, press them lightly into the surface of the compost, rather than covering them with more compost.

4 Lightly water the seed tray before covering it with a sheet of clear glass or plastic wrap, and a sheet of newspaper if required (the paper provides shade to prevent the compost from drying out).

When to transplant

You can tell when a seedling is ready to be transplanted because it will have developed its first true leaves. Prior to that stage in its development, the seedling develops its seed leaves (known as cotyledons). These swell on germination to force the seed coat to split open, but the true pair of leaves that appear next indicate that the plant is now strong enough to handle life outdoors. At this point, the plant will withstand the shock of transplantation more easily.

Hardening off

Normally, the seedlings are placed in a cold frame outdoors, in which the ventilation is progressively increased over 10 days or so until the seedlings are fully acclimatized. If you do not have a cold frame, put the seedlings outdoors during the day only and bring them in again at night. Then, once the nights are less cold, you can leave them outside overnight before transplanting them into their final outdoor positions.

Hardening off (left) *Once the seedlings have been transplanted into individual pots or cells and are growing strongly, they can be hardened off to acclimatize them to life outdoors.*

Sowing outdoors

You can sow seeds of many hardy plants, including hardy annuals, directly into their flowering positions once the soil warms up in spring. If you sow seeds directly into the soil, you must

SOWING SEEDS OUTDOORS (BROADCAST)
Broadcast sowing is a useful technique for hardy annuals, salad vegetables such as radishes and spring onions, and green manure crops such as comfrey or mustard.

1 *Rake the soil to form a finely tilled seed bed, remove any large stones, and break down lumps of earth. This will leave the soil with a fine layer on the top surface.*

2 *Pour a few of the seeds from the packet into the palm of your hand.*

3 *Sow the seeds by scattering them evenly over the soil surface. Sow from a height of about 1 ft. above soil level.*

4 *Lightly rake over the seed bed in at least two different directions to incorporate the seeds into the soil and to avoid gathering them into clusters. Label the seed bed.*

make sure that a finely tilled soil is created by raking it over to remove any lumps or pebbles. Such lumps prevent the seeds from reaching the light, thereby cutting down on the number that successfully germinate.

How deep to sow

Most seeds need to be covered with twice their own depth of soil, so the finer the seeds, the closer to the surface they are sown.

Broadcast or drills?

Annuals are not too fussy about the nutrient content of the soil and will thrive in poor ground, but all seeds need a free-draining soil that is fine in quality, with any stones or pebbles removed. If you sow the seeds broadcast (literally, spread about, rather than in any order), the danger is that you will then not be able to distinguish between the seedlings and young weeds. If you sow in neat rows, or drills, it is easier to see what to remove and what to preserve. Remember to label your rows carefully, otherwise a month later you will have no idea what you sowed where.

Sowing seeds outdoors is to some degree a hit-or-miss operation, because changing weather conditions can easily destroy an entire crop of seedlings—for example, if it rains very heavily after sowing. For this reason, it is a good idea to plan any such planting for random infilling, so that your overall design is not spoiled if the plants fail to flourish in some areas.

THINNING SEEDLINGS

Seeds are often sown slightly thicker than required to allow for losses. At some stage, these seedlings will need to be thinned out.

Remove sections of unwanted seedlings with a hoe to leave small, manageable groups. Then thin out the groups of seedlings by hand, carefully removing the unwanted seedlings and leaving the strongest one at each position, or "station."

SOWING SEEDS OUTDOORS (DRILL)

Drill sowing is a good technique for growing various annuals and perennials, as well as most vegetables, allowing you to see immediately when seeds have germinated and to remove weed seedlings from between the drills easily.

1 *Rake the soil to form a finely tilled seed bed, break up large lumps of earth, and remove any large stones. Mark out the rows with a garden line (keeping it taut).*

2 *Using a draw hoe or cane, make a groove in the soil to form the seed drill.*

3 *Sow the seeds thinly into the drill by hand, aiming for a set distance between the seeds. Never sow them directly from the packet.*

4 *Using a rake, draw the soil back into the drill, covering the seeds. Gently pat the soil firm over the seeds using the back of the rake.*

Taking cuttings

The process of taking cuttings allows you to grow a replica of the parent plant. Various parts of the plant—shoots, roots, and leaves— can be used for this purpose; which part you choose depends on the nature of that particular plant.

Fleshy stems

Plants with extremely fleshy stems can be encouraged to root in water. Place the cut stem of the plant in a jar of water and wait for roots to appear. When they start to emerge, pot the stem in the normal way.

The most efficient method of propagating shrubs is to take cuttings of the shoots (stem cuttings). Inserted into a prepared medium, these will root at the base, and a replica of the parent will grow. Cuttings can be taken at different times and from shoots at different stages of development.

Softwood cuttings

These are the youngest shoots, from which cuttings are taken from the tips in spring and early summer. These cuttings tend to root more easily than other types, so this method is widely used for plants that are difficult to propagate from mature cuttings. Humidity, warmth, and moisture are very important during the rooting period, and a closed propagating case is therefore advised.

Semi-ripe cuttings

These are taken in late summer or early autumn from the current year's growth. They do not root as readily as softwood cuttings, but their survival rate is better, as they are less inclined to wilt.

Hardwood cuttings

These are taken in autumn or winter, when the shoots are about a year old, and are rooted outdoors or in a cold frame. They will not root readily unless hormone rooting powder is applied to the wound; root formation can be slow, but most cuttings will have rooted by the following spring.

TAKING SOFTWOOD CUTTINGS

A wide range of plants—including buddlejas, forsythias, weigelas, and many others—will root very quickly and easily from softwood cuttings, many of them forming new roots in just a few weeks.

1 *Collect the stem tips—which are the fastest-growing part—and store them in a moist plastic bag.*

2 *Fill a container with an open, free-draining compost and firm it down, tapping the tray to level it.*

3 *Trim the stem base to below a node (leaf joint) and remove the lower leaves.*

4 *Dip the stem into rooting powder and insert it into the compost to just below its lowest leaves. Water.*

TAKING HARDWOOD CUTTINGS

This technique is suitable for propagating a wide range of deciduous trees, shrubs, and bush fruits.

It is probably the simplest and cheapest method of propagating plants from cuttings.

1 *Prepare the ground by forking it over and roughly leveling it, before adding a base dressing of general-purpose fertilizer.*

2 *Cover the soil with black plastic, burying the edges. Insert the tines of a fork vertically through the plastic into the soil.*

3 *Remove healthy current-season shoots. Trim into 10-in. lengths, making the top cut above a bud and the bottom cut below.*

4 *Gently push the cuttings, base first, vertically through the holes in the plastic into the soil below, with the bottom two-thirds in the soil.*

Types of cutting

Cuttings can be taken at various points when separating the shoot from the parent plant.

Stem cuttings are cut straight across the stem, just below the tip—this is usually where the current season's growth begins.

Heel cuttings are created by pulling off a sideshoot so that it brings a sliver of the stem (the heel) with it.

Basal cuttings are prepared from new shoots that are growing from the crown of a plant, mainly hardy perennials. Remove these cuttings when they are about 2 in. high, as close to the crown as possible.

Looking after cuttings

The cuttings need special care in the early stages in order to encourage new roots to form.

Special compost (a mix of equal parts of peat and sharp sand), warmth, light, and moisture are all required. The danger with many cuttings is that they will dry out before they have made roots, so some kind of transparent cover is necessary. Professionals use mist propagation units, but a cut-down clear plastic bottle will serve the purpose of retaining much-needed moisture and humidity around cuttings in a pot. A heated propagating case is the ideal piece of equipment for rooting cuttings.

Since some cuttings can take up to six months to root, the temptation is often to pull them up and inspect them before the process is complete. You can usually tell when the plants have rooted, as one or two small new leaves will appear on the stem, and it is only then that you should decide to plant the cutting.

Planting

Once the cutting has developed an independent root system, you can plant it into an individual pot—a 3½-in. pot is about the right size for one season, until the plant is growing strongly and can be planted out in its permanent position. However, very small cuttings that are planted directly into borders are easy to overlook or pull up by accident, so it can be worth tending your young plants' for another year before planting them out.

Once the cutting is growing strongly, nip out the growing tip. This encourages the sideshoots to develop, giving the plant a more bushy appearance.

Rooting powder

When applied to the cut end, this hormone preparation increases the rooting capacity of the cutting. Dip the base of the cutting in the powder and then blow away any surplus.

Root and leaf cuttings

In addition to cuttings made from new shoots, some plants can be propagated from other parts as well, in particular the roots and the leaves. The sections of root or leaf are placed in or on an appropriate growing medium so that they can develop new roots and shoots.

Some plants produce very short stems and shoots, which can make taking cuttings very awkward, so another part of the plant has to be used.

Root cuttings

Plants that produce shoots directly from their roots—for example, acanthus (*Acanthus*) and sumac (*Rhus*)—can be increased by taking root cuttings. These cuttings are normally taken in late autumn or during early winter while the plant is dormant.

How you deal with the cuttings depends on the type of root system of the plant. Thicker roots should normally be cut into sections 2–3 in. long, while thinner roots should be cut into longer sections up to 4 in. long. It is important that you make a different cut at each end of thick roots so that you know which way up to plant them: make a straight cut at the top of the root (nearest the stem) and a slanted cut at the other end.

Prepare a tray or pots of compost containing a mixture of peat and vermiculite. Insert the slanting ends of the roots into the compost. Cover with grit and then water well. Alternatively, use sand to cover the cuttings.

With thin roots that are too delicate to insert upright, lay the roots on the surface of the compost. Cover with grit, as before, and then water well.

Root cuttings can be propagated in a cold frame and potted when new shoots appear in spring.

TAKING ROOT CUTTINGS

Some plants produce very short stems and shoots, which can make taking cuttings very awkward, so another part of the plant has to be used. The roots of many herbaceous plants and alpines, and a number of trees, shrubs, and climbers, can be used for propagation.

1 *After carefully digging up the roots of the plant that is to be propagated, wash them to remove as much soil as possible before you begin.*

2 *Cut thick roots into sections 2–3 in. long with a flat cut at the top and a slanted cut at the bottom—this will become the planted end.*

3 *Insert the root cuttings by gently pushing the slanted ends into a pot of compost so that the top of each cutting is level with the surface.*

4 *Cover with grit, which allows air to reach the top of each cutting without letting them dry out and also ensures good drainage.*

Leaf cuttings

Some plants can be propagated from their leaves. Notable among these are African violets (*Saintpaulia*), Cape primroses (*Streptocarpus*), and begonias (*Begonia*). The new plants will develop either from the base of the leaf (the leaf petiole) or from one of the veins that runs across the leaves. The compost should be a mixture of multipurpose compost and sharp sand (roughly two parts to one part). The addition of sand makes rotting less likely.

African violets are easily propagated by removing a couple of leaves from the parent plant with the stalk attached and then inserting the stalk of each leaf into a small pot of cutting compost, so that the base of the leaf touches the compost. Cover the pot with an upturned clear plastic bottle or plastic bag and leave in a warm place, out of direct sunlight. Small plantlets will form at the base of the leaves. Once they grow large enough, you can remove the plantlets and plant them individually. Some succulents, such as crassulas (*Crassula*), can be propagated in the same way by removing a couple of leaves from the parent plant, but you should allow a day or so for the wound to callus over before inserting each leaf into the cutting compost.

Larger leaves, such as those of cape primroses, can be cut into sections to be used for propagation. Plantlets will form where the cut surface of a vein is in contact with the compost (see below). To keep the leaf cuttings moist, cover the tray or pot with a clear plastic bag and seal. Alternatively, all types of leaf cutting can be rooted in a propagating case.

TAKING LEAF CUTTINGS

It is possible to propagate some plants by cutting and planting their leaves in a pot or tray of compost. New plantlets grow from either the base of the leaf or the veins that run across it. Cape primrose (*Streptocarpus*) is shown here.

1 *Lay the leaf upside down. Use a sharp knife to cut along the leaf close to the thick fleshy midrib, to leave two sections of leaf blade. Discard the midrib.*

2 *If you are dealing with particularly long leaf strips, cut them into halves or thirds so that they will fit comfortably into a tray or pot of compost.*

3 *Insert the strips so that the cut surface is just below the top of the compost. Lightly firm the compost, water, and leave on a warm windowsill or in a propagator.*

Layering plants

Layering is one of the easiest methods of propagation, and it has the added advantage of being more or less foolproof. It is used primarily as a way of increasing a wide range of shrubs, trees, and climbers, and can also be used for propagating some soft fruits.

Layering, in which new plants are encouraged to grow from the stems of the parent plant while these are still attached, makes use of the natural tendency to produce new roots (known as adventitious roots) where a wound occurs in the cambium of the plant (the layer immediately under the bark). You can make use of this tendency by cutting through the outer part of the stem and ensuring that the wound is placed in contact with soil that is then kept sufficiently moist. Layering can be done either by pegging down a cut shoot or by wrapping the cut area with sphagnum moss that is wrapped in a clear plastic bag. There are several different methods of layering, each suitable for use with plants displaying particular characteristics.

Simple layering

This method works well with shrubs or trees with flexible stems. Using a sharp knife, cut a tongue into the wood tissue about halfway through, then peg the cut side so that it is in contact with the soil. A small mound of compost placed at the contact point will encourage rooting.

Serpentine layering

This is used for climbers such as clematis or wisteria. Several cuts are made along the shoot and pegged down, so that a number of new plantlets form.

Tip layering

This method of layering is used for the genus *Rubus* (wild brambles), including blackberries, which will form new plants where

SIMPLE LAYERING

The most basic form of layering is "simple layering", where a soft, flexible shoot is bent down to touch the soil. If rooting is successful, this shoot can then be separated from the parent plant so that it can grow on independently.

1 *Select a suitable shoot and gently bend it down to soil level to see where the hole should be dug.*

2 *Remove any leaves at about 12 in. from the tip. Cut a 1½-in. "tongue" half into the stem.*

3 *Dig a shallow hole, so that the side nearest the parent plant slopes at 45 degrees and the other is vertical.*

4 *Lay the wounded section into the bottom of the hole. Peg into place with a wire hoop. Cover with soil.*

For this method of layering, you will need a small, clear plastic bag with the bottom removed,

a sharp garden knife, a matchstick, a couple of ties, and a small amount of sphagnum moss.

1 *Cut the bottom off a plastic bag to make a tube and slide it over the leaves. This holds the leaves out of the way.*

2 *Further down, make an upward cut into the stem, penetrating halfway through. Wedge the cut open with a clean matchstick.*

3 *Slide the plastic tube down the stem so that the wounded area is in the center of the bag. Tie the bottom firmly around the stem.*

4 *Pack the plastic bag with moist sphagnum moss until it is full and tie the top of the bag firmly around the stem with string.*

the tips of the shoots touch the soil. These plants will often do this without help from the gardener. All you need to do is make sure that the tip of the shoot is buried shallowly in the soil.

Air layering

This is a useful method of layering for plants with stems that are not very flexible. You can use either the basic layering (above) cut or the stem girdling technique (below) for air layering. The secret of the method lies in creating a sealed pocket of growing medium around the cut area of your plant, which then encourages new roots to form.

This method involves damaging the stem of the parent plant in various ways to encourage new roots to form.

This technique can be used when carrying out air layering.

1 *Tightly twist a piece of thin wire until it cuts into the bark. This will encourage roots to form.*

2 *Twist the stem until the bark splits. As the stem heals, roots may form around the damaged area.*

3 *Remove a narrow ring of bark. This will encourage roots to form around the damaged area.*

4 *Make an angled cut into the stem, creating a wound which may form roots as the stem heals.*

Dividing plants

You can increase perennials by simply breaking up the clumps of adult specimens, while young bulbs can be removed from the parent bulb and potted to grow on into new plants.

What type of perennial to choose? (above) *A perennial that produces new growth from its base is an excellent choice for division.*

Perennials

In addition to taking basal cuttings, you can increase many clump-forming herbaceous perennials by dividing up the clumps. This not only creates useful new plants, but also revitalizes the existing ones, in which the center will tend to die out as the new growth pushes outward from the crown. Small clumps of not particularly fibrous-rooted plants can be divided relatively easily by digging up the entire plant and then pulling it apart in your hands. Stronger-growing plants with an established root system will need a degree of brute force applied to split them. The normal method is to insert two forks back to back through the clump and work the tines of the forks apart to lever apart the roots.

Generally, plants are best divided in autumn once they have become dormant, as the plants then have a break before new growth starts in spring.

Replant the divided plants right away, either in pots or directly into their flowering positions. Most divided plants will flower again the following year.

Some plants simplify the task of propagation by producing runners with small plantlets on the end, or, in the case of tolmieas (*Tolmiea*), little plantlets at the base of the leaves, which can be removed and planted.

DIVISION

Many plants can be divided easily to provide you with new stock.
This method also ensures that plants remain vigorous and free-flowering.

1 *Using a garden fork, lift the plant out of the soil and wash it clean with a hosepipe to remove as much soil as possible.*

2 *Push two hand forks into the middle of the clump back to back and pull them apart to split the clump into smaller sections.*

3 *Break down each section into small individual plants with several roots and a few shoots or buds to each piece; these can then be replanted.*

Bulbs

Bulbs can be lifted and divided to increase the numbers grown. Those that flower poorly will benefit from being divided. Most bulbs are best lifted and divided when they become dormant, and the period for this will vary depending on the flowering time of the particular bulb. Exceptions to this rule are snowdrops and winter aconites (*Eranthis*), which are best divided "in the green": just after flowering has finished but before the leaves die down. Nerines, too, are best divided in the spring rather than waiting until the leaves have died down.

When dividing bulbs, remove any small offsets (which form the next generation of flowers) from the parent bulb. Those that are nearly the same size as the parent bulb can be planted in their permanent positions in the garden. Smaller ones are best planted in pots, because these will not flower until they have reached maturity.

Some bulbs, including some lilies and alliums, produce small bulbs on sections of the stem. You can remove these, treating them in exactly the same way as you would the offsets that form on the bulb itself.

Plants with rhizomes, corms, and tubers

Plants that grow from these can be propagated by cutting the rhizomes, corms, or tubers into pieces, ensuring that there is a growing bud on each from which the new plant will sprout. Among the plants that can be propagated in this way are irises and dahlias.

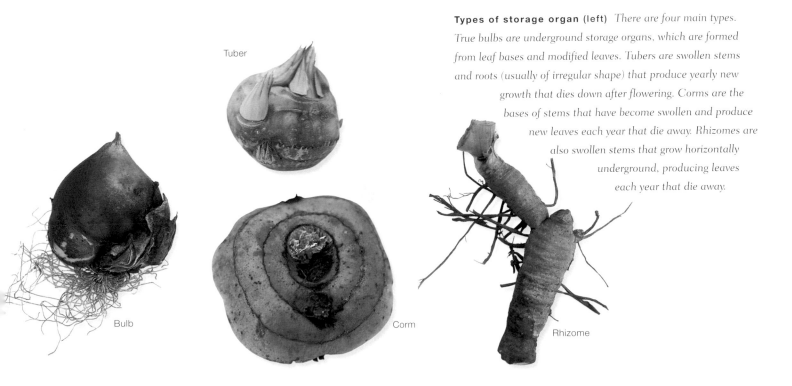

Types of storage organ (left) *There are four main types. True bulbs are underground storage organs, which are formed from leaf bases and modified leaves. Tubers are swollen stems and roots (usually of irregular shape) that produce yearly new growth that dies down after flowering. Corms are the bases of stems that have become swollen and produce new leaves each year that die away. Rhizomes are also swollen stems that grow horizontally underground, producing leaves each year that die away.*

Tuber

Bulb

Corm

Rhizome

Grafting

This is a fascinating method of reproducing plants that involves joining two separate plants together to grow as one. It is a useful method for plants that are very slow or difficult to root from cuttings or that do not grow well on their own roots.

Simple grafting (below)

You will be able to restock your greenhouse or garden with a multitude of your favorite woody plants once you have mastered the skill of grafting.

The lower part of the graft (the rootstock) will form the root system of the new plant, and it should be as closely related to the top part (the scion) as possible for the graft to work. For example, a basic rootstock for grafting roses can be propagated as a hardwood cutting from a wild rose or a sucker from a garden rose. The scion is a section of stem taken from the plant that is to be increased in numbers. If the graft is successful, the two plants will grow together almost seamlessly and give the appearance of being a single plant.

Over the years, a number of different types of graft have evolved for individual plants or groups of plants, but many of these are both complicated and, in a number of cases, totally unnecessary. It is possible to propagate most plants with just one or two of the simplest grafts. Any gardener armed with a sharp, good-quality knife, and with plenty of practice beforehand, should be able to graft plants together. If you want to have a go at grafting but do not have a specialty knife, try using a cheap general-purpose knife to make the cuts. Should you want to pursue grafting, the grafting knife is the next step.

Some woody plants can be difficult to propagate by the conventional means of taking cuttings (see pages 126–127). Among the plants that are commonly grafted are roses (in which a vigorous rose adds strength to a less vigorous new variety, for example) and fruit trees, such as apples and pears (*Pyrus*) (where a dwarfing rootstock, say, will result in a small tree).

SUCKERS

Suckers occur when the rootstock of a grafted plant starts to produce shoots from the area below the graft union.

If suckers are allowed to grow unchecked, they will start to compete with the grafted plant to which they are joined. Unfortunately, because the rootstock is usually more vigorous than the cultivar grafted onto it, the growth of these suckers will outstrip that of the grafted plant, usually resulting in the death of the grafted plant. Suckers must be removed at an early stage by simply pulling them out.

ROSE GRAFTING

Tools and materials

- cutting from a rose rootstock
- sharp knife
- shears
- semi-ripe shoot from rose cultivar
- rubber band
- pot and compost
- plastic bag

1 *Start hardwood cuttings, taken from one-year-old shoots of a rose rootstock, into growth in a warm greenhouse in midwinter. Remove the lower buds, then heel in to a soil bed. Graft in spring, when semi-ripe shoots of the rose you want to propagate are available. Prepare the rootstock by cutting it down to 6 in.*

2 *Make a single shallow, upward-slanting cut 1½ in. long at the top of the rootstock, thereby exposing the plant tissue responsible for healing (the cambium), which allows the stock and scion to heal together.*

3 *Select a semi-ripe shoot about 3 in. long from the rose cultivar you want. Remove all of the leaves apart from the uppermost one, to form the scion.*

4 *Make a single downward-slanting cut approximately 1½ in. long on the bottom section of the scion, just behind a bud. This cut will expose the cambium.*

5 *Gently place the two sections of plant together, so that the cut surfaces match. When they are correctly positioned, carefully bind the graft with a rubber band. This will hold the graft firmly until the two sections join.*

6 *Place the graft into a pot of compost. Water it well, cover with a plastic bag, and place on a warm windowsill until the graft has taken.*

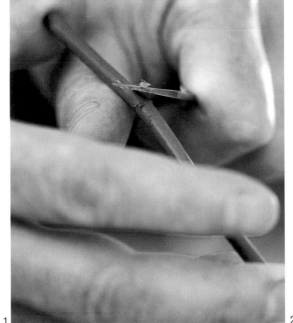

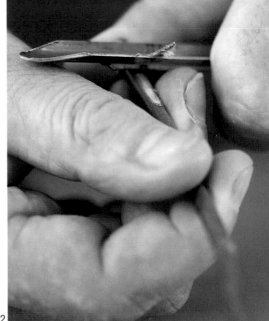

1

2

3
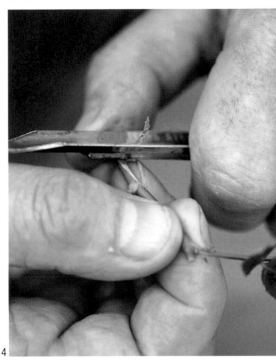

4

5

6

Garden
maintenance

Caring for your garden

It is important to be realistic about the amount of time you can give to your garden, because the reality almost always exceeds the plan. The time you will need to spend tending your garden not only depends on its style and content, but also varies from season to season.

In a traditional garden, with a modest lawn and a small vegetable patch surrounded by borders of shrubs and perennials, the most time-consuming seasons are spring (when the planting and much of the pruning are carried out) and autumn (when you will be occupied with digging and tidying up). However, if the summer is very dry, then you may spend quite a lot of time watering, especially if you have plenty of plants in containers. The lawn will require regular mowing regardless of the weather—ideally once a week.

Another factor is your own preference: if you like to keep the garden in almost military order, with nothing out of place, then clearly it will take almost double the time that a more relaxed approach would demand. Whichever group you belong to, for efficiency's sake it will always be worth ensuring that the tools you use are cleaned before being put away and are hung up or stored in a specific place. Nothing is more annoying than losing, again, your only pair of shears, and it may well be worth investing in a gardener's belt, or some other device with large pockets, in order to keep them safe.

Wooden surfaces

In addition to the work required to keep the plants in good shape, you will also need to keep the hard surfaces in your yard in good condition. Any softwood in the garden needs to be protected against the ravages of the weather

Cleaning tools (above) *To keep tools in good condition, it is important to clean off any soil and grime after use. Scrape off the thicker layers before wiping the surfaces with an oily cloth.*

Oiling moving parts (above) *All the joints on your tools should be treated with oil regularly to keep them in good working order and to prevent excessive wear and tear.*

Treating wooden tools (above) *Wooden shafts should be kept clean and treated with linseed oil at least once a year. This prevents the joints from drying out and the wood from splitting.*

and occasional new coats of preservative will be required. For most pretreated woods, linseed oil offers an efficient form of protection, feeding the wood as it preserves it. A good time to treat the wood is in early winter on a fine, reasonably warm day, after the autumn's gardening tasks have been completed. The wood will then be protected against the winter rains and frosts.

Wooden decks, particularly in wet climates, will need occasional scrubbing with a stiff-bristled brush and an algicide to remove any accumulated (and slippery) green slime. Hardwood decks need not be treated, but softwood will need to be treated with preservative once a year.

Gravel and paving

If you have areas of gravel, even if you have laid a membrane or plastic sheet underneath it, you

Raking gravel (above) *A rake with widely spaced tines is ideal for removing leaves from gravel without disturbing the underlying surface.*

Cleaning wooden surfaces (above and left)
Wooden areas such as decks will gradually accumulate dirt and grime. This encourages algae to grow on the wood. Scrubbing the deck with a solution of mild detergent once a year can help to control this problem. In areas of high rainfall, decking requires more frequent treatment, using an algicide to remove slimy deposits.

may need to apply weedkiller or remove any emerging weeds by hand. Once every three years or so you may need to top up the gravel.

Paved areas of the garden will need sweeping occasionally (but more frequently during the fall, if there are deciduous trees nearby), and a hose-down once in a while to remove the inevitable build-up of dirt. You can recycle any leaves that have fallen onto paved areas of your garden by bagging them up and allowing them to rot down into valuable compost or leaf mold (see pages 54–55).

Plants

Looking after your plants will involve you primarily in feeding and watering (see pages 142–147), and also in pruning (see pages 152–163). In addition to these basic tasks, you will also need to support some of your plants, particularly climbers, to

prevent them from flopping over (see pages 164–165). To prolong the flowering season of any plant, it pays to remove any dead or dying flowerheads so that the plant does not set seed (which will automatically prevent it from making any additional blooms). Deadheading is a task that should be carried out regularly throughout the flowering season, although you will find that it needs to be done most frequently during summer.

·With most gardening chores, it pays to spend small, regular periods of time in the garden—perhaps half an hour every other day—rather than trying to cram in everything during the weekend. You can deal with small chores such as deadheading and watering as you walk around the garden. Pruning is also best done this way, as and when individual plants have finished flowering, rather than in a once- or twice-yearly hit.

Water features

If you have a pond in your garden you should find it relatively easy to maintain, but occasionally you will have to clean it out to remove any leaves and other debris that may have built up in the base of the pond. No pond should be installed near deciduous trees. If yours is in this position, you will have to cover it with a net during autumn to catch the fallen leaves.

If you have water plants in the pond, you will need to check regularly to see if they have become too big for their pots. If so, they will need to be potted into larger containers (or, alternately, you can prune their roots). Autumn is a good time to do this. If you have a butyl pond liner, be very careful not to damage it while carrying out maintenance tasks like these.

Tranquil haven (above) *A pond can be a precious asset to your garden, so it is well worth carrying out maintenance tasks to keep it looking its best.*

You must take any fish out of the pond before you attempt to carry out any maintenance. Remove them using a net and keep them in a shady spot in a container filled with pond water. Leave the pond to settle for at least 24 hours before you return the fish to their home. If necessary, use a specially formulated water-balancing chemical to improve the quality of the water.

In really cold weather, you may need to prevent your pond from freezing over. If you do not deal with this problem, gases may build

Protecting water features (above) *A lightweight ball can help to prevent your pond or water feature from freezing over. This is vital if you have fish or other pondlife.*

CLEANING A POND

Your pond should be cleaned to remove debris that has accumulated throughout the year. Before cleaning, any beneficial creatures, such as water snails, should be placed in a shallow tray of water so that they can be reintroduced to the pond once you have finished.

1 *Empty the pond by bailing it out with a bucket, or pump the water out by attaching a hose to the pump outlet.*

2 *Remove any soil, mud, and plant debris from the bottom of the pond. Put pond animals in a tray of water.*

3 *Using a stiff brush, scrub the sides of the pond, applying a weak solution of sterilizing agent.*

4 *Clean the sides and bottom with a powerful water jet. Allow the pond surface to dry, then refill.*

up under the ice, causing the fish to suffocate. The best solution is to install an electric pond heater to keep the water at a steady temperature. However, for this you will need a permanent outdoor electricity supply that conforms to safety standards—this includes specially insulated cable and socket. It is advisable to consult a qualified electrician.

This solution can prove expensive, but is an important investment if you have a lot of fish or if your pond is stocked with expensive breeds. If you cannot afford this, you can float a ball on the surface of the pond—the movement of the ball is supposed to prevent ice from forming. This method is not infallible, and you may not want to take the risk if you have fish, but it can help to protect water plants. Generally, lighter balls work best—ping-pong or tennis balls are ideal.

Winter maintenance for plants

Your winter maintenance tasks will depend on the severity of the local climate and the kind of plants you grow. If you live in a marginal climate, which occasionally experiences hard winters, you will probably be tempted to grow slightly tender plants, which will then need some form of extra protection during any cold snaps. If you are unsure whether your chosen plants are sufficiently hardy for your climate, it is always wise to grow them in containers, since you can then wheel them indoors for a short period in winter, or at least move them to a more sheltered spot during the worst of the weather. Otherwise, the best means of

protecting your plants is to wrap the base of the plant (or the whole container, if it is housed in one) in burlap, or even the bubble wrap used for greenhouse insulation. This will provide at least some protection against the elements.

General winter tasks

Just because the garden is largely dormant, this does not mean that there is nothing to do once your preparatory tasks are complete.

The gardening lull in winter offers the ideal opportunity to clean up the garden shed and store all your equipment neatly. You can also use this time to oil and sharpen the blades of saws, pruners, cylinder lawn mowers and garden knives.

Preparing for winter (left)

Frost-tender plants will need to be well wrapped in winter to prevent frost damage. Wrap container-grown plants and their pots in burlap or bubble wrap. Cover the crowns of tender perennials with straw.

SHARPENING A KNIFE

Knives used for gardening are ideal for a whole range of tasks from taking cuttings to cutting string. Whatever they are used for, the blades should always be kept very sharp.

Use a moistened oilstone to sharpen your knife. Hold the blade at an angle of 25 degrees and push it gently along the oilstone until it is sharp. Only the factory-sharpened edge needs to be treated in this way.

Watering

Like us, plants are primarily composed of water—around 90 percent of their mass— which performs the vital function of moving nutrients around the plant. Desert plants have adapted to cope without water for considerable periods of time, but most plants will wilt quite rapidly unless the water supply is replenished frequently.

For optimum plant performance, the supply of water should be fairly regular and definitely at those periods when the plant is programmed to expect it—otherwise, even if the plant manages to survive, it will experience various growth problems.

The job of the gardener is to help nature along at those times when, for one reason or another, the climate does not behave as expected. However, it is a wise gardener who also understands that they will create less work for themselves if they choose to grow plants that survive in the average rainfall conditions of their climate, rather than hankering after plants from wetter climes that will require constant watering.

Preventing moisture loss

No one wants to spend all their time watering, so it makes sense to explore ways to reduce moisture loss. The most effective method of minimizing water loss is through mulching—covering the surface of the soil with a layer of porous material that will help to prevent evaporation. In larger gardens, you can spread plastic sheeting over the beds, topped with a layer of organic material. Gravel is also a useful mulch, particularly for small areas such as containers or pots.

MULCHING

Mulching the surface of the soil helps to conserve moisture. You can use inorganic substances, such as gravel, or those that add nutrients, such as homemade compost, bark chips, or straw. The mulch will need to be replaced every year or so.

Gravel *Membranes, such as woven plastic or plastic sheeting, are effective but look unsightly. Cover with ornamental gravel.*

Organic mulches *Shredded bark or wood chips, will compost if in contact with the soil. Fungal molds may grow—these do not harm plants.*

The right depth *To provide good weed control and prevent moisture loss from the soil, organic mulches should be 2–4 in. deep.*

Water delivery

There is a wide a range of watering equipment available (see pages 74–75), but you need to choose those items most suited to your needs and your style of gardening. You will almost certainly need a watering can and a garden hose. If you have a lawn and your climate suffers from dry spells, you would be well advised to invest in a lawn sprinkler as well. If you are away from home a lot in the summer, consider installing a water sprinkler system that is operated by a moisture sensor, which activates the system when the soil becomes too dry.

There is a wide range of special irrigation systems designed to cope with all kinds of garden layout, and your choice will be dictated by your circumstances.

The two most common forms of irrigation are the basic "leaky pipe" system and more elaborately designed systems with valves and nozzles that deliver water to specific areas.

How to water

Although this sounds absolutely basic, a great many gardeners do not water their plants efficiently, wasting large quantities of water in the process. The point of watering is to ensure that the moisture reaches as far as the plant's roots. It follows that water needs to be directed toward these, and also that it is directed for long enough to seep through the layers of soil to moisten these roots. A gentle, regular supply over a longer period is much more effective than lots of water poured on too quickly.

When to water

Avoid watering in the heat of the day. Many plants are susceptible to leaf scorch if the leaves are soaked when in strong sun. Also, some water will evaporate before it can penetrate the soil.

If you have timed watering devices, set the timer to early morning or late evening.

Special watering needs

If you grow plants in containers, you will have to pay special attention to their need for moisture. Terra-cotta pots are very porous and moisture quickly evaporates. You can help preserve the moisture content of the compost by mulching the top of the pots with gravel. Hanging baskets are especially vulnerable to moisture loss. In really hot weather, water them twice a day.

Reviving a wilted plant (above) *Plunge the plant into a bucket of water until bubbles stop rising to the surface.*

SPECIAL WATERING NEEDS

Plants growing in full sun (except those originating from Mediterranean or hot climates) need to be watered more frequently than those in shade. Plants with larger leaves require more water than those with smaller leaves, and plants in containers dry out particularly fast.

Small leaves *Small-leaved plants need less watering than those with large leaves, but all container plants need frequent watering.*

Large leaves *The large surface area of these leaves means that moisture is lost quickly. Position the plant so that watering is easy.*

Containers *Position containers in groups. This makes watering less of a chore, especially in hot weather when frequent watering is required.*

Using a soaker hose system

During the height of summer, the job of watering the garden can seem never-ending, and half an hour after the hose has been put away the plants look dry again. By installing a soaker hose system around your garden, you can help to minimize the work involved.

You can limit the time spent watering by making sure the plants actually get the water intended for them, delivered to the place from which they can benefit most. This is particularly important if your water is metered.

Sprays may only soak the surface before the water starts to evaporate or run into the drains.

Low-level watering systems (pipes laid along the ground) delivers the water very close to the plants' roots and requires only a low-pressure water supply. This means that large areas can be watered at low pressure, because the water only seeps out of the pipe when the pipe is full; this slow, steady delivery allows the water to penetrate the soil with little evaporation. This system can be activated by a timing device, so that the garden can be watered even when there is no one at home. Set it for dawn watering; night watering provides the ideal conditions for nocturnal slugs and snails.

In a larger garden, install the soaker hose in an area where the plants are most vulnerable. To avoid wasting water, you need to find ways to conserve water in the garden. Try to choose plants that survive with minimal watering. However, if you have a vegetable garden, for example, where regular and copious watering is essential, you will have to install a suitable watering system.

Remember to install a water butt so that you can catch any rainwater and deliver it to the areas or plants that need it most. For example, acid-loving plants in containers should be watered with rainwater rather than tap water if the latter has a lot of lime in it (you will know this if limescale is a problem).

Watering the roots (above) *A soaker hose system allows water to get straight to the plants' roots, where it is most needed.*

FINAL CHECK

Before switching on the system, check the pipe carefully.

It is important to even out any twists or kinks in the pipe. If these are left, the pipe will "snake" or creep as it fills with water, or in some instances, water flow may be restricted.

INSTALLING A SOAKER HOSE

Tools and materials

- heavy-gauge plastic-coated wire
- good-quality knife
- broom handle
- vice or work bench
- soaker hose
- container
- timing device (optional)

1 *Cut sections of heavy-gauge plastic-coated wire into 10 in. lengths. Bend these sections until they are roughly straight and, using a broom handle and a vise or work bench, trap the middle of the wire to prevent it from moving.*

2 *Bend the wire around the broom handle twice to form a loose spiral, so that the top of the wire peg can be "threaded" over the soaker hose at any point along its length.*

3 *Thread the wire loops onto the seephose and lay out the piping to get the maximum amount of water possible to each plant (for established shrubs, position the pipe within 6–12 in. of the base).*

4 *Peg the pipe into position and connect it to a water supply, such as a hose with connectors. Gently turn on the tap to allow the water to flow through the pipes, and check carefully for any large, unintended leaks.*

5 *About two-thirds of the way along the run of pipe, insert a container into the soil below the pipe so that its rim is level with the soil surface. This can be used to measure the water flow per hour, lifting up the container slightly to check.*

6 *To make the system fully automatic, a battery-powered timing device can be fitted to the water supply. This will make it possible for the watering system to work even when you are on vacation.*

Feeding

Before feeding your plants, you need to decide whether or not you wish to follow organic principles. If you do, you will need to use organic fertilizers only. These are obtained from "natural" waste of plants and animals: rotted-down leaves and plants, or the excrement (often with bedding) of animals and birds (mostly horses and chickens, because the mix of manure to bedding is not too rich).

Whether or not you choose to limit yourself to organic feeds is a matter of personal choice. If you are happy using ordinary fertilizers, there are some suitable for every plant and situation. If you do choose to use manure as an organic feed, it will need time to rot down before being applied to the soil. The bulk supplied by the bedding helps to improve the soil structure; it also dilutes the quantities of nitrogen in the manure itself.

Because of this, bulky plant foods are normally added in autumn, to give them time to break down over winter. Feeding programs with fertilizers usually begin in early spring, when most plants are emerging from winter dormancy. They are then fed throughout the growing period. Watering is essential during this time, as the feeds need to be absorbed into the water that the plant takes up. Applications are usually given about once a month.

Plant "pick-me-ups"

In addition to regular feeds, you will also need plant "pick-me-ups" from time to time. These boost plant vigor at certain times, such as during the flowering or fruiting periods. They are the plant equivalent of a vitamin drink. These are most rapidly absorbed in liquid form, and you can make your own organic "teas" if you wish. The most well known is "blackjack," a concoction made from rotted animal manure.

MAKING BLACKJACK

Blackjack is an excellent, nutritious plant "pick-me-up," which is very useful during flowering or fruiting periods. Although it is not sweet-smelling, your plants will be very grateful for an application.

1 *To create blackjack, you will first need a quantity of animal manure that has been well rotted down.*

2 *Add some soot (which provides nitrogen) and wood ash (good for potassium) to the manure. Put the mixture into a plastic-net bag.*

3 *Seal the bag carefully and suspend in a barrel of rainwater. Leave it in position for several weeks.*

4 *Once the solution is ready, decant it as required into a watering can, diluting it to the color of weak tea, and apply it to your plants.*

MAKING STRAW COMPOST

Old straw makes excellent bulky organic matter to incorporate into the soil to help improve drainage, moisture retention, and general fertility.

Alternatively, it can be used as an organic mulch; spread it over the soil surface to preserve moisture and suppress weeds.

This layer will be gradually incorporated into the soil by the activity of worms, bacteria, and other soil-borne organisms.

1 *Cover the base of the area with 12 in. of loose straw. Soak the straw with water.*

2 *Sprinkle a light covering of nitrogenous fertilizer over the straw to speed up decomposition.*

3 *Add another 12in. layer of loose straw to the stack, water it and add more fertilizer.*

4 *As the straw decomposes, it becomes covered in a white mold and resembles well-rotted manure.*

Feeding edible plants

When you are growing edible plants with very specific needs, the feeding program must be both well considered and balanced. In general, edible plants need particular nutrients at specific stages of development, especially when producing fruit.

In spring, supply your edible plants with a base dressing (see page 201) that contains plenty of nitrogen and phosphorus. At the secondary stage of growth, the plants can be given a boost with a top dressing (see page 201) of similar nutrients. Later, when the plant is producing fruit, for example, you can give it another extra boost of nutrients using a liquid feed containing plenty of potassium. You can use an organic preparation, such as blackjack (see opposite), or a propriety feed, such as a tomato fertilizer, a popular feed that is useful as a "pick-me-up" for all types of plants.

Composting straw

You can add straw to your existing compost heap, or allow it to rot down in a heap of its own. To do this, make up a heap of straw in layers about 6 in. deep. As you add each layer, water it and sprinkle with a nitrogen-rich fertilizer. Over the next few months, periodically turn over the heap, turning in toward the middle. After this, the compost should be ready to add to the soil as a bulk feed.

Foliar feeds

These liquid feeds are extremely useful for adding a quick burst of nutrients when your plants are in full growth. Liquid feeds are usually easier to apply than granular fertilizers, and the plants often respond quite quickly to such treatment. Concentrated foliar feeds can be purchased in liquid or powder form and then diluted according to the specific manufacturer's instructions.

Spray leaves in either the morning or evening, but not in full sun, as they may scorch. Most feeding will be needed prior to flowering or fruiting. The composition of feed will be determined accordingly: for example, fruiting plants need more potassium than flowers. Do not apply the feed during wet weather or when rain is forecast, as it may be washed away before it gets to work. You can direct foliar feeds to areas of the plant that need an extra boost.

Granular feed (above) *Avoid touching foliage with granular feeds, because they can scorch the plant.*

Foliar feed (left) *Apply foliar feeds directly to the leaves, paying special attention to any areas that look in particular need of help.*

Weeding

Every gardener faces an ongoing struggle against unwanted plants—
weeds—that always grow much more vigorously than those that
have been carefully selected. Whatever your style of gardening,
you will spend some time weeding.

There is no real definition of a weed except that, in gardening terms, it is a plant in the wrong place! Some garden perennials self-seed so vigorously that they become weeds; other plants grow too exuberantly because the conditions simply happen to be absolutely right for them. Some so-called weeds—stinging nettles, for example—benefit wildlife and should be tolerated (in controlled circumstances) just for that purpose. A patch of nettles behind the garden shed does not affect the look of your garden and provides valuable food for the caterpillars. On the other hand, the gardener needs to guard diligently against long tap-rooted perennial weeds, such as thistles, docks, and dandelions, and spreaders, such as ground elder and couch grass, which will regrow from the tiniest piece of root.

You can employ various tactics to suppress and eliminate weeds, including some drastic means involving chemicals (such as glyphosate); undoubtedly, though, the best way to weed is laboriously, by hand, with great patience.

Clearing ground

Virgin ground must be cleared of all perennial weeds before any attempt is made to grow ornamental or edible plants. Failure to do so adequately, or with sufficient care, will cause considerable problems later on, as the roots of the more rampant weeds will render any attempt to tend the garden plants virtually impossible.

In order to clear the ground, you will need to dig over the soil and then patiently fork through it, picking out every piece of root. You can only do this on fairly heavy soil when the conditions are right: if the ground is too wet, the roots will remain stuck in a ball of soil, and you will not be able to separate them. The best time for such thorough weeding is usually two or three days after the last rain, because if the ground is too dry, a similar problem occurs, only this time the soil is rock hard.

Periodically, you will come across weeds that have a particularly determined root system, usually those with one large, long tap root which appears unending. Thistles and dandelions are common offenders in this category. The only solution for these is to loosen the soil around the root until you can remove it.

DEALING WITH PERENNIAL WEEDS

When you have removed perennial weeds, take them away from the ground you are clearing before allowing them to dry thoroughly and then discarding them. Never add perennial weeds to the compost heap.

1 *Established perennial weeds can be very difficult to eradicate, because the smallest piece of root can develop into a new plant.*

2 *Use a garden fork to work over an area and gently ease the roots out so that they are not broken.*

3 *Using a glove (especially for prickly weeds like thistles), pull the weeds out of the soil with as much root as possible.*

Many of the most troublesome lawn weeds are those which have a rosette or spreading habit and a long tap root.

If you spot them early, they can be removed with a sharp knife, or a blade with a forked tip called a 'daisy grubber'.

1 *Start by inserting the tip of the blade into the soil at a steep angle, about 2 in. away from the center of the weed.*

2 *Push the blade into the soil toward the weed to a depth of about 6 in. Try not to cut through the root, or it will regrow.*

3 *Lever the blade upward to remove the weed and root. For soft soil, rest the base of the blade on a block of wood to stop it sinking.*

4 *Once you have finished, collect the weeds and dispose of them. Do not add them to your compost heap.*

Annual weeds

On cultivated land, you will inevitably find a fresh crop of annual weeds when warmth and rain combine to encourage seeds to germinate. This is one of the main reasons you need to tackle weeds promptly, to remove them before they flower and set seed.

Your best time to deal with these weeds is when they are approximately 2 in. high. The quickest way for you to remove them on a vegetable plot is with a hoe, a long-handled tool with a short blade (see page 61). The short blade allows you to run the hoe between rows of vegetables, for example, removing any annual weeds that spring up between the crops without disturbing the principal plants.

In extremely densely packed flower borders, you will find that the best method is to hand weed using a small border fork. Depending on the size of your garden and the amount of bare soil in it, from late spring to midsummer, you will have to spend some time each week weeding.

You will discover that it pays to keep bare soil covered by mulching it with organic or inorganic matter such as bark chips or gravel, or growing some groundcovering plants over the top.

If you have traditional borders, you will spend a considerable amount of your gardening time weeding.

Weed killers are available, but for planted areas, the safest method is to weed by hand.

1 *Long, trailing annual weeds can be removed by gathering up the top growth and then pulling up the root system to clear the area.*

2 *For small groups of weed seedlings, use an onion hoe to chop out the weeds.*

3 *For small weeds that have a tap root, use a hand fork to ease the whole root out of the ground without breaking it.*

CREATIVE MULCHING

It is all too easy to be put off by the idea of garden maintenance. It is true that some essential tasks are neither interesting nor much fun, but this is not always so. The apparently dull task of mulching your soil can be an opportunity to think creatively and add a personal decorative touch to your garden.

Covering the bare soil of the garden with some kind of mulch (inorganic or organic matter that helps to conserve moisture and suppress weeds) is one of the most important labor-saving devices in the garden. The choice of materials is very wide: some are just attractive, while others, although less attractive, help to cut down the work involved in weeding

and watering. Among the commonly used inorganic materials are pebbles, shells, gravel and sand, and black plastic (best covered with something more aesthetically pleasing). Among the best organic materials are bark chips, composted straw (not very attractive, but useful in the vegetable garden) and various animal waste and straw combinations.

Any layer of mulch needs to be thick enough to help prevent weeds from germinating and moisture evaporating (normally about 3–4 in.), and those that are heavy enough not to blow around last the longest. You can use more than one material to cover the surface, and interesting patterns can be created with different-sized gravel and pebbles.

Mulches are usually in position for a long time, if not indefinitely, so think about how the materials will affect the look of your garden. Inorganic materials can have a dramatic impact on the color scheme and feel. Look for unusual shapes and textures, such as sea shells, slate, or attractive pebbles, and choose colors to enhance your plants: slate-grays and blues can look marvelous against bright green foliage, for example. You can also incorporate elements that have special relevance to you—such as stone from your local area. The key is to achieve a look with which you are happy, and not to despair that your garden needs to be covered over. Let your creative side loose and your mulched beds can be beautiful.

Pruning

This technique causes more consternation among gardeners than any other. The whole point of pruning is to improve the plant's shape or performance and also to control growth. In order to do this, you need to have some understanding of basic botany.

Once you grasp the principles, you will be able to relate the techniques to a range of different plants in your garden.

You also need to be aware that books on pruning have mainly been written by dedicated enthusiasts determined to get the absolute maximum performance from the plant. If you are not looking for show quality but simply a reasonable performance from the particular plant, you can be less stringent about your pruning techniques.

Controlling vigour

If your main goal in pruning is to control a plant's excessive growth, you might need instead to consider the suitability of the plant for its setting. Why grow a giant that puts on large amounts of growth each year if you do not have the space to let it have its head? A hedge of Leyland cypresses that have had their tops chopped off is a pitiful sight, since they do not look attractive once they have lost their conical shape. If you want a 6-ft. high hedge,

you are better off exercising patience and choosing slower-growing plants that can be kept to this height without too much difficulty.

In fact, with many shrubs, pruning *promotes* rather than reduces growth; so although you may succeed in reducing the size of the shrub in the season you prune it, the next year you may be faced with an even more vigorous specimen that bears more shoots.

Principles of pruning

The main thing to understand is that plants have a built-in reproductive system that works as follows: if you cut off the plant's leading shoot (from which it will eventually form flowers and seeds), you set in a motion a secondary system, whereby the branches lower down are galvanized into activity to do the work of the removed leading shoot. As you can probably visualize, this then changes the shape of the plant from one with a strong, tall central stem to one with a more branching appearance, which you may prefer.

If you follow this principle on an apple tree, you will find that if you remove the leading shoot, you

Close-up of well-pruned stem (below) *Twining stems of plants such as wisteria can only twist around supports of up to 1 in. diameter and need to be tied to thicker supports that they are unable to grip.*

Well-pruned climber (right) *Cut all ties and prune out any unwanted wood before tying the stems into place.*

DEADHEADING

If you remove dead flowers regularly, thereby preventing them from forming seeds, you will encourage sideshoots to flower.

Trimming spent flowers *Remove these using either a good pair of garden scissors or sharp shears. This will improve the appearance of the plant and prolong the flowering season, because new buds are encouraged to form.*

get more secondary shoots. If the fruit grows on these secondary shoots, you increase the opportunity for more fruit to grow. The same applies to plants grown for their flowers: you increase the shooting ability of the plant and inevitably increase its flowering performance. In order to create a strong framework of branches, you need to prune every year.

When to prune

Some shrubs produce their flowers on the current season's new wood, others on the wood made in previous seasons. To make matters more complicated, not every species in a particular genus performs in the same way. For example, in the Buddleia genus, orange ball tree (*Buddleia globosa*) needs barely any pruning, summer lilac (*B. davidii*) flowers on new season's wood and should be pruned in early spring, and fountain butterflybush (*B. alternifolia*) flowers on the previous year's wood and should be pruned after flowering in summer. The right timing is crucial to ensuring that you promote the growth of the new shoots that will bear the current season's flowers.

The best times to prune, therefore, are after flowering on any plant that will flower the following year on the growth made this year; for plants that flower on the current season's growth, no later than the end of winter or early spring. If you get this timing the wrong way round, and prune a plant that flowers on the previous season's growth in late winter or early spring, you will remove the current season's crop of flowers and have to wait a year for the next display.

Reasons for pruning

The major reasons for pruning a tree or shrub are to increase the fruiting or flowering performance or to improve the health and vigor of a plant. It is also done to make the shape of the plant more pleasing.

Plants that have been subjected to difficult growing conditions tend to be more prone to disease, and these problems can also be introduced by injury. It therefore makes good sense to prune back hard if the plant has suffered because of the climate or as a result of some other problem, and to remove broken or damaged shoots before any viral or infectious diseases can take advantage of the exposed tissue. Such shoots are best removed close to the main stem in a cut that is angled outwards, to allow any water to drain off rather than soak into the plant.

Young apple tree (below)
A well-staked young tree, showing the unpruned growth put on during the first year after planting.

Pruning trees and shrubs

The main goal when growing trees and shrubs is to create a really good shape that both looks attractive and also encourages air circulation around the branches, because this helps to counteract disease. If you are growing fruit trees, pruning can also be used to improve the quality and quantity of fruit produced.

Many trees and shrubs have a naturally balanced, attractive habit and the advantage of requiring only a little pruning. Generally, evergreens belong in this category and require far less pruning than their deciduous counterparts; this may be something to consider when deciding which trees and shrubs you want to include in your garden, especially if the time you have to dedicate to maintenance is limited.

Tree pruning

By and large, major tree pruning is best left to tree surgeons. The main reason for this is that if you get it wrong, you are left with an eyesore. The branches are also large and heavy, and you can injure yourself or a bystander, if you make a mistake. The general rule should be that if you have a well-established, mature tree of a reasonable size, you should consult a tree surgeon. However, removing diseased or damaged branches from smaller trees is well within the capabilities of most gardeners.

Deciduous trees are normally pruned in late autumn or winter, when they are dormant. This applies especially to birch (*Betula*) and maple: the sap will bleed if these trees are pruned during the growing season, so

PRUNING GROUPS

Plants are pruned according to their pruning group. Plants in group 1 are deciduous shrubs that require little pruning when mature. Plants in group 2 are deciduous shrubs that flower on the previous season's growth and are pruned after flowering. Plants in group 3 bear flowers on the current season's growth and are pruned in early spring.

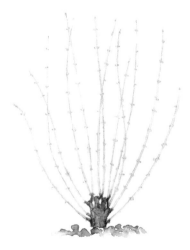

Group 1 (above) *Plants in this group require no regular pruning other than removing any dead, diseased, or dying wood when it appears, and lightly pruning the old flowering shoots.*

Group 2 (above) *These plants require pruning to remove old flower-bearing wood straight after flowering has finished, giving as much time as possible for next year's flowers to grow.*

Group 3 (above) *Plants in this group are pruned hard in early spring, back to a framework of older wood from which the new shoots will emerge.*

prune them when they are fully dormant. When the trees are young, pruning will help to establish a balanced shape. For more mature trees, you should only prune to maintain the shape you have and to encourage growth. Removing any thin or crossing branches from the main structure of the tree will allow light and air into the center of the framework.

Some evergreen trees, such as some magnolias, do not need to be pruned at all. If they do need pruning, it should be done in late spring. If the tree is immature, you can encourage a strong central stem by training a vertical shoot upward and removing competing leaders. With well-established evergreens, simply remove any weak or unshapely branches by cutting back to a healthy shoot.

Shaping shrubs

Most deciduous shrubs will gradually become weaker and less attractive if left to their own devices. Getting a good open shape is an important element in pruning shrubs. The main goal is to remove any branches that cross over and rub each other, because these will almost certainly allow diseases to penetrate the plant. You also need to encourage the branches to fan outward, rather than turn inward. To do this, you should make any pruning cuts just above outward-facing buds. If the buds grow in pairs, though, simply cut the stem straight across just above the pair.

In addition to the cosmetic benefits of pruning, you will also encourage the shrub to flower, and you may even prolong its life.

CORRECTING UNEVEN GROWTH

Many plants grow unevenly if there is one principal light source that is not overhead. To correct this, prune the shrub as shown here.

Unbalanced growth (left)
Prune the less strongly growing side of the shrub more heavily. This encourages new growth on the weaker side to balance the shape.

New, even growth (right)
Once you have evened out the shrub, continue pruning in the appropriate manner, according to its pruning group.

PRUNING AN EVERGREEN

Generally speaking, evergreens need little pruning compared with deciduous shrubs.

However, as with all shrubs, young plants benefit from encouragement to form a good branching structure and evenly spaced lateral stems. In the first year after planting, prune the leading shoot to encourage a stronger system of sideshoots to form. Thereafter, you only need to remove weak or damaged shoots, or clip the bush lightly all over.

Pruned camellia (right) *A young camellia that has been pruned to encourage the sideshoots to grow more strongly.*

PRUNING TIMES FOR COMMON DECIDUOUS SHRUBS

Spring

Buddleja davidii

Caryopteris × clandonensis

Ceanothus 'Gloire de Versailles'

Cornus alba

Cotinus

Fuchsia (hardy cultivars)

Hydrangea paniculata

Lavatera

Perovskia

Sorbaria

Spiraea japonica

Summer

Chaenomeles

Deutzia

Exochorda

Kerria

Kolkwitzia

Philadelphus

Ribes sanguineum

Stephanandra

Syringa

Weigela

Pruning and training climbers

Climbing plants pose more pruning problems than shrubs, because in addition to the normal pruning requirements you need to make sure that the climbers grow in the direction you prefer and do not wander off into the neighbor's garden or away from the rest of your scheme.

Most climbing plants have a natural tendency to reach for the light, with the result that they flower at the top of increasingly long stems, which may not be the look you intended. You may also prefer to prevent the plant from heading straight for the roof of the house and filling the gutters. Your view of the flowers then becomes rather limited, so the chief aim when pruning and training climbers is to persuade the plant to produce flowering stems lower down where they can be appreciated. Generally, this is done by creating a fan shape and encouraging the spread of horizontal branches, as opposed to purely vertical ones.

Some climbers are notoriously vigorous and demand quite considerable pruning effort. For this reason, wisteria is not a plant for the faint-hearted gardener (see below). The Bhukara fleeceflower (*Polygonum baldschuanicum*) is frequently recommended for covering unsightly views quickly, but its common name is "mile-a-minute," and this is really not much of an exaggeration; it is best to avoid this plant unless you are prepared to spend a lot of time pruning.

How climbers grow

The amount of work demanded of the gardener depends on the natural habit of the plant. Some climbers attach themselves to any support with no help from the gardener. These are the plants that have aerial roots or small suckers that fix on to any surface. Others, such as many rambling roses, will scramble over suitable supports using the thorns on their stems.

Wisteria stem (above)

If twining stems are allowed to wrap around one another, the inner stems may become strangled as a result of the pressure exerted by the outer ones.

PRUNING WISTERIA

These vigorous climbers need to be cut back fairly severely.

Young lateral shoots not needed for the framework of the plant are cut back annually in midwinter.

1 *Start by untwining any tangled shoots and stems. These may need to be cut out in sections to prevent other shoots from being damaged.*

2 *Space the remaining shoots to give an even covering over as much of the support as possible. Tie shoots to be used as part of the plant's framework into position.*

3 *Cut back long lateral growths which are not to be used as part of the framework to just above a bud, 6–8 in. from where they emerge from the stem.*

4 *Tie as many shoots as possible into a horizontal position, to help to cover the frame and encourage flowering. Fix the ties into a figure-eight around the stem and supports.*

PRUNING CLEMATIS

Clematis are deservedly popular, but tend to confuse the amateur pruner.
The key is to understand their flowering habit.

Year 1 pruning
To encourage a stronger, more bushy habit, cut back newly planted clematis to two buds.

Year 2 pruning *Shorten the growths to about half, cutting back to a pair of strong buds. Do this in mid- to late winter. Train in any new stems to horizontal wires.*

Year 3 pruning *Prune group 1 clematis (spring-flowering) in midsummer to within two or three buds of the framework. Prune group 2 (summer- and autumn-flowering on new wood) down to the lowest pair of strong buds in early spring. For group 3, cut one-third of the stems to within 1 ft. of the ground.*

The largest number of climbers belong to the twining group, and these do their work through twining tendrils, leaf petioles, or stems. The latter group need suitable poles or wires around which they can weave themselves, with enough space in between the supports for them to bend their entire stems around them. In contrast, plants that climb using twining tendrils or leaf petioles can support themselves happily on thin wires that are relatively closely spaced.

In their formative year or years, most twining climbers need the gardener's help in order to establish themselves on their support. It is therefore important to tie them in loosely to the support structure, using ties that are both soft enough and loose enough not to damage any delicate stems.

CLEMATIS GROUPS

If you wish, you can have a clematis in flower almost all year round, but the appropriate pruning treatment for each type depends on their flowering season. Botanists have grouped them accordingly, and this will help you determine the pruning season.

Group 1 clematis flower in spring on the previous year's growth, and should be pruned immediately after flowering.

C. alpina
C. armandii
C. cirrhosa
C. macropetala
C. montana

Group 2 clematis flower in early summer on the previous year's shoots, and again in late summer and autumn on the current season's growth, so prune them in early spring.

Large-flowered cultivars, including:
'Barbara Dibley'
'Elsa Spath'
'Lasurstern'
'Marie Boisselot'
'Nelly Moser'
'The President'
'Vyvyan Pennell'

Group 3 are the late-flowering clematis that bloom on the current season's growth, and they, too, should be pruned in early spring.

Late-flowering species and hybrids, including:
'Comtesse de Bouchaud'
'Ernest Markham'
'Gipsy Queen'
'Hagley Hybrid'
'Jackmanii'
'Niobe'
'Perle d'Azur'
C. tangutica
'Ville de Lyon'
C. viticella

Pruning and training roses

One of the all-time favorite plants, popular in many styles of gardens, roses are actually often ill-treated by the gardener, due to a lack of understanding of their needs. There are many different types of roses, as breeders over the centuries have perfected hybrids of many different kinds, and the different types perform in different ways. To get the best out of the roses in your garden, you need to know which group your rose belongs to, as this will determine the right way to treat it. The different groups of roses include; bush roses (hybrid tea and floribunda), shrub and species roses, climbers, and ramblers. Climbers flower at least twice a year, ramblers only once.

Most bush and shrub roses form a fairly wide-spreading plant about 5 ft. tall. Generally speaking, they require no special pruning different from any other deciduous, summer-flowering shrub. You can prune them in late autumn or very early spring.

Climbing roses

Climbing roses are popular but their pruning needs cause many headaches. There are several different groups, each demanding different pruning techniques.

The first group is the ramblers, which are vigorous, flower on old wood, and produce new canes from the base. Generally, the best system of

PRUNING A RAMBLER

The best time to prune rambling roses is in late summer, when the old flowering shoots can still be seen and the new shoots are growing rapidly.

1 *After flowering in summer, remove some of the older, unproductive stems with a saw. Cut long sections into smaller pieces in order to do this.*

2 *Trim back the young growths to four or five buds. These will produce new shoots that carry the following year's flowers.*

3 *Tie in some of the long, vigorous shoots with string. These will act as replacements for the old growths you removed.*

REJUVENATING A ROSE

Left to their own devices, roses that are neglected and left unpruned will usually flower for many years, but eventually the plant becomes a tangled mass of dead stems and diseased leaves with small, badly shaped flowers.

Fortunately, most roses are tough and will respond well to severe (rejuvenation) pruning.

Removing suckers (above) *It is important to remove suckers from the rootstock before pruning.*

Cutting back (above) *Cut damaged wood and half the live stems to ground level.*

Frame (above) *Cut side shoots on remaining stems to three or four buds, leaving a frame to support new growth.*

New growth (above) *As the plant grows, the new stems may need thinning out to prevent overcrowding.*

pruning is simply to cut out the old wood from the base (about one-third each year in winter), encouraging the new wood to grow and flower. A subsidiary group of ramblers produces few new stems, so these are normally pruned back in late summer to a framework where a new leader is developing. Repeat-flowering ramblers flower on new shoots. They are normally pruned in early autumn by removing all but 6 in. of the laterals that have flowered.

Another group of pillar roses are pruned similarly in late autumn, but some of the oldest stems will need to be cut out and some of the new lateral growth pruned back to improve the shape. Finally, the species roses, such as *Rosa filipes* 'Kiftsgate', are so vigorous that pruning defeats most people. Plant them where they have space to wander!

Bush roses

Hybrid teas and floribunda roses are pruned in late spring, cutting back new shoots to 6 in. and shortening laterals on remaining wood. On older plants, some old wood may need to be removed.

Standard roses

Roses that are grown as standards have been trained with a crown of spreading stems. These stems then form a flowering canopy above the long clear stem.

Suckers (left) *Remove any suckering shoots by carefully digging the soil from the base of the sucker and tearing the sucker away by hand. This will rip out not only the sucker stem, but also all of the dormant buds around its base.*

Root pruning

Root pruning is sometimes used to control very vigorous trees and shrubs and to make them produce more flowers. The technique is particularly useful for over-vigorous fruit trees that are producing growth at the expense of fruit; however, this is not a very common problem, because so many varieties are grown on dwarfing rootstocks.

This pruning technique works because certain chemicals that occur in the roots of plants actually influence the rate of growth and the spread of the branches. By removing sections of root, the manufacture and supply of these chemicals is restricted, which in turn has the effect of curtailing the development and extension of the branches.

If you are growing vigorous plants in containers, you may need to trim back the roots to keep the plant at a manageable size. The aim when doing this is to remove only one-third of the roots. More drastic pruning than this is likely to cause permanent damage to the plant. If the plant is exceptionally vigorous, it may not be suitable for container growing. The frequency with which you will have to carry out root pruning depends entirely on the speed of growth of the plant. The best time to root-prune a container plant is fall, when the plant is dormant.

If you are root pruning a tree, the best time to do this is in fall or winter. The technique is simple. All you need to do is mark out an area in a circle around the circumference of the tree immediately below the current spread of the canopy. This will then limit the future size of the canopy to this, because there is a direct relationship between root spread and canopy size. If you then dig a trench around the circumference of this circle and sever the main roots, you effectively stop further spread of the tree for a period of three or four years.

Firming the soil (right)

After pruning the roots, make sure that the surrounding soil is tamped in well.

ROOT PRUNING

Tools and materials

- garden twine
- awl or twig
- spade
- pruning saw or shears

1 *Loosely tie a good length of garden twine to the trunk of the tree, and tie the other end to an awl or sharp twig.*

2 *Moving back from the tree, pull the twine taut until you are standing just outside the canopy. Then, using the twine like a compass, mark out a circle on the ground immediately below the spread of the canopy.*

3 *Using the circle you have marked out as a guide, dig a trench around the tree. This should be about 18 in. wide and 2 ft. deep.*

4 *Set aside the topsoil as you dig, because you will need to replace it later.*

5 *Carefully expose all of the thick tree roots. Using a pruning saw or shears, cut out entire sections of exposed roots. This will prevent the canopy from extending any farther.*

6 *Finally, refill the trench around the tree with topsoil. Firm it in well using the heel of your boot or shoe.*

Maintaining hedges

The main purpose of clipping is to produce a hedge of the desired height and width that is well furnished with growth over the entire surface. If a hedge is pruned and trimmed correctly in the early stages of development, there is no need for it to exceed 2½ ft. in width—this applies to even the most vigorous species of hedging plants.

Limiting the width of the hedge is particularly important; the wider the hedge is allowed to become, the more difficult it is to trim (especially the top) and the more space it occupies. The sloping angle of the hedge is called the "batter." Creating this batter will expose all parts of the hedge to the light and stop parts of it from dying; this is especially important at the base.

Clipped hedges should always be narrower at the top than at the base to make trimming easier. If the hedge is wider at the top than at the base, it is prone to damage by strong winds, because it is top-heavy and the branches are opened up. If the top is flat, snow settling and accumulating on the top of the hedge can cause the branches to splay out, resulting in considerable damage to the branches. This is a much greater problem with evergreen species, because they can collect large quantities of snow and ice in winter. The answer is to have a rounded top to the hedge.

Low hedging (below) *This hedge must be kept low or it will obscure the plants on either side of the border.*

TIP

When the hedge has reached its required height, cut the top down to 1 ft. below this height. The top of the hedge will then grow bushy and strong as it responds to pruning. You will not see any woody stumps from the pruning cuts or sections of bare stem, because they will be hidden by the new growth.

EVERGREEN HEDGES

For broad-leaved evergreen hedges to look really good after trimming, they should be clipped to remove any damaged leaves.

Any leaves that are cut in half by shears or a hedge trimmer will usually turn yellow and die within a few weeks. The cut edges of these leaves are very susceptible to fungal attacks, which may spread into the healthy tissue.

TRIMMING A HEDGE

Tools and materials

- hedge trimmer or shears
- posts or canes
- garden twine
- pruning saw or shears

1 *Start at the bottom to establish the ideal width required, and then work upward, allowing the clippings to fall out of the way as they are cut. This makes it easier to see where to cut next.*

2 *When cutting with an electric hedge trimmer, cut upward in a sweeping, arc-like motion, and keep the cutting blade parallel to the hedge. Only cut what can be reached comfortably without stretching.*

3 *To achieve a level top to the hedge, insert two posts or tall canes into the ground beside (or inside) the hedge and stretch a length of twine taut between them at a predetermined height.*

4 *If you need to cut around a corner, insert a third post and stretch the twine around to continue the line. It is important to make sure that the line stays at the correct height throughout. You can also use this technique to create a sloping hedge if you like.*

5 *Cut the hedge in sections, checking the line at regular intervals to ensure the correct level is achieved neatly all along the top. Use twine that is brightly colored, as this makes it much easier to follow the line without cutting through it.*

6 *For thicker stems, use a pruning saw rather than a hedge trimmer, because the trimmer may jam while cutting through thick stems.*

1

2

3

4

5

6

Supporting plants

A number of your plants will need support of one form or another, either to keep them upright and protect them from strong winds and rain while they are young and not yet established, or simply to display their flowers to best advantage.

The plants most in need of support are soft-stemmed perennials and climbing plants. You may also need to support plants that have particularly heavy flowerheads. Young plants will often benefit from some sort of additional support. The type of support required will be determined by the habit of the plant.

TYPES OF STAKES

Below are the basic stakes available.

Stout wood stakes (for trees) with pointed ends for driving into the soil can be bought in varying sizes to suit the size of the tree. They must be driven well into the ground to provide a suitable anchor, and they must be positioned close to the plant.

Bamboo canes are suitable for perennials and small shrubs. Buy small stoppers to put on the cane ends to prevent eye injuries.

Link stakes are metal stakes that can be linked together to form a circle. These are suitable for staking clumps of perennials.

Supporting perennials, bulbs, and annuals

Soft-stemmed herbaceous plants will require help to ensure that the wind does not cause delicate stems to snap, particularly when they are in flower. There are various staking options, and much depends on the setting for the plants. In a border, where the plants are quite closely packed, the supports will not show and you can use supports that have little aesthetic appeal. Link stakes, which slot into each other to form a ring around the plant, are useful for this kind of job.

For plants in containers, which are normally on show, more attractive forms of staking are useful. You can use branching twigs inserted around the edge of

Free-standing supports (above)
Here, Clematis x durandii is growing over a free-standing hoop.

Individual supports (right)
Tall, heavy-headed perennials like delphiniums warrant individual stakes.

SUPPORTING A TREE

Most trees and shrubs only need staking or tying immediately after planting. This helps them establish
more rapidly by keeping the rootball firmly in place until new roots can spread out into the surrounding soil.
Here, a vertical stake is used; an alternative method using a slanting stake is shown on page 115.

1 *First, position the stake so that it is no more than 2–3 in. from the plant. Hammer it in until the top is about 6–8 in. above ground level.*

2 *Next, tie the tree to the stake, putting a spacer between the plant and the stake to prevent the stake from damaging the bark.*

3 *Position the tie about 1½ in. below the top of the stake. This will prevent the stem from flexing in the wind and hitting the top of the stake. Use a nail to fasten the tie to the stake.*

the container; these look more attractive than either link stakes or bamboo canes held together with string. Alternately, you can make your own supporting cage from supple stems such as dogwood or willow. Insert about eight stems around the edge of the pot and tie them at the top with raffia to make a feature of the support. This also works well with heavy-headed flowers that tend to flop over, such as hyacinths.

Supporting climbers

These need a variety of supports, ranging from simple wooden trellis to a system of wires secured on a fence or wall with vine eyes (see page 116). It is important to make sure that there is enough space for any twining climbers to wrap around the support, and it is always a good idea to attach any

trellis about 2 in. away from the wall. This will allow air to circulate freely around the plant.

Demountable trellises are extremely useful on painted walls, because they allow you to lay the trellis flat on the ground when you need to repaint. Hinges at the base of the trellis and catches at the top make this possible.

Supporting young plants

Young plants often need some kind of support to get established. Young trees should always be staked when planting to ensure that rocking winds do not disturb the roots and slow down growth. It also ensures that a strong vertical stem develops.

Climbers are best started with a small fan trellis to spread out the principal leading shoots and establish the eventual direction.

Young trees (above) *These benefit from support until they are well-established. This tie is too low down the stake—see pictures above.*

Pests

There are many pests that can affect the plants in your garden adversely. Some are broad-spectrum pests, attacking a whole range of plants; others are programmed to attack only certain species. The following is not an exhaustive list of every known pest, but covers some of those most commonly found. Control suggestions are given where possible.

Aphids (above) *These sap-sucking insects can be green, brown, or black.*

Caterpillars (below) *These larvae of butterflies and moths do particular damage to foliage, flowers, and seedpods.*

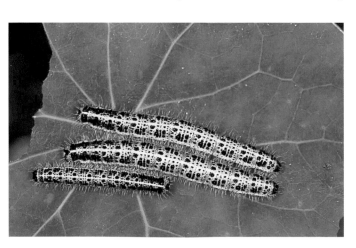

The most important element in pest control is to check your plants frequently and try to combat any infestation fast, before it has time really to catch hold. Some insects will simply cause a measure of damage to one plant; others will quickly destroy a whole crop. However, in general it is not in nature's interest to destroy the host plant, so most predator problems are annoyances rather than catastrophic. You will need to decide whether to treat problems organically or use chemical solutions.

Aphids

Aphids are green, brown, or black winged insects (occasionally in other colors, too) that suck the sap from new shoots. Warning signs of an aphid infestation include distorted shoot tips and new leaves. Aphids leave a sticky coating (honeydew), sometimes with accompanying black mold.

If you wish to treat an infestation organically, spray the plant with an insecticidal soap or simply wipe the aphids off the areas. For a chemical solution, try using a systemic insecticide, such as permethrin, at regular intervals.

Caterpillars

These are larvae of butterflies and moths. They have tubular bodies in different colors. Look out for holes in foliage, flowers, and seedpods. They can strip a whole

Earwig (above) *Small, shiny brown insects with pincerlike tails, they leave circular holes or notches in leaves and flowers.*

plant. Remove the pests by hand, or spray with permethrin if you prefer a chemical solution.

Earwigs

Earwigs are small, shiny brown insects with pincerlike tails that leave circular holes or notches in leaves and flowers. Balance upturned, straw-filled pots on canes. Leave them overnight and remove the pots (and trapped earwigs) in the morning. You can also spray with permethrin.

Spittlebugs

These small green insects suck sap and can be identified by frothy bubbles on the leaves and

Spittlebug (above) *Small, green, sap-sucking insects, these leave a bubble of froth on leaves and stems.*

Leaf miner (above) *These larvae can be identified by the lines left on leaves as they tunnel through them.*

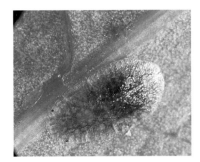

Scale insect (above) *These tiny insects produce a blister-like bump on leaves and stems.*

stems. Wipe the pests off by hand or spray with systemic insecticide if really necessary; otherwise, you can ignore spittlebugs.

Leaf miners

These tiny insect larvae tunnel through leaves and create wiggly lines. This is an aesthetic problem rather than a damaging pest. Remove affected leaves or, for a chemical solution, spray with malathion when first sighted.

Red spider mite

Red spider mites are tiny sap-sucking insects that cause stunted, curled, and finely mottled leaves. Keeping plants moist, particularly the undersides of the leaves, helps to prevent attacks. For an organic option, spray with an insecticidal soap. In greenhouses, use *Phytoseiulus*

persimilis as a biologicial control, or spray with malathion for a chemical solution.

Scale insects

These are tiny insects resembling brown, blister-like bumps on leaves and stems. Look for stunted growth and yellowed leaves, as well as a sticky coating on the lower leaves, sometimes with sooty mold. Introduce *Metaphycus* as a biological control, or spray with malathion at regular intervals in late spring and early summer.

Slugs and snails

These slimy molluscs feed at night or after rain. Holes appear in leaves, and stems may be stripped. Look for a silvery trail on the ground around the plant. Collect slugs and snails at night, or use sunken traps of beer to drown them. Apply a copper band to containers. For a chemical option, use slug pellets around the bases of plants. Biological control is also available using nematodes.

Red spider mite (left) *Tiny sap-sucking insects on the underside of leaves cause stunted, mottled foliage.*

Slugs and snails (above and left) *These leave a trail of slime and can do considerable damage, stripping leaves and stems.*

Thrips

These tiny, brownish-black insects gather on the upper surfaces of leaves and thrive in hot, dry conditions. They affect a wide range of ornamental and edible plants, in particular peas and onions. They produce a silvery discoloration with black dots on the upper leaf surfaces. Regular misting with water helps prevent attacks, and several chemicals can be used.

Thrips (below) *These affect a wide range of plants, producing a silver discoloration of the leaves.*

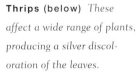

Diseases

Just like humans, plants are prone to diseases, particularly when they are not in good general health. The key to dealing with diseases is to do your best to ensure that your plants are provided with the optimum conditions in which to survive and thrive.

If you care for your plants, giving them the nutrients and conditions they need, they will be more resistant to diseases. Irregular feeding and watering will cause the plants stress, making them more susceptible. Another common feature of disease-prone plants is poor pruning cuts, where the tissue has been torn rather than cut through cleanly. This makes the site that much more attractive to invading organisms.

Some plants are tougher and more naturally resistant than others. Most do best when the environment they are grown in matches closely that of their natural habitat.

While chemical controls are often effective, a quick response using an organic treatment will often serve the same purpose; check your plants regularly for signs of good or ill health and act swiftly if you find a problem.

Botrytis (gray mold)

Look for discolored, yellowing leaves. Eventually the plant, or part of it, becomes covered with gray felt. Prune out affected parts and discard them. Improving air circulation around the plant will help. Spray with chlorothalonil when symptoms appear.

Canker (above) *This causes pitted areas of bark to form, primarily on fruit trees.*

Canker

This disease principally affects fruit trees. Pitted areas of bark can lead to stem dieback. Prune out affected branches; treat wounds with proprietary wound paint. Avoid susceptible fruit varieties.

Nectria canker

This fungus is most commonly found on dead wood, but it also affects live tissue, covering bark with small pink blisters. Prune out affected stems and discard.

Downy mildew

This is a fungus affecting leaves and stems. Symptoms include

Nectria canker (above) *Small pink blisters on the trunks and branches of trees indicate nectria canker.*

Downy mildew (above) *This is a fungal disease which causes discoloration on the underside of leaves.*

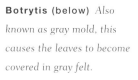

Botrytis (below) *Also known as gray mold, this causes the leaves to become covered in gray felt.*

Root rot (far left) *The first indication of root rot is often wilting of the upper parts of the plant.*

Rust (left) *A fungal disease that produces bright orange spots on the upper and under sides of leaves.*

discolored yellowing leaves with gray-white patches on the undersides. Improve air circulation and use resistant varieties where possible. For chemical control, spray with mancozeb. Remove and discard badly affected plants.

Fire blight

This bacterial disease affects trees and shrubs in the rose family. It attacks the soft tissue, causing blackened flowers, shriveled young shoots, and browning, wilting leaves. Remove and discard any affected plants. There is no known cure.

Powdery mildew

Look for floury white patches on leaves, distorted shoots, and premature leaf fall. Prune out the affected stems; if you wish to use chemicals, spray with fungicide at the first signs of infection.

Root rot

Often caused by poor growing conditions, such as wet or waterlogged soil or compost, the roots rot away and the top part of the plant wilts and dies. The situation can be improved by better drainage. Root rot can also often be caused by waterlogging and using unsterilized compost when planting in containers.

Rust

This is a fungal disease that particularly affects roses. Symptoms include bright orange spots on both the upper and lower sides of the leaves. Improve air circulation around the plant by pruning. For chemical control, spray regularly with mancozeb.

Viruses

Viruses are usually spread by sap-sucking insects. Look out particularly for distorted leaves and shoots, and yellow mottling or streaking on the leaves. There is no cure for viral infection. Remove and discard any plants that have been affected.

Powdery mildew (below left)
White patches on leaves and shoots indicate powdery mildew.

Viruses (below) *There are many viral disorders, spread mainly by sap-sucking insects.*

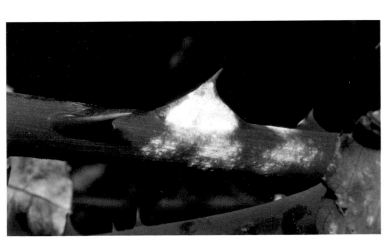

Maintaining a water feature

If running water is an element of your water feature, you will need to service the pumping system regularly in order to avoid blockages and other problems. In still ponds, you will need to clean out debris from the base every few years—more often if your pond is near deciduous trees.

Small water features

(below) *These can be very peaceful and are safer than ponds, especially if you have young children.*

Water features are incredibly popular. Running water has a soothing sound and provides movement and interest. Not everyone has a garden large enough to support a pond, or indeed wants one, as ponds can require a considerable amount of maintenance.

Ponds are not a good idea if there are young children in the family. However, it is possible to have a water feature which is perfectly safe with even very young children playing nearby. Smaller water features, such as child-friendly bubble fountains, will create interest and movement in the garden and require little or no maintenance. When the pump is going and water is running over the stones, some water will be lost through evaporation; check the level in the reservoir once a week throughout the summer. It is also important to keep in mind that the pump will need to be checked at least once a year (and preferably twice) to make sure that it is not clogged with silt and debris from the reservoir. However, even this can be reduced if you are prepared to pay slightly more for a pump that is "self-cleaning," giving you all the advantages of moving water with none of the drawbacks.

Every few years, the water feature will need to be drained to remove accumulated debris from around the pump. If weeds and algae have been a persistent problem, consider flushing a chemical algicide through the system to eradicate them, or install an ultraviolet filter to clean the water as it passes through.

LENGTHENING THE LIFE OF THE FILTER

A homemade solution involving a section of old panty hose will extend the life of your pond filter.

To give extra protection to the pump and reduce the risk of damage, simply cover the filter with a section cut from old panty hose. The fine mesh will block many of the particles that might otherwise block the filter. Remember that the filter may still need regular cleaning if the water is particularly dirty.

CLEANING A WATER FEATURE

1 Start by removing the outlet of the water feature—in this case, an urn—and place the latter carefully to one side (this will usually expose the water supply pipe).

2 Remove all the stones and pebbles from the surface of the water reservoir and place them in a container.

3 Lift the supporting grid off the reservoir to reveal the pump beneath.

4 Remove the filter from the pump and wash it thoroughly to remove any trapped debris. The best way to remove any sediment is to soak the filter and squeeze out the water, forcing the sediment out at the same time.

5 Wash the pebbles that cover the water reservoir using a hose. This will remove any accumulated dirt and debris before it is washed into the reservoir.

6 Clean the water outlet by scrubbing it with a coarse cloth. Finally, reassemble the water feature and test the pump.

Growing in containers

Container gardening

Containers open up a world of possibilities to the gardener. Owners of small gardens can plant pots that take advantage of even the tiniest space and that can be moved around as required. Whatever the size of your garden, you can use containers to decorate every surface, including walls and steps, or even to create a roof garden.

Seasonal plantings

(below) *Plan your plants so that you have some permanent structure (in the form of evergreens) with a changing seasonal display to add the high notes. These parrot tulips from spring can be replaced in summer with lilies, for example, and nerines in fall.*

To those with only limited space or who live in high-rise settings with balconies and roof terraces, planting in containers is the obvious solution. In fact, gardening in containers is not very different from traditional gardening; however, you do need to be aware that, unlike plants in the traditional garden, which can largely rely on nature for their basic needs, container-grown plants are heavily dependent on you. You will need to provide extra nutrients

regularly and, because containers dry out very quickly in hot weather, make sure that they receive regular and adequate quantities of water. Fast-growing plants will rapidly outgrow their containers, and you will either need to repot them every year or so or, once they reach the optimum size, prune the roots, which will slow growth. Otherwise, pruning, propagating, supporting, and general maintenance are the same as for soil-grown plants.

You can grow almost anything in containers, from edible plants to water-loving ones. You can even grow trees, but they will never reach the size they would in an unrestricted situation, simply because you will not be able to provide a container large enough for the full root span. While you are not obliged to opt for slow-growing trees and shrubs, it will mean less work for you if you do. Likewise, selecting drought-tolerant plants will cut down on

ROOTBALL RATIO
Choose the right pot for the plant and keep everything in proportion.

The best container size for any plant is one that is roughly 2 in. larger than the diameter of the rootball and roughly 4 in. deeper. After a year or so, depending on speed of growth, you will need to repot the plant into a larger container. Do not think that planting a small plant in a much larger container is a time-saving solution, as plants do best in containers only slightly larger than their rootball. Check regularly that the roots are not growing through the base of the pot. If they are, it is time to repot.

Using available space (left)
Here, a flight of steps is emphasized with a row of clipped box shapes.

Groupings (below) *Matching materials and shapes help give unity and form to the container planting.*

Country garden containers (below) *Lush and naturalistic container plants bring an area of hard surfacing to life in this traditional garden.*

the chore of watering in summer. Make sure that the compost is suitable for the plants you want to grow, and choose waterproof containers for any water plants.

If you have a bigger garden, containers provide the ideal opportunity to grow plants that would not normally flourish in your soil. Rhododendrons, for example, like acidic soil; if you live in an alkaline area, the easiest way to grow lime-hating plants is in containers filled with acidic compost.

Aesthetics

Many of the same principles apply to the design of a container-based garden as to that of a traditional one. Make sure that you have a good mix of evergreen and deciduous plants; build up displays, using staging if necessary, to provide color and interest at several levels; and choose some good foliage plants to provide either a backdrop to the flower color or relief from it. Evergreens clipped

into formal shapes provide structure in a container display. Box, privet, myrtle, holly, rosemary, and lavender are all ideal, although any evergreen with relatively small leaves will do.

SITING CONTAINERS

- *On balconies and roof terraces, place the heaviest containers over the major supports.*
- *Make sure that containers on windowsills cannot topple off in high winds. Add a lip support to the sill; chain windowboxes to the walls.*
- *Expensive containers (and topiary) can tempt thieves. Secure pots and plants with chains.*
- *Raise containers above wooden surfaces with "pot feet" or supports.*
- *Where possible, group containers for ease of maintenance.*

Choosing containers

The range of container types is vast, but if you wish to create a harmonious-looking display you will need to pay attention to the size and shape of the containers and the materials from which they are made. A mismatched selection of pots can look messy and unattractive. The container is at least as important as the plant, and just as much on view, so do not skimp on quality.

A splash of color (below)
Containers are not just for traditional gardens. Here the vibrant colors of the flowers and containers are in keeping with the bright blue wall.

Terra-cotta and stone are the most attractive options, along with metal and good-quality wood. Plastic, while lightweight and convenient, tends to look flimsy, and pure white is so bright that it dominates the planting scheme. Wire containers are a good lightweight alternative to plastic, although you will have to line them with moss to ensure that the compost stays in place. If you must go for plastic, buy it in dark green, or paint the containers with attractive "art" shades—sage-green, dusty blue, or soft violet—that provide an attractive foil for the plants.

Choosing a size

Container sizes vary from huge half-barrels to tiny wall pots, and you can find both free-standing containers and those specially constructed to hang from either walls or brackets. For the more imaginative, containers can be custom-made or adapted from all kinds of household relics, from old metal colanders to bread bins.

If you are planning to grow edible plants in containers, then depth can be an important consideration, since plants that are eaten for their roots will need space in which to develop them. Some purpose-made containers can be purchased for specific plants. For example, strawberry planters make economical use of space. They consist of a series of small planting pockets in the sides of a terra-cotta container, which allows you to grow the maximum yield of strawberries from a container that takes up little floor space. Growing bags containing specially formulated compost for tomatoes and other nutrient-hungry plants are another option, but in a small garden where the container is clearly visible from the windows of the house it might be more aesthetically pleasing to disguise these plastic bags with a wooden surround or something similar.

Harmonious colors (above)
A large traditional earthenware container provides a home for a spring planting of tulips.

Futuristic planting (above) *This uncompromisingly modern setting features a symmetrical display of pots filled with bamboo, giving it an Asian feel.*

Setting the scene (right) *Staging provides the opportunity to vary the height of the plants, regardless of the size of the containers.*

Weight is an important consideration for balconies and roof terraces. You not only have the weight of the container to take into account but also that of its contents, which will be particularly heavy when wet. Before using weighty containers on a balcony or roof terrace, consult a structural engineer for advice on what to purchase and where to site it.

If you have very little room to spare in your garden, you can use hanging baskets or wall pots, suspending them on heavy-duty brackets or hooks and pulleys. Remember, however, that these containers tend to dry out extremely quickly due to the large surface area that is exposed, and hanging baskets require watering twice a day in very hot weather.

Grouping containers

If you vary the size and scale of the containers, you will improve the look of the plants. Staggered planting heights allow you to appreciate the flowers of all the plants, which might otherwise be hidden behind each other. You can purchase containers in a range of sizes, and several sizes in a single material usually look good together.

Choosing a shape (below) *Wide, shallow containers are useful for small-growing plants, such as alpines and small herbs.*

Deep containers (left) *These are ideal for large bulbs, perennials, shrubs, and small trees. Containers made from good-quality materials, with textural interest, provide a focal point even when the plants are not in flower.*

Composts for containers

You will have to purchase a compost to use in your containers. Most plants survive perfectly well in a multipurpose growing medium, but a few that enjoy acidic conditions in nature will require specially formulated compost with a higher than normal level of acidity.

Improving drainage

(below) *Most bulbs, such as these tulips, will grow well in multipurpose compost but prefer a free-draining situation, so add a layer of pebbles to the base before you plant.*

If you are growing plants in containers, it is your responsibility to provide the medium in which they can thrive. The constraint of containment means that you have to provide a mixture that is ideally suited to the plants, and you must make sure that nutrients stay at appropriate levels throughout the plant's life. This ensures that the plant will display maximum vigor, resistance to pests and diseases, and produce the best-quality foliage, flowers, and fruit. If you are growing edible plants, the medium in which they are to be planted is even more important, since maximum yields will only be produced by plants that have been properly fed and nourished throughout their lifetime.

You can take the easy route and purchase the growing medium ready-mixed, or, if you have the time, knowledge and space available, you can mix your own. Whether or not you choose to do this, it is worth gaining an understanding of what the various mixes do and which plants grow best in which mixes.

Compost formulations

A series of compost mixes to cover a wide range of planting circumstances was devised by the John Innes Horticultural Institute, and these were numbered. These composts are referred to as JI followed by the appropriate number.

COMPOSTS FOR CONTAINERS

There is a range of suitable growing mediums for containers, including some peat-free substances that are kinder to the environment than traditional peat-based versions.

Multipurpose

Acidic

Organic

Loam-based

JI potting compost No. 1 is used for fine-rooted, slow-growing plants such as alpines, for seedlings, or for plants that are recovering. It is composed of a mixture of 7 parts loam, 3 parts peat, and 2 parts coarse sand, to which a small amount of powdered chalk or ground limestone and JI alkaline fertilizer has been added. This mixture is alkaline in nature (from the addition of the chalk).

John Innes No. 2 is a multipurpose formulation used for plants of average vigor and for most fruit and vegetables, but with double the quantity of chalk/limestone and fertilizer added.

John Innes No. 3 is for fast-growing plants such as tomatoes or sweet peas, and it contains three times the amount of chalk/limestone and fertilizer.

Although peat was once the most widely used component of compost, its extraction is now frowned upon, as it damages the delicate ecosystem of the peat bogs from which it is cut. Various peat substitutes have been developed, including coconut fiber (coir). This has very little nutritional value, however, so other elements are added to produce an appropriate growing medium.

For vegetables, bags of ready-mixed compost are particularly popular. Known as growing bags, various formulations are available to suit different kinds· of plants. Most are about 3 ft. long and 1 ft. wide. They will provide sufficient compost for about three tomato plants or half a dozen lettuce or strawberry plants. However, because the bags are relatively shallow (about 4 in. deep), they are unsuitable for deep-rooted plants such as root vegetables, for example. On the other hand, summer annuals often grow well in them.

Storing and using composts

Compost loses its nutritional value over time. Try to use up your compost within one growing season, and remember to close the bag when you are finished with it.

Keep in mind that although the compost you have bought or mixed may be appropriate for the plant now, frequent watering with water that has a high lime content will, in time, render it too alkaline for some acid-loving plants, and they may turn yellow and sickly looking. You can correct this by applying a solution of iron sequestral or repotting the plants in a specially created, more acidic environment.

Growing bags (above) *Growing bags are particularly useful for edible plants such as tomatoes, because the compost in the bag is formulated specifically for nutrient-hungry plants like these.*

MIXING CONTAINER COMPOST

If you decide to make up your own compost, you will need a reasonable space in which to mix the ingredients. Container-grown plants will benefit from a good, loam-based compost mixed with a measured amount of alkaline fertilizer to keep the plants in good condition. It is easy to mix this up yourself.

1 *Loam-based composts consist of 7 parts sterilized loam, 3 parts medium-grade sphagnum moss peat, 2 parts coarse sand, plus a balanced (alkaline) fertilizer.*

2 *Start by thoroughly mixing the loam, peat, and sand together until they form a uniform mixture. Then draw up the resulting compost into a heap.*

3 *Sprinkle the alkaline fertilizer over the heap of compost and mix it in until there is no visible trace of the fertilizer—the compost is now ready for use.*

Feeding and watering

Failing to feed and water your plants regularly causes them stress, which in turn puts them at increased risk of contracting diseases and being attacked by pests. Container plants need frequent watering and a good supply of nutrients if they are to thrive.

The health and strength of your container-grown plants are totally dependent on your ability to provide them with the right nutrients at the appropriate time. Efficient, sensible methods of feeding and watering are a vital part of container gardening.

It is important to understand that plants have a growing season (broadly speaking, spring and summer) and a dormant period (usually fall and winter). Feeding and watering needs differ according to the season, with the greatest concentration required during the period of active growth.

Although your outdoor plants will receive the normal allocation of natural rainfall, containers do tend to dry out rapidly, particularly in hot weather. Some containers have less insulation than others, and the speed of the drying-out process will be determined by the material from which the container is made. Terra-cotta, a traditional material for containers, causes the compost to lose moisture fast, stone and plastic less quickly.

Feeding

The more bulky forms of plant food are not suitable for containers, since there is inadequate space for the plant to use them. You will therefore need to rely on more concentrated forms of feed. These feeds are available in various forms, as follows.

Slow-release food granules

These can be added to the compost as a top dressing. Their chief advantage is that they release small quantities of plant food into the soil at regular intervals over several months. They will only do their work in moist compost, so be sure to water regularly and do not allow the compost to dry out. Over-watering, on the other hand, is likely to wash away plant foods, so if there are periods of heavy rain, make sure you top up the feed more frequently than usual.

Liquid feeds

These feeds are bought as concentrates, to which water is added according to the manufacturer's instructions. The mixture that results is then applied to the compost. Liquid feeds come in a range of formulations: some are multipurpose with a balanced range of potassium, nitrogen, and phosphorus for general foliage, flower and fruit formation; others have been formulated specifically to encourage a particular aspect of growth, such as fruit formation.

Foliar feeds

These are largely used as a pick-me-up for a plant and are applied directly to the leaves. They are often used to correct mineral deficiencies in the soil.

Foliar feeds have the benefit of being quick-acting, and can be used where diseases or disorders have damaged the plant and rapid recovery is required.

APPLYING LIQUID FEEDS

When applying these feeds, it is essential to read the manufacturer's instructions carefully before you begin.

1 *Always mix the concentrated feed with water so that it is correctly diluted. This will reduce the risk of damage to the roots when the fertilizer is applied.*

2 *Add the liquid feed to the container as part of the watering regime. Try to avoid splashing any of the solution onto the plants' foliage, because this may lead to leaf scorch.*

FERTILIZER RELEASE RATES	
Fertilizer type	Plant response
Slow-release	14–21 days
Quick-acting	7–10 days
Liquid feed	5–7 days
Foliar feed	3–4 days

Watering

Since containers dry out quickly, any watering program must be comprehensive and systematic. Plants will become stressed if watering is irregular or if the compost is allowed to dry out for periods of time; the watering plan should be organized to deliver water to the plants at least twice a week in spring and three times a week in summer. Plants with an exceptionally high transpiration rate, such as lettuces (*Lactuca*), may need to be watered once a day at these times.

Water the plants either early in the morning or in the evening when the sun has gone down. Less water will be lost though evaporation and you avoid the risk of scorching the leaves, which happens when wet leaves are exposed to strong sunlight.

Hanging baskets

These are notoriously susceptible to drying out, and in hot weather they will probably need to be watered twice a day. Unless you have had the foresight to suspend the hanging baskets on a pulley system, you will have to construct some kind of hose attachment to enable you to water them. Smaller quantities of water delivered over a longer period of time do the job more thoroughly and encourage the compost to absorb the water. If the compost has dried out, the water runoff will be considerable if you apply it too vigorously.

Preventing water loss

One way to cut down on watering is to mulch the surface of the compost with gravel or bark chips. Anything that cuts down on the surface area of the compost that is exposed to drying winds will improve its water-retaining abilities. Grouping plants together will also help reduce moisture loss. For vulnerable plants, a tray partially filled with pebbles to which water has been added can be used as a stand for the plants. (This is also a good system to use for periods when you may not be able to water as frequently).

Water-retaining granules can be added to the compost of particularly susceptible plants. These fill with water, swelling to several times their size, and release the water slowly into the compost. Another solution is to create a gravity-wick watering system. Position a bucket of water containing a length (or lengths) of capillary matting on a shelf above the pots and anchor the other end of the wick to the compost to deliver the water.

EMERGENCIES

If you do allow a plant to dry out to the point of wilting, you can usually revive it by giving it a long, cool drink.

1 *Plunge the entire container into water, and hold it down so that the compost is beneath the water level.*

2 *Keep the container submerged until any air bubbles stop rising. Remove and allow to drain. The plant should revive.*

CONSIDERING CONTAINERS

As with all gardening, when using containers you need to think in terms of the overall look, as if you were decorating one of the rooms in your home. The multitude of styles and colors of containers and plants available can completely transform the look of a garden, so consider the finished effect before you buy.

Planning a planting scheme for any container garden simply requires a little forethought. The pots as well as the plants play a major role in the final appearance, and you need to pay attention to container shape, texture, and color to ensure that your chosen pot complements the textures, forms, and colors of the plants. If you can create interesting contrasts or

subtle harmonies, it will help to unite the display. Look for plants with exciting form—deep-colored, interestingly shaped foliage, for example—and match this to plain or patterned containers in good-quality materials. You can also paint or decorate your containers to provide additional interest, but keep the patterns clean and simple. In fact, simplicity is the

key to success. Then combine the containers and plants in ways that produce the greatest possible display of visible flowers and foliage.

The array of container materials and shapes has increased greatly in the last few years, with a range of inexpensive and particularly beautiful handmade pots from the Far East now available. Glazed or unglazed terra-cotta pots abound, as do those with textured surfaces.

Containers are wonderful for changing the mood or defining the style of a specific area. You could use metallic pots to achieve a futuristic look, or traditional wooden baskets to convey a cottage garden atmosphere. Why not use one or two really large specimens in containers to create a stunning focal point? Try architectural plants, such as agaves and phormiums (*Phormium*), or even a cactus if your climate will allow. Use a simple flower or pot color that coordinates with your garden furniture to enhance a seating area, or introduce some fragrant plants to enjoy as you relax, such as tobacco, lavender, or scented-leaved pelargoniums.

Hanging baskets

Suspending plants in baskets from brackets, pergola frames, or other overhead supports gives you more scope for planting. The baskets themselves can vary greatly in form and size, from simple wire constructions to recycled metal colanders.

Foliage and flowers

(below) *The abundant foliage of this geranium helps to disguise the compost in the basket, while the flowers contribute color.*

Hanging baskets filled with plants are ideal for growing even more varieties when space is at a premium, and they can be filled with a range of bright, cheery bedding and trailing plants. The basket is the most common type of hanging container, and it is usually made from heavy-gauge wire that has been coated in plastic or a solid plastic bowl with drainage holes; other materials such as willow or moss baskets are sometimes available, as well.

The choice of compost is a matter of personal preference. Loam-free composts are based on peat or an alternative and are favored by many gardeners. They are light but tend to dry out very quickly and can be difficult to rewet. Loam-based composts, such as John Innes No. 2, can be very heavy when watered but retain moisture well.

Both types of compost will usually last for just one season, and a moss lining can only be used once. However, the hanging basket itself can be reused for many years to come.

Bedding and other tender plants are the favorites for planting in hanging baskets, for two main reasons: their bright and colorful display throughout the summer, and the fact that their relatively short lifecycle fits in very well with the one- or two- season display expected from a hanging basket. However, some of the plants, such as fuchsias and geraniums, can be over-wintered or propagated from cuttings to provide plants for the same hanging basket the following year.

TEMPORARY SUPPORT

Most baskets come with the chains already linked to them. The following is a neat way to keep them out of the way while you work.

Insert a bamboo cane into the center of the basket and then tie the suspending hook for the chains to the cane. Remove the cane when you have finished planting the basket, and hang the hook from a sturdy, well-fixed support. Remember that the weight of a newly watered, planted basket is considerable.

PLANTING A HANGING BASKET

Tools and materials

- hanging basket
- large plant pot
- sphagnum moss
- compost
- water-retaining granules (optional)
- plants

1 *Start by placing the basket upright on top of a large empty plant pot. This will hold the basket in position so that it can be filled without rolling around on the work surface. Line the lower half of the basket with a layer of sphagnum moss.*

2 *Press this layer of moss firmly against the wire mesh of the basket before adding compost to the same level as the moss lining. Add water-retaining granules if you wish, following the manufacturer's instructions.*

3 *Insert the first layer of plants into the basket by passing the roots through the mesh around the sides of the basket, and resting the roots on the compost, with the tops of the plants hanging down the outside of the basket.*

4 *Line the top half of the basket with a layer of sphagnum moss before adding compost, but leaving sufficient space for plants. Insert the second layer of plants into the basket.*

5 *Position the largest plants in the center of the basket, but angle them slightly outward over the rim of the basket.*

6 *Add smaller plants around the edge of the basket before topping up the compost so that it is almost level with the rim (but leave room for watering). Hang the basket in its desired position and water thoroughly.*

Year-round displays

It is important to get the best value from your containers throughout the year, especially if space is at a premium. You will need a combination of plants—shrubs, climbers, perennials (including bulbs), and annuals. Ideally, some of the shrubs and climbers will have evergreen foliage, so that they provide a backbone of permanent plants for more fleeting displays of color.

You need a range of foliage forms (spiky, hand-shaped, small, variegated, and so on) and a flowering period that ideally lasts from early spring right through to winter. Not least among the attributes you might want to enjoy throughout the year is scent, since the perfume of plants wafting through open windows is one of the greatest delights of gardening. It is not difficult to choose scented plants for every season, although there are many more in evidence during spring and summer than you can find in fall and winter. However, nothing beats the unexpected pleasure of the heady scent produced by the almost inconspicuous flowers of elaeagnus in autumn or spring, or the rich perfume of scented daphnes in midwinter.

You can extend the flowering season in a single container by underplanting perennials (which come into leaf in late spring) with early-flowering bulbs, such as daffodils, squills, and crocuses. However, in practice it is easier to devote specific containers to timed displays and then group the containers so that at least one has something of interest to offer at any given season.

Year-round interest (above) *Creating a mixed group of foliage and flowering plants will help to prolong the season of interest. Here, the foliage of blue fescue (Festuca glauca), hostas, and alumroot provide a foil for the geraniums.*

Topiary (above) *Containers with sculptural evergreens, such as dwarf cypresses or simple topiary boxwood or yew, will provide year-round interest.*

	annuals	perennials/bulbs	shrubs/climbers
SCENTED PLANTS FOR DIFFERENT SEASONS			
Spring		*Hyacinthus* (hybrids), *Narcissus* (many), *Viola odorata*	*Clematis armandii, Skimmia × confusa* 'Kew Green', *Viburnum × burkwoodii*
Summer	*Heliotropium, Lathyrus odoratus, Malcolmia maritima, Nicotiana* (hybrids), *Pelargonium* 'Graveolens'	*Dianthus* 'Doris', *Erysimum cheiri, Hosta* 'Honeybells', *Lilium regale, Thymus*	*Genista aetnensis, Jasminum officinale, Lavandula, Lonicera, Rosa* (most), *Trachelospermum jasminoides, Wisteria sinensis*
Fall			*Elaeagnus × ebbingei*
Winter		*Iris unguicularis*	*Chimonanthus praecox, Daphne mezereum, Hamamelis mollis, Sarcococca hookeriana*

You will get the most from your space by looking for out-of-season attributes in the plants you choose, so that you do not have to replant containers or bring in new ones at different times of the year. These features include the attractive hips or berries that follow on from the flowers in some roses; seedheads, such as those of the late-flowering golden virginsbower; the brilliant fall foliage color of Virginia creeper (*Parthenocissus henryana*); and the wonderful scarlet leaves of the small cutleaf Japanese maple (*Acer palmatum* 'Atropurpureum Dissectum').

WINDOW BOXES

It is a good idea to plan any window box planting to create displays that look attractive at different times of the year.

In spring, small bulbs are ideal: crocuses and dwarf narcissus, combined with early primulas; in summer, try dwarf wallflowers or cosmos with miniature lavenders and thymes; in early autumn, dwarf chrysanthemums can replace the wallflowers, and in winter replant with heathers and hardy cyclamen.

Summer planting (above) *Sun-drenched areas are ideal for cheerful displays, such as these African daisies (Osteospermum). Once the weather gets colder, you can introduce more hardy plants.*

Using supports

Where space is at a premium, vertical gardening (growing plants upward rather than sideways) allows you to incorporate new features that overcome space limitations. You can try arches, tripods, and wigwams. These support the plants and let them develop fully without taking up much room in the garden or on the patio.

Sweet pea wigwam (above) *You will be amazed how quickly young sweet peas shoot upward and cover the wigwam frame with exquisite little flowers.*

If you want to grow climbing plants through supports, there are a number of factors you will need to consider before you place the plants in position.

Ideally, the structure should be chosen to suit the plants it will support—this is especially important for plants that have twining stems or tendrils. There is a limit to the diameter of the support around which a plant can twine and grip happily—this is usually about the thickness of an ordinary bamboo cane. If the support you have chosen has a larger diameter than this, you will need to use extra ties or training in addition to the structure itself. Also, if the supports are too thick the climbing plants will tend to cling to each other rather than to the support. Slender supports such as hazel and willow twigs or bamboo canes are ideal for supporting plants such as sweet peas. They are strong enough to support the weight of the plants and thin enough to become totally obscured by foliage and flowers as the plants become established and cover the support completely.

SUPPORTING SMALLER PLANTS

Supports do not only benefit climbers but also weak-stemmed annuals and perennials.

Perennials such as daisies and geraniums benefit from some form of ring staking. The plants will eventually bush out, disguising the support. Other useful staking devices are twiggy bits of brushwood inserted around the perimeter of a pot, or metal linked stakes that fit together to provide a containing girdle.

PLANTING A WIGWAM

Tools and materials

- container
- drill
- newspaper
- compost
- ready-made plant wigwam
- piece of waste wood
- sweet peas

1 Start by selecting a suitable container. If necessary, make some drainage holes in the base (at least one 1 in. hole for every 1 ft. diameter of the container's base).

2 Line the base of the container with sheets of newspaper to prevent the compost from running out of the drainage holes when it is first watered. The paper will rot away within a couple of weeks, but by then the compost will have packed down.

3 When the compost is up to the required level in the container, place the wigwam in a central position, pushing it lightly into the compost.

4 Using a piece of wood as a scribe, mark a line in the compost around the outside of the wigwam legs.

5 Remove the wigwam frame and gently remove the sweet pea plants from their pots ready for planting.

6 Plant the sweet peas into the compost, positioning them so that they are about 4 in. inside the line marked in the compost. Replace the wigwam frame in its original position and press firmly into place.

1

2

3

4

5

6

Edible container plants

Growing edible plants in containers is not at all difficult, but you will need a sunny site for almost all vegetables and soft fruits. Climbers and tall plants, such as beans, tomatoes, peas, and cucumbers, make the most of relatively small areas of ground space.

The containers need a depth of at least 12 in.—more for some root crops, such as potatoes. Generally, you should allow 6½ pints of compost per plant to encourage a reasonable yield. Small plants, such as certain herbs, radishes, and spring onions, can be planted in among larger ones. Underplant tomatoes with lettuce—the oak-leaved red and green 'Lollo' types are ideal and very decorative.

Some plants are easier to grow in containers than others. It is best to avoid cauliflower, sweet corn, celery, peas, parsnips, and rutabagas. Among the easiest crops are many kinds of lettuce, runner beans, radishes, spring onions, beets, tomatoes, outdoor cucumbers, zucchini, Swiss chard, potatoes, and carrots. Eggplants, peppers, and chilies are not difficult but require warmer temperatures and more

sun to ripen. Strawberries, raspberries, and blueberries are among the easiest fruit to grow. Fruit trees, such as specially designed "family" apple trees which have two or three varieties on one dwarf rootstock, are ideal.

Ready-made growing bags filled with compost containing appropriate fertilizers are ideal for temporary crops with fairly shallow root systems, including tomatoes and lettuces. If you are

THE YEAR-ROUND EDIBLE CONTAINER GARDEN

Spring

Radishes, spring onions

Summer

Lettuces, beets, zucchini, Swiss chard, carrots, potatoes, eggplants, peppers, chilies, runner beans, French beans, strawberries, raspberries, cucumbers, tomatoes

Autumn

Apples, carrots, blackberries, raspberries (autumn-fruiting), runner beans

Winter

Lamb's lettuce

Herb corner (above) *It is easy to create a potted herb garden in a sheltered spot. Here, lemon balm (Melissa officinalis), sage, and mint (Mentha) create an attractive foliage display against a wall and provide a feast of herbs for the kitchen.*

short of space, you can train cucumbers and tomatoes up strings against a sunny wall.

Cultivation

Start sowing seeds for tender vegetables in early spring under glass, hardening them off and planting out once the danger of frost has passed. Feed and water all vegetables in containers regularly, and keep a constant eye out for pests and diseases. With only a small crop to worry about, you can usually remove any pests manually.

Containers are prone to drying out and watering is therefore of prime importance; most vegetables are composed of 90 percent water and will suffer very quickly in drought conditions. To keep all types of fruits and vegetables growing well, the water supply must be adequate and regular.

It is also well worth devoting a couple of windowboxes to various culinary herbs: parsley (*Petroselinum*), thyme (there are many attractive forms), basil (*Ocimum*), chervil (*Anthriscus cerefolium*), chives (*Allium schoenoprasum*), and coriander (*Coriandum sativum*) are all ideal. Larger pots can be planted with rosemary or bay and trained to create attractive topiaries.

It is a good idea to make several sowings of the same vegetable, a week or so apart. Not only will you extend the length of the season over which they can be harvested, but you are creating an insurance policy against pest and disease damage.

Potted garden (top) *Here, a group of plain metallic pots makes up a thoroughly modern kitchen garden.*

Salad crops (above) *A wide variety of salad crops will grow well in containers, including many varieties of lettuce. Here, the bright green foliage contrasts with a warm terra-cotta container.*

Planting a strawberry pot

Strawberries are very popular soft fruits for the summer and fall; delicious as they are, however, they do have a number of drawbacks. If they are grown in the garden, they need plenty of space, and even then they will spread as far as they can reach, with the young plants (runners) rooting as they go.

**Space-saving ideas
(below)** *You can plant a number of strawberry plants together in a wall container. Planted in a vegetable patch, they would require a great deal of space.*

As strawberries are low-growing perennials, they lie on the ground as they ripen, making them a tasty snack for slugs, snails, and a range of other passing feeders. It also means that strawberries can be awkward to harvest, because they are so low down and hidden by their canopy of leaves that you have to stoop and search to find them.

As a convenient alternative to growing them in soil, it is worth considering planting your strawberries in containers such as pots, tubs or hanging baskets, or even on the wall or fence in a "track pot." This is a series of small and medium-sized containers assembled on a plastic strip and anchored to a wall, providing a vertical cascade of plants arranged on several different levels and taking up almost no space whatsoever. As the fruits develop, they remain clean and out of the reach of most pests.

Best of all, they are easy to pick, because they hang down clear of the leaves. In this type of container, if the plants are kept well fed and watered they can crop for up to four years before they need to be replaced or repotted.

There is a wide range of strawberry varieties, some early, some mid-season, and some late fruiting. After fruiting the plants will make runners with small plantlets. If you remove these and pot them up, you will have a continual supply of new plants with which to replace the older ones.

Assembling strawberry pots (above) *Individual track pots are clipped onto the supporting brackets in a series and fixed to a wall or fence to create a cascade effect when planted.*

PLANTING A TRACK POT

Tools and materials

- suitable track pot
- compost
- strawberry plants
- drill
- wall plugs
- screws
- screwdriver

1 *Start by three-quarters filling the pot segment with compost. Position the young strawberry plant in it, firming gently and adding more compost as required.*

2 *Repeat this process until all of the pot segments have been filled. Small segments will have room for just one plant, large ones will have room for three.*

3 *On a suitable wall or fence, drill the holes to anchor the "track" (onto which the pot segments will fit), and use wall plugs and screws to fasten the track vertically onto the wall.*

4 *Fit the pot segments onto the track so that the interlocking grooves match (be careful to arrange each pot segment so that the plants get as much room and light as possible).*

5 *Slide the pot segments down the track until each settles onto the segment below, so that they interlock to form a solid column.*

6 *Once the column of pot segments has been fully assembled and locked together, water the plants thoroughly until water drains out of the lowest pot segment.*

Container topiary

Increasingly popular in urban settings, topiary specimens grown in pots can add great style to a balcony or terrace. Pairs of matching topiary pots—pyramids or spheres—add a touch of elegance to any formal area of the garden and help to offset less formal flowering displays.

Topiary is attractive, but the plants are very slow-growing. However, if you grow a plant to a small height this is less of a problem, so topiary pots are an ideal way of including these plants in your garden.

One of the easiest plants to grow from cuttings is American boxwood; it roots readily if you simply remove a young shoot from the parent plant with a little heel of bark any time from spring through summer. All you need to do is plant this in a small individual pot with a mixture of compost and sand, and keep it well watered. Within three months, your cutting will have formed a strong root system. If you take a dozen cuttings and plant them in individual pots, you will rapidly acquire the material for an attractive window-ledge display of matching box pots. Alternatively, a small, clear-stemmed standard boxwood tree will make an eye-catching focal point.

If you do not have the time or patience to create traditional topiary shapes using slow-growing plants, you can create the effect of topiary using fast-growing evergreen climbing plants such as ivy trained over a wire frame. In just a little over one season, you can achieve a similar effect to several years' growth of boxwood, for example. However, frequent clipping will be required to persuade the plants to keep the intended shape, so this is only an option if you have the time to maintain your topiary.

Ivy topiary (left) *Keep the completed sphere neat by trimming wayward shoots.*

GROWING A TOPIARY SPHERE

Tools and materials

- ivy plants
- container
- 2 hanging baskets of equal size
- garden wire

1 *Choose an ivy with trailing shoots, which will cover the sphere quickly.*

2 *Plant two or three well-branched ivies in a suitable container. Space the plants evenly around the container so that they will produce good balanced growth.*

3 *Examine the plants and remove any dead or damaged growth and any discolored leaves. Also, pinch out the final 1 in. of growth from each shoot to encourage sideshoots to develop.*

4 *Tease out all the shoots and splay them around the rim of the container. Leave the shorter shoots in an upright position, so that they can grow up through the support structure.*

5 *Make a support for the ivy by wiring together the two hanging baskets to create a sphere. Place the sphere onto the rim of the container, and thread the plant's shoots through the mesh of the globe. Over the next seven to ten days, all the leaves will turn to face the light, so you will need to turn the container regularly to ensure even growth.*

6 *As the ivy grows and starts branching, it will gradually cover the entire surface of the globe.*

The kitchen garden

Growing your own produce

Growing your own vegetables, fruits, and herbs is becoming an increasingly popular pastime, particularly because it allows you to grow your produce organically if you wish. You do not need a huge plot of land—you can grow an interesting range of edible plants in an area no bigger than 10 sq. ft. If you live in an apartment with a terrace, you can even grow your plants in containers with equally good results.

All fruits and vegetables, and almost all herbs, need plenty of sunlight to ripen, and your kitchen garden must be in the sunniest part of the plot. It makes good sense to grow the produce that is expensive in the grocery store or that you eat raw, when flavor is all-important. For that reason, salad crops are a particularly good choice for the small kitchen garden. Equally, a range of culinary herbs is especially useful and not particularly hard work or difficult to grow. Growing edible plants requires more regular and systematic attention than growing ornamental plants, if you are to produce a worthwhile crop. The principal season for planting and sowing is early and mid-spring, with sowings continuing into the summer. The ground itself will need to be prepared thoroughly in the autumn, ensuring that the soil is sufficiently worked and fertile to produce a good crop. Once the growing season starts, you must weed the area regularly; otherwise, these unwanted plants will draw the nutrients away from your intended crop.

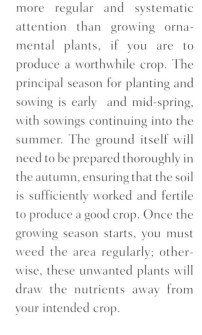

Artichokes (far left) *Artichokes taste good, and the flowers add an attractive splash of color to the vegetable garden.*

Lettuces (top left) *You can grow many kitchen-garden crops in containers. These bright green lettuces contrast well with the terra-cotta pot.*

Bronze fennel (left) *You can use your kitchen garden to grow crops of herbs or more unusual fruits and vegetables. The delicate leaves of this Foeniculum vulgare 'Bronze fennel' are decorative as well as delicious.*

Gardening organically

Nowhere is the principle of organic gardening more relevant than in the kitchen garden; it has become a source of interest to many of us who are alarmed by the pesticides that have been used in commercial food production since the mid-20th century.

Organic gardens risk losing more produce to pests and diseases, but sensible management can minimize these risks. Healthy plants are less susceptible to disease, so ensure that the soil is in top condition and the plants watered and fed adequately.

Encourage beneficial insects by ensuring that their host plants are grown nearby. A few piles of old tiles or wood will encourage ground beetles. Grow a range of nectar-producing flowers close to the kitchen garden. A small herb garden with a thyme bed, a rosemary bush, and some dill (*Anethum graveolens*), fennel, marjoram (*Origanum*), mint, and parsley will provide you with useful culinary herbs and attract bees and hoverflies to your garden. Cottage garden flowers attract a wide range of insects, but modern varieties, particularly those with double flowers, are often sterile and do not produce pollen, nectar, or seeds.

Protecting your fruit with netting and your vegetables with cloches or fleece will help to ensure that more of the produce remains for you.

Adding visual interest (above) *These narrow plots make it easy to tend the crops. The taller plants add visual interest as well as fruit.*

Mixing crops and flowers (below) *The traditional garden that mixes crops and garden flowers is known as a potager. Here, marigolds have been used to add color to this geometric garden.*

Making a plan

It is important to plan your kitchen garden well, in order to prevent a buildup of pests and diseases in the soil and to ensure you make the best use of space. Planting in relatively small blocks makes tending the plants less of a chore and means that you do not damage the soil structure by tramping over it in the process.

Vegetables are prone to a range of pests and diseases. One of the ways to cut down on these problems is to rotate the crops—that is, move the different families of crops around on the plot so that the same types (root, leaf, legume, and fruiting) are not grown successively in the same place. This will deny soil borne from pests the chance to build up in the way they do if the same plants are grown in the same area year after year. One of the easiest crop-rotation schemes is a four-year one, based on certain families of plants (the members of which attract the same pests) being grown in designated areas and then moved each year to a different one. It pays to alternate nitrogen-fixing legumes (peas and beans) with nitrogen-loving crops such as lettuces and tomatoes.

Although most vegetable crops are rotated, a few, such as rhubarb or asparagus, are best left in position. There should also be a permanent place for a fruit-growing area (trees and/or bush fruit) and herbs, both in sunny and sheltered positions. Site the compost heap close to the vegetable-growing area for ease of working.

Garden layout

It is best to grow the plants in small blocks so that you do not have to trample over the soil in order to tend the plants. Although long rows have been employed traditionally (because they maximize the yield from the space available), this only works if the soil is in top condition. If you have compacted it by walking over it, the result will be a smaller crop. It is therefore much easier to make narrow paths upon which you can walk or trundle a wheelbarrow between small blocks and rows of vegetables.

Paths can be made from trodden-down soil or, to save

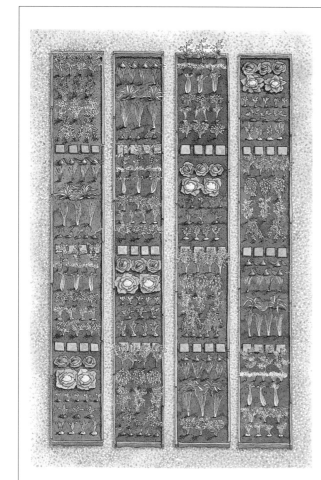

CROP ROTATION

To avoid a buildup of pests and diseases in the soil, vary the positions of your crops. This rotation is normally planned over a three- or four-year period.

YEAR 1 bed 1 legumes: broad beans, peas, runner beans; **bed 2** onions: bulb onions, garlic, leeks, salad onions, shallots; **bed 3** roots and miscellaneous: carrots, celery, parsnips, peppers, potatoes, tomatoes; **bed 4** brassicas: cabbage, cauliflower, radish, rutabaga, turnip

YEAR 2 bed 1 onions: bulb onions, garlic, leeks, salad onions, shallots; **bed 2** roots and miscellaneous: carrots, celery, parsnips, peppers, potatoes, tomatoes; **bed 3** brassicas: cabbage, cauliflower, radish, rutabaga, turnip; **bed 4** legumes: broad beans, peas, runner beans

YEAR 3 bed 1 roots and miscellaneous: carrots, celery, parsnips, peppers, potatoes, tomatoes; **bed 2** brassicas: cabbage, cauliflower, radish, rutabaga, turnip; **bed 3** legumes: broad beans, peas, runner beans; **bed 4** onions: bulb onions, garlic, leeks, salad onions, shallots

YEAR 4 bed 1 brassicas: cabbage, cauliflower, radish, rutabaga , turnip; **bed 2** legumes: broad beans, peas, runner beans; **bed 3** onions: bulb onions, garlic, leeks, salad onions, shallots; **bed 4** roots and miscellaneous: carrots, celery, parsnips, peppers, potatoes, tomatoes

weeding, strips of old carpet. The latter is not particularly attractive to look at, but it certainly saves a great deal of work.

Preparing the soil

Vegetables are particularly hungry for certain nutrients, and you will fail to produce a decent crop unless you improve the soil sufficiently in advance. The best time to do this is in the fall, after the current year's harvest has been picked. Dig over the plot and add generous quantities of organic manure (but not on plots where root crops will be grown), which will improve not only the nutrient content, but also the texture of the soil. In heavy clay soil, this addition of bulky organic material is essential. Check the acid/alkaline balance of the soil with a testing kit, since vegetables tend to grow well within a fairly narrow range—around pH 6.5–7.5.

Vegetables vary in their need for nutrients, and they have to absorb these in balanced amounts. Suitable fertilizers can be purchased in bags or cartons and applied in several different ways: as a base dressing in spring a few weeks before planting; as a booster during growth as a top dressing to the soil; or as a supplementary liquid foliar feed to the leaves if necessary.

BASE DRESSING

Base dressings of fertilizer are applied to the soil before the plants or seeds occupy the site. This helps to maximize the nutrients in the soil that will be available to the young plants.

1 *First, sprinkle a measure of the appropriate fertilizer onto prepared soil in the area you intend to plant or sow.*

2 *Incorporate the fertilizer into the top few inches of soil using a garden or wooden rake.*

TOP DRESSING

Most vegetables grow relatively quickly and will almost certainly need an extra feed during the growing season. A top dressing of fertilizer applied around the plants will help to increase both bulk and yield.

1 *First, carefully sprinkle the fertilizer onto the soil around the plants. Make sure the fertilizer does not land on the foliage, as it will burn it.*

2 *Use a hoe or tined cultivator to incorporate the fertilizer into the soil. Do not cultivate too deeply, or some plant roots may be damaged.*

Well-planned potager (above) *A well-planned garden is easy to maintain and also looks good. This potager contains a wealth of crops, but the clear paths and edged beds minimize the amount of time you will spend trampling on your soil when tending your plants. The geometric layout is also pleasing to the eye.*

Drainage and raised beds

Getting the best from your vegetable garden means dealing with any potential soil problems at the outset. One of the key issues (in an area of heavy soil) is to avoid waterlogging. Another key is to make sure that you are not so overwhelmed with weeding that you cannot attend to your crops.

SOAKAWAY

Check your drainage by digging a test pit. You may find you need to build a soakaway.

A very poorly drained soil may need a gulley (a herringbone-pattern drainage system formed with land drainage pipes) leading to the main pipe, to draw water to a soakaway pit. Fill the pit almost to the top with rubble, covering the last 6 in. with sand and garden soil. The pipe must be sufficiently slanted to drain the water.

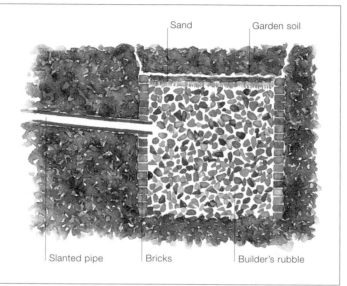

Sand   Garden soil

Slanted pipe   Bricks   Builder's rubble

USING BLACK PLASTIC SHEETS

Black plastic sheeting will help to seal moisture into the soil.

1 *Start by clearing and leveling the area before planting begins. Place a sheet of heavy-gauge black plastic over the area and use a shovel to push the edges at least 6 in. deep into the soil.*

2 *Use your foot to seal the soil around the edges of the plastic, making sure the plastic is stretched as tightly as possible.*

3 *Using a sharp knife, cut a cross in the plastic where each plant is to be placed. Fold back the flaps of plastic and dig out a hole large enough for the rootball of the plant. Insert the plant and firm the soil into place around it.*

There are various ways to ensure that your vegetable garden is more productive and that you get the maximum yield for the minimum effort. Not only do you need to make sure that the soil is well nourished, but it must also drain well.

The vegetable-growing season tends to start all at once in mid-spring. If you haven't managed to dig over your beds in autumn, you will suddenly find yourself with nothing close to enough time to dig, sow and plant. Anything you can do to cut down on the work will be a great help.

Raised beds

Heavy clay soil will present a problem in spring if the ground is waterlogged, and while you need to make every effort to add organic matter to the soil to open it up, it also makes sense to raise the beds and create drainage channels if you can.

Ideally, the raised beds should be narrow enough (about 4–5 ft.) for you to tend them without having to walk on them, which compacts the soil; the beds should stand approximately 9 in. above the surrounding soil surface, and they should be edged with boards to prevent the soil

Cottage garden bed (right) *The soil in raised beds does not have to be very high. Here, a low, retaining edge encloses a riot of color and form reminiscent of the traditional cottage garden.*

from slipping back onto the paths. Much higher raised beds can be created to avoid the necessity of bending down or to allow them to be tended from a wheelchair.

Mulching and improving the soil

Once the soil has been dug over in autumn, you can cover the area with black plastic sheeting, which should be weighted down at the edges. This will prevent weeds from seeding themselves until you are ready to sow in spring. If you raise plants indoors or in seed beds outdoors, you can then plant through the plastic. This acts as a mulch, so that evaporation is reduced and the moisture content of the soil remains more constant. Some crops do particularly well planted in this way, notably strawberries, courgettes and onions. However, if you do this, remember that when you water it needs to be done more thoroughly than usual. This method is also a short cut to weeding, a chore that can occupy a good half of the gardener's time during the growing season, so it is ideal if your gardening time is limited.

If you find that your soil drains too freely and you are constantly having to water your plants, you will need to add plenty of bulky organic matter to it to improve its water-retaining abilities and to ensure that the plants manage to take up the nutrients properly.

Mixed planting (below) *Following in the tradition of creating potagers, here lettuces and nasturtiums coexist in a raised bed.*

Deep cultivation

Any soil cultivation deeper than 8–10 in. can be regarded as a form of deep cultivation. Deep digging is a practice that can be beneficial to heavy and compacted soils, as it can aid drainage as well as improve conditions in the root zone.

The top 6 in. of the soil is the most biologically active, containing a thriving, organically rich community of beneficial organisms such as bacteria, fungi, insects, and worms. These organisms will feed on the organic matter and plant debris in the soil, breaking them down into forms which are available as food for the resident plants. Incorporating organic matter such as garden compost or rotted manure into this zone, or just below it, will improve natural soil fertility, as well as placing nutrients close to the roots and improving the texture of the soil. An additional benefit is that the decomposing organic matter is very good at retaining moisture close to the plants' roots, a factor that can be hugely advantageous during dry summer conditions. Burying the manure or compost in the bottom of a trench during digging (providing it is not buried too deep) will encourage deeper-rooting plants.

An alternative method involves digging before spreading manure or compost over the freshly dug surface, allowing worms, beetles, and other soil dwellers to draw it into the loose soil. This will keep much of the added soil nutrients just below the soil surface, which is useful for naturally shallow-rooted plants.

If you are preparing virgin ground, you will need to remove all the perennial weeds first. You can either cover the area to be dug with old carpet or black plastic sheeting about six months in advance of digging so that the weeds die back, or use a spade to slice the layer of weeds off at the roots, making it easier to dig.

All perennial weed roots must be removed during digging—otherwise they will re-sprout (even from the smallest piece). In ground that is very heavily infested, it may pay to dig over the ground twice.

Growing leeks (right) *The 'Musselburgh' variety is a very hardy vegetable, but it needs deep, rich soil in order for the long white shanks of the leeks to swell.*

DIGGING AND ADDING MANURE

Tools and materials

- garden twine
- spade
- 2 wheelbarrows
- well-rotted manure or garden compost

1 *Dig the vegetable plot in autumn. Start at one end by taking out a trench across the width of the plot to the width of the spade blade, and up to 1 ft. deep. Use a piece of twine pulled taut to ensure a straight trench.*

2 *Remove another trench immediately beside the first to give you a trench about the width of two spade blades, or approximately 2 ft. The wide trench makes adding the organic matter easier.*

3 *Move the soil from the first wide trench to the end of the plot in a wheelbarrow and place it to one side. This will be used to fill the final trench.*

4 *Load the bulky organic matter—such as garden compost or well-rotted farmyard or stable manure—into another wheelbarrow and move it into position, ready to add to the bottom of each trench.*

5 *Spread a 2–3 in. deep layer of the organic matter over the bottom of the first trench. Make sure it is spread to an even depth.*

6 *Next, dig a second wide trench immediately behind the first one. Move the soil from this forward into the first trench, covering the bulky organic matter. Make sure you turn each spadeful of soil over completely, so that the original soil surface is buried. Add bulky organic matter to the second trench, as before. Continue digging the plot in this way, and fill the final trench with the soil from the first.*

Vegetable-growing techniques

When sowing and planting fruits and vegetables, you will need to carry out a range of special tasks. It is worth taking time to learn about kitchen gardening techniques, because putting in a little extra effort at the beginning will enable you to give your plants a good start.

The vegetable gardening year begins in the autumn, when you need to dig over the soil and add any bulky manure or compost in time for it to rot down well before the chief planting time in the spring.

Sowing seeds

The time at which you sow your vegetables will depend on whether they are fast- or slow-maturing, and whether or not they are hardy. Tender plants that mature slowly, such as tomatoes, peppers, and eggplants, are sown indoors in warmth several weeks before the last frosts in the region. They are then hardened off gradually in a cold frame and transplanted into their planting positions once all danger of frost has passed. Hardy vegetables can be sown outside, and you can make successional sowings every week or so to extend the harvesting period.

If you sow vegetable seeds in place, you will need to thin out the surplus plants to ensure the remaining ones grow to their full size. This is especially important with fine seeds, but vegetables from larger seeds, such as carrots, lettuces, parsnips, radishes, and beets, will also need thinning. Instead of throwing away the thinnings—use some of them in salads.

"Earthing up"

Some vegetables need to be "earthed up" to grow properly—that is, have soil drawn up around the base of the plant. Those, like leeks and celery, that are grown for their blanched stems, need to be earthed up for this purpose (although this does not apply to self-blanching celery). Others, like potatoes, that grow from sideshoots below the surface of the soil, must be earthed up to prevent the tubers from turning green (if they do, they are toxic and must not be eaten).

Support and protection

Plants that have weak stems or a climbing habit will require some kind of support. Among these are cucumbers, tomatoes (tall varieties), peas, and beans. The form of support will be determined by the plant's habit. Beans, which are vigorous growers, will need 6 ft. canes tied together in a wigwam shape or in a row. The

TRANSPLANTING YOUNG PLANTS

Once plants raised in a seed bed become sufficiently large (cabbages are shown here), you will need to transplant them to allow them enough space to carry on growing steadily.

1 *Lift seedlings to be transplanted carefully; hold the leaves rather than the stem—it is liable to bruise easily.*

2 *Make a hole in the new position with a dibble and insert the plant, firming down the soil around it. Water the plant in well.*

SUPPORTING BEANS

In order to encourage runner beans to grow upward, they will need some sort of support structure. Canes are ideal for this.

DIGGING A TRENCH

Vegetables such as beans tend to perform better when they are grown over a prepared trench, which will help to retain moisture.

1 *Insert the canes at least 6 in. into the ground at appropriate planting distances, and plant about 2 in. to the side of each supporting cane.*

2 *The plant will twine itself around the cane until it reaches the top. You can then pinch out the leading shoot to prevent further growth.*

1 *Well in advance of planting, dig a narrow trench where the beans are to be planted. Fill the trench with well-rotted garden compost.*

2 *Return the soil, leaving it slightly ridged. Allow it to settle, without firming, before the beans are planted or seeds are sown.*

canes must be anchored firmly, because the weight with a full crop is considerable. Tomatoes are best supported with a single stout bamboo cane. Cucumbers can be trained flat to a trellis panel. With any fast-growing climbing vegetables, you will need to pinch out the growing point once enough fruiting trusses have formed, and you may have to remove some of the leaves from the sideshoots so that the fruit can ripen.

Plants that are vulnerable to attacks from flying pests will benefit from being grown in a plastic tunnel, or covered with fleece (a form of net). This will also help to protect them against cold. However, those plants that are insect-pollinated must have the covers removed once they flower in order to set fruit.

TRAINING CUCUMBERS

Training cucumbers not only gives them support, but can actually encourage the plants to grow more strongly.

1 *Cucumbers can be supported easily by lowering a string from an overhead anchor point and fastening it to the base of the plant stem. As the stem grows, twist it around the string to keep the plant upright.*

2 *Because the plant is now supported by the string, it has no need to produce clinging tendrils with which to support itself. These can be removed, so that more of the plant's energy goes into producing flowers and fruit.*

Fruit

One of the greatest pleasures of gardening is to be able to eat fruit straight from the bush or tree. Nothing beats the flavor of sun-warmed fruit fresh from the garden. You can grow soft fruit (strawberries), vine fruit (grapes, kiwi), cane and bush fruits (raspberries, currants, blueberries), or many tree fruits, from the traditional (apples and pears) to the more exotic (peaches and cherries).

All fruit requires sunshine to ripen; some of the more tender trees, such as peaches, require a warm spot, ideally against a sunny wall, and shelter from prevailing winds.

To encourage the best crops, you will need to feed your fruiting plants regularly and well with potassium-rich fertilizers; if you want to ensure that pests do not decimate your crops, you may require help from chemicals. If, however, you prefer to garden organically, there are a number of preventative measures you can take, but you may need to resign yourself to some losses.

Getting started

If you are growing your first fruit, the easiest to grow successfully in the soft fruit category are strawberries and rhubarb; among cane and bush fruits, none is particularly difficult to grow, so you can choose from raspberries, currants, gooseberries, blackberries, and blueberries (although the latter do need acidic soil). Of the tree fruit, apples, plums, and pears are likely to be the most successful. Tender tree fruit,

Blackberries (below)
Blackberries are easy to grow but very vigorous, so regular pruning and tying in is needed to keep them under control.

Growing peaches (above) *Peach trees need a warm, sunny wall to ensure a crop. The trees blossom early and are susceptible to frost damage.*

CANE FRUIT

Raspberries fruit well provided you
feed them generously and prune out
the old wood after fruiting.

BUSH FRUIT

Currants are easy to grow, and produce
an excellent yield with relatively little attention.
Make sure you pick them on a cool, dry day.

1 *Pick the fruits by gripping them gently between fingers and thumb, before gently pulling them away from their central core or "plug."*

2 *As soon as these fruits have been harvested, they should be taken into a cool, shaded place to allow them to cool down gradually—this will help to extend their storage life.*

1 *To harvest currants, hold the truss of fruits in one hand and remove the individual strings of currants with the other.*

2 *Place the harvested currants in a cool, shaded container and keep it covered while you pick the rest of the fruit.*

such as peaches, apricots, and nectarines, require much more care and appropriate conditions if you are to succeed. Of the vining fruit, grapes are not difficult to grow but do need expert pruning to ensure maximum yield.

Soft fruit

Strawberries are often grown in a slightly raised bed through black plastic sheeting. They are highly susceptible to slug and snail damage, and the fruits are easily bruised. Put down a mulch of straw, both to deter slugs and snails and to keep the fruit off the soil. Strawberry plants normally fruit well for 2–3 years, but if you pot up the plantlets that form each year on the runners, you will have young replacement plants.

Rhubarb likes a rich soil, so make sure you dig in a lot of well-rotted manure. Provided it is kept watered, it will reward you in spring with plenty of tender young shoots and is largely pest- and disease-free.

Cane and bush fruit

For raspberries and blackberries (cane fruits) you will need a supporting framework on which to train the stems. Vertical poles with horizontal wires strung between them are normally used for this purpose. With raspberries, which fruit on the new season's wood, you will need to cut down the old fruited canes after cropping and train the new growths against the supports. Currants and gooseberries grow as free-standing bushes and require relatively little pruning. Blueberries are easy to grow and are tolerant of some shade, but they need an acidic soil. If you do not have such soil, you can grow them easily in containers filled with acidic compost.

Prune bush fruit to ensure that the plant has an open, airy center. Shorten the sideshoots of gooseberries to one or two buds.

Tree fruit

Even in a small space, you can still have one or two fruit trees. You can opt for family trees (in which several cultivars are grafted onto one rootstock) or choose a single dwarf cultivar. These can be grown successfully in containers, so even a balcony can support one or two fruit trees, if you wish.

With tree fruit, you will need to prune carefully to encourage fruiting shoots to form, and to make sure that enough air and sunlight reach the ripening fruit.

Protecting your crops

You are not alone in enjoying fruit fresh from the branch or bush: so do many animals, birds, and insects, and much of your work when growing involves making sure that you get at least some share of your chosen crop!

Fruit cages (below)

Lightweight structures such as this provide ideal protection for fruiting trees and bushes, and they do not look out of place in the kitchen garden.

It is an unfortunate fact that human beings are not the only ones who find crops of fruits and vegetables attractive and tasty. All too often, the wildlife we encourage to feed on slugs and insects also find ripening fruits and berries very appealing. Even if they only nibble or peck at the fruit, this will leave an open wound that can attract second-ary feeders (such as wasps) or leave the fruit prone to fungal and bacterial infection that may then spread to other fruits.

Birds rely on their sense of smell, rather than color, to tell them when fruit is ripening, and they will often strip the fruit from one plant before moving on to the next.

It is important to put some form of protection over the fruit before it starts to ripen, rather than waiting until it has been attacked. For a large area, you can use a bird scarer, provided it is not too noisy, or use several in combination, as the birds quickly become used to a single type.

Individual plants or small areas of fruits and vegetables can be protected quite efficiently using small-mesh plastic. This forms an effective barrier, but it must be held on a frame above the plants rather than draped over them. If it is in contact with the crop, the birds can simply perch on a shoot and peck through to feed.

A special fruit cage—consisting of a permanent frame-work over which the netting is tightly stretched to avoid trap-ping birds—is the best solution for protecting fruit bushes and small trees.

Fruit cages (below)

Lightweight structures such as this provide ideal protection for fruiting trees and bushes, and they do not look out of place in the kitchen garden.

SECURING THE NETTING

It is vital that birds cannot get underneath your protective cages, so take simple measures to prevent this.

Large areas of netting can be difficult to secure. Cut a 4 in. section of garden hose and split it open vertically. Wrap the sections of hose around the supporting framework, trapping the netting securely underneath. Repeat as many times as necessary. The larger your structure, the more sections of hose you will need.

ERECTING A FRUIT CAGE

Tools and materials

- heavy-gauge wire
- wire cutters
- vice
- heavy-duty bamboo canes
- drill
- small-mesh netting (plastic)
- garden twine
- wire pins

1 Start by cutting some lengths of heavy-gauge wire into 8 in. sections and bending them in a vice to form a right angle with two 4 in. sides. Then, select some stout bamboo canes to act as the supports for the netting (choose canes about 3 ft. taller than the crop being protected).

2 Insert the support canes into the ground, about 2 ft. deep to keep the structure stable, with a distance of 6–10 ft. between them. Once all the upright supports have been inserted, the lateral supports can be added to the structure. Join these to the upright supports by inserting the wire right angles into the ends of the canes.

3 For any intermediate supports, drill the canes and push a wire right angle through the holes before slotting them into the upright.

4 When the support structure is complete, the netting can be draped over the structure, starting with the roof and moving on to the sides and ends.

5 Attach the netting to the supports using garden twine.

6 Stretch the net tightly over the supports to prevent any sagging, and fix the bottom of the netting into the soil using wire pins. Rolling the bottom of the netting around a cane helps to keep the net taut and makes pinning it into position easier.

Herbs

Herbs have great advantages, both for our health and our enjoyment of food. It is well worth growing a few culinary herbs, and perhaps a few medicinal ones, too, for good measure. In the garden, they are wonderfully aromatic, and many are evergreen.

Herb gardens have been popular since medieval times. The wonderful scents and attractive foliage of these plants make them ideal for symmetrically designed gardens, from tiny plots to large, complex knot gardens. Traditionally, these gardens are edged with low boxwood hedges (*Buxus sempervirens* 'Suffruticosa'), which provide a neat evergreen surround.

Many herbs originate in warm climates, particularly in the Mediterranean region; consequently, not all are hardy. Among the best culinary herbs for temperate climates are thyme, sage, rosemary, bay, mint, tarragon (*Artemisia dracunculus*), chervil, chives, dill, parsley, and marjoram. Basil is usually grown as an annual, because it is tender, but it does very well in small pots on the windowsill.

Herbs are relatively easy to grow, but most need a sunny position to do well (mint needs shade). They take up relatively little space, and a good number will do well even in very small containers, so there is nothing to stop you from growing some culinary herbs—even if you only have a windowbox.

Many herbs prefer light, free-draining soil, so if your soil tends to be heavy, you will need to work in plenty of organic matter and a quantity of sand to make its structure more open.

A choice of herbs

Of the medicinal and flowering herbs, lavender is one of the most popular. It lends itself to being grown as a low hedge (the evergreen, silvery leaves being a year-round feature) or a small standard. There are many species and varieties, all wonderfully scented. French lavender (*Lavandula stoechas*) has curiously shaped purplish heads; English lavender (*Lavandula angustifolia*) is generally the most fragrant—it is used for potpourri, oils, and scenting linen.

Traditional potager (left) *This is a practical and decorative mixture of vegetables and herbs in geometric beds.*

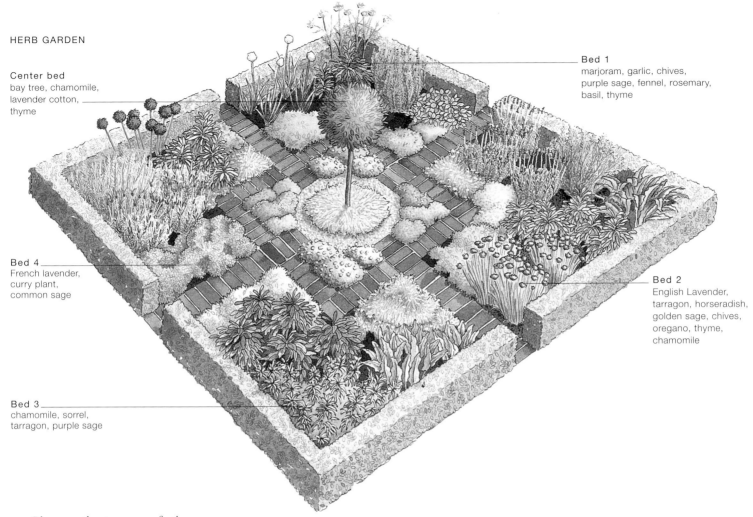

Center bed
bay tree, chamomile,
lavender cotton,
thyme

Bed 1
marjoram, garlic, chives,
purple sage, fennel, rosemary,
basil, thyme

Bed 4
French lavender,
curry plant,
common sage

Bed 2
English Lavender,
tarragon, horseradish,
golden sage, chives,
oregano, thyme,
chamomile

Bed 3
chamomile, sorrel,
tarragon, purple sage

Chamomile is one of the most popular medicinal herbs, and it is reasonably easy to grow. It is often used as a substitute for grass (in the variety 'Treneague') to make a small lawn in a formal garden that has a wonderfully springy, aromatic scent.

Herbs present a variety of interesting foliage attributes, with many different leaf colors available. Thymes, mints, marjorams and sages all include unusual cultivars. The different species and varieties of mint offer distinct scents and tastes.

You can even shape a number of evergreen shrubby herbs into topiary (see pages 96–97). For example, bay trees can be pruned to create classic standards or pyramids.

CONTAINING MINT

Mint grows very easily and so is popular with gardeners. However, if left uncontained, it can run rampant, growing well beyond its intended area.

1 *Mint can be very invasive and extremely difficult to control once it has colonized an area of the garden. This problem can be avoided by planting the mint into a container, such as this clay drainage pipe.*

2 *Plunge the drainage pipe containing the mint into a garden border to a depth of about 1 ft. deep. This will allow the mint to grow in controlled isolation.*

The vegetable garden calendar

One of the most difficult aspects of running a kitchen garden is remembering what to do when. All too often, you only remember that you should have sown the seeds of a particular vegetable well into the season, and if you leave it too late you will miss the best time of year for growth.

The times of greatest activity in the vegetable garden are spring and summer. You need to plan carefully to ensure that you find the time to sow, transplant, weed, and harvest during these busy periods. You may find that mulching the surface of the soil with black plastic helps to cut down on weeding (see page 203), and thereby reduce the workload.

The chart here provides you with an outline of what will be needed when, but the detailed planning depends very much on the particular plants you want to grow. It is a good idea to keep a notebook to record the performance of plants and when certain tasks must be carried out.

Remember that even in the quieter periods, there are still jobs to be done. As well as preparing the ground for the following year's planting, you can use the winter months to check on your crops and do the maintenance tasks that can be so difficult to fit in during the spring and summer. A cold or rainy day can provide the perfect opportunity to reorganize the shed, oil and sharpen knives or other equipment, or simply sit back with a gardening book or some seed catalogs and enjoy a spell of armchair gardening.

Early spring

- Sprout potatoes indoors.
- Sow vegetables such as broad beans and runner beans indoors.
- Sow vegetables such as kohlrabi and spring onions outdoors.
- Force rhubarb by covering with an upturned bucket.
- Harvest the last of your overwintered vegetables, such as lamb's lettuce, Brussels sprouts, winter cabbage, leeks and parsnips.
- Plant onions.
- Prepare any beds that you failed to dig over in autumn.
- Add straw or bulky manure to give soil good texture.
- Check over any stored vegetables for signs of rotting.

Mid-spring

- Continue on sowing seed successionally for the vegetables already mentioned.
- Start sowing seed indoors for eggplants, peppers, outdoor tomatoes, and lettuce.
- Plant rhubarb, shallots, onions and garlic.
- Start to trim grass edges.
- Plant potatoes.
- Cover early fruit blossoms with fleece to offer protection against any remaining frosts.
- Cover early-cropping soft fruit.

Late spring

- Continue sowing eggplants, sweetcorn, French and runner beans, cucumbers, zucchini, and tomatoes indoors.
- Sow all hardier vegetables outdoors, including Brussels sprouts, cabbages, kale, carrots, leeks, parsnip, peas, Swiss chard, and turnips.
- Plant lettuces outdoors under cloches.
- Start to hoe and weed between rows of crops.
- Plant the earliest potatoes.
- Harvest spring cabbages, leeks, spring onions, parsley, overwintered salad plants, and spinach.

Early summer

- Harden off and transplant bean, tomato, cucumber, pepper, and eggplant seedlings, and cloche the more tender plants such as sweet corn, peppers, eggplants, and tomatoes.
- Sow directly outdoors crops such as carrots, beets, peas, zucchini, lettuce, radishes, and argula.
- Plant Jerusalem artichokes.

- Continue weeding regularly.
- Mow grass paths and trim edges.
- Plant potatoes.
- Stake peas and beans.
- Watch out for pests, such as blackfly, on broad beans.
- Make small successional sowings of salad plants.
- Harvest rhubarb, broad beans, autumn-sown onions, radishes, spinach and turnips.

Midsummer

- Harvest vegetables such as broad beans, lettuces, radishes, zucchini, beets, and spring onions.
- Harvest strawberries, raspberries, gooseberries, and currants.
- Tie in shoots of outdoor tomatoes and cucumbers. Stake peppers and eggplants.
- Water, mulch, and feed all crops as necessary.
- Thin fruits on apple trees.
- Pinch out growing points of runner beans.
- Top-dress vegetables with fertilizer.
- Remove excess foliage from tomato plants.
- Watch out for flying pests, and use fleece for susceptible crops.
- Hoe regularly to keep weeds under control.
- Cover with black plastic any areas of soil that have not been planted, to keep weeds at bay.
- Trim surrounding hedges.

Late summer

- Lift onions and shallots when the tops have died down.
- Thin fruits on fruit trees as necessary.

- Summer-prune trained fruit trees.
- Net fruit crops against birds.
- Harvest herbs.
- Feed tomatoes regularly.
- Harvest beans, peas, potatoes, beetroot, cabbages, carrots, outdoor cucumbers, tomatoes, sweet corn, lettuces, garlic, and zucchini.
- Harvest plums, blackberries, blueberries, and late-fruiting strawberries and raspberries.

Early autumn

- Dig up any vegetables that have finished cropping, and compost the leaves and stalks.
- Harvest tomatoes, peppers, eggplants, zucchini, beans, lettuces, and salad greens.
- Store potatoes.
- Harvest apples and pears.
- Cloche any tomatoes, peppers and eggplants that have not yet ripened.
- Plant onions for an early spring crop.
- Order farmyard manure.

Mid-autumn

- Start to dig over the plot, incorporating well-rotted manure and compost.
- Plant leeks.
- Plant cabbages for spring.
- Prune black currants.
- Tidy up strawberries; remove and replant runners.
- Plant new raspberry canes and trim old ones.
- Clean, sort, and store stakes that are no longer needed.
- Compost tomato and bean plants.
- Store fruit on wooden racks in a cool, airy place.

Late autumn

- Continue digging over the ground.
- Sow broad beans for over-wintering.
- Plant onions.
- Plant herb containers for winter use.
- Cloche salad vegetables for winter use.
- Lift and store root crops for winter use.
- Prune blackberry and gooseberry plants.
- If legal in your area, burn all garden material that cannot be added to the compost heap and use the resulting ash for potassium fertilizer.
- Make the last cut of any grass.
- String onions and garlic.
- Plant fruit trees.

Winter

- Continue to dig if weather permits.
- Check the acidity of the soil using a kit. Add lime if necessary for any brassicas.
- Lift leeks and parsnips.
- Harvest spinach.
- Check fruit and vegetable stores for signs of rotting and remove any affected specimens.
- Plant hedges.
- Order seed catalogs, then prepare your seed order.
- Protect any overwintering vegetables with cloches.
- Tidy the garden shed and sharpen all blades.
- Oil mowers and other equipment with moving parts.
- Check the structure of the garden shed and carry out any repairs as required.
- Plant garlic.

Harvesting chives (above)
Harvest chives by snipping off the top half of each shoot. Chives are ideal for use in salads and baked potatoes.

Storing potatoes (above)
Be sure to store harvested potatoes in a dry, dark place.

THE FRUITS OF YOUR LABOR

Home-grown fruit, vegetables, and herbs taste delicious and give the grower a great sense of achievement. But if "growing your own" conjures up images of "digging for victory" or tending vast plots of land, then think again. Home-grown produce is undergoing a renaissance in popularity.

Concerns about food safety, a demand for better-quality produce, and an increased awareness of the importance of fresh fruits and vegetables in our diet have made kitchen gardening fashionable again. After all, the way to be certain that your food has not been fed chemical fertilizers or sprayed with pesticides is to grow it yourself. The upsurge of interest in the

flavor of fruits and vegetables and the expansion of organic gardening have led to a much wider range of varieties being introduced. Rather than competing with the low-cost, everyday produce available in the grocery store, many gardeners are taking the opportunity to grow unusual or rediscovered varieties of fruits, vegetables, and herbs.

"Heirloom" seeds of old varieties are now available. Among the wealth of unusual plants available, you can find purple-podded beans, yellow carrots, and even striped tomatoes, to name just a few. Look out for, and aim to grow, at least one or two of these different kinds, even if it is simply as an experiment alongside the more tried and true varieties.

By encouraging diversity and helping to ensure that old varieties do not fall into disuse, you are also helping to ensure that you pass on a much greater choice to your children. If you have trouble finding the more unusual varieties, organic organizations, such as the Henry Doubleday Research Association, keep seed libraries. When growing unusual vegetables, record the sowing, transplanting, and harvesting times, as well as the yield, so that you can compare the performance with those of more commonly grown varieties.

You may also find that your culinary interest is reawakened. There is nothing like really fresh produce to inspire you to be creative in the kitchen.

Extending the season

It can be very useful to extend the warm season so you can grow plants that would not normally survive or grow well in lower temperatures. To do this, you need to insulate the plants from cold while still providing them plenty of daylight. Cold frames and cloches are the easiest means by which to accomplish this. A permanent greenhouse (see pages 222–223) is essential if you want to grow larger plants.

There are various types of cloches and cold frames you can use in the kitchen garden. A cold frame typically has wooden sides and a glass top, which is then lifted to tend the plants. A cloche is a glass or plastic cover. It can take various forms, including tunnel, tent, or bell shapes.

Cold frames

Early cold frames were made of wood, but these days, aluminum is the material of choice for most people, because it is light and inexpensive. You can usually buy cold frames to assemble at home. They let in more light than the traditional wooden or brick cold frame but can blow over in high winds unless firmly anchored.

You need to choose a size that is appropriate for the purpose you have in mind. If you are growing taller plants in pots, you may need to raise the sides of the cold frame on bricks. Remember that cold frames are not frost-proof, although they provide some protection. In severe weather, and depending on how frost-tender the crops are, you will have to provide additional insulation. This can take the form of either bubble wrap inserted in the frame against the sides, or burlap tied around the frame in exceptionally cold weather.

Once the temperature rises up and the weather alternates

Warming the soil (below)
Covering the soil with black plastic sheeting will warm it up and allow you to plant crops such as potatoes earlier than usual. Cut crosses in the plastic through which to plant.

Raising plants early (right) *Tender plants, such as geraniums, can be raised early by transplanting seedlings grown indoors to covered frames in the garden.*

between warm and cold, the problem is that the cold frame overheats. Cold frames should have some form of ventilation incorporated—simply propping open the hinged lid or leaving the sliding top slightly ajar will do the trick.

Although horticultural glass is the best glazing material to use for cold frames (it transmits light well and provides the best insulation), it is not a good idea where children and animals use the garden. For safety's sake, use plastic instead.

For a permanently positioned cold frame, you need to choose an appropriate site. Ideally, it should make the most of the light in winter, so choose a sunny site. Lightweight aluminum frames can be moved around the garden to take advantage of the best light. This also ensures that you make the best use of the soil.

Cloches

These come in various forms and shapes, but there are two basic structures: tent-shaped (with a pitched roof) and tunnel-shaped (with a rounded roof)—there are various permutations of these. The material can be either glass (see the warning left about children) or plastic. If your cloche is tunnel-shaped or you have a row of tent cloches, remember that end pieces are necessary to prevent wind funneling through the tunnel or row and killing off the plants.

You can buy cloches or, if you prefer, it is possible to improvise and make your own.

Small individual cloches can be made simply from plastic bottles with the bases cut off. These provide useful protection for small tender plants, and also create an effective barrier against slugs and snails.

Remember that in many instances cloches enable you to get two crops a year out of the same plot, but you must ensure that the soil is fertilized adequately to support such a high yield.

Homemade cloches (above)
Plastic bottles with the bases removed are an inexpensive means of protecting individual plants.

Making a cloche

Cloches can easily be constructed on any sheltered area of the garden and are ideal for giving plants an early start in the spring. They can often promote growth up to three weeks ahead of unprotected plants. This type of temporary shelter can be important for protecting early vegetables and low-growing fruits such as strawberries from late spring frosts.

Seedlings under a cloche (below) *Young, tender plants benefit from the protection of a cloche. As well as affording shelter from the elements; it provides a barrier against pests.*

A ready-to-use tunnel cloche can be constructed quite simply, by cutting 3 ft. wide sections of rigid, galvanized wire mesh (about 3 in. squares), bending each one over to form a semi-circle, and tying each end with a 28-in. length of wire or plastic string. These cloches have the advantage of being mobile.

Some gardeners are reluctant to use a cloche, because they can look quite forbidding and difficult to use. However, if the cloche is well constructed and positioned, it should be quite easy to maintain your plants within it. When you need to tend your plants, simply lift up the plastic covering and remove the wire mesh. As a precaution on sites that are particularly windy, it is best to position the tunnel so that one end faces squarely into the prevailing wind. This will present a much smaller surface area to the wind than if the cloche is positioned side-on, making it less vulnerable. It is also much easier to reinforce the smaller ends of the tunnel than the sides.

You can even customize your homemade cloche to suit the current weather conditions in your garden. By using different types of covering materials, the same structure can be used to offer protection from several degrees of frost in the spring. When the plants are older, the covering can be changed to different grades of netting to provide the plants with protection against attack by birds.

For this type of construction, the most expensive item at the outset will be the wire mesh sections that form the basis of the cloche. However, it is well worth buying good-quality wire, because it will last you for anything up to 20 years. The plastic covering should last for two or three years.

MAKING A CLOCHE

Tools and materials

- rigid, galvanized wire mesh and wire or plastic string
- clear plastic sheeting
- wooden battens
- drill
- nails or plastic pins
- general-purpose knife or scissors

1 *Place the prepared wire mesh sections over the plants to be protected (in this case, strawberries), with the plants occupying the central position within the cloche.*

2 *Position the sections together with their ends touching, adding as many sections as necessary to cover the row of plants.*

3 *Take a sheet of clear plastic, unfold it, and spread it out over the wire mesh carefully so that it does not tear. Allow at least 2 ft. of surplus plastic at each end of the cloche.*

4 *At the sides of the cloche, lay down sections of ¾ x 1½ in. wooden batten drilled with holes at 1 ft. intervals. Position these at the edges of the plastic.*

5 *Anchor the plastic along one side of the cloche by pushing 6 in. nails or plastic pins through the holes and plastic into the soil below.*

6 *Stretch the plastic taut on the remaining side of the cloche and pin it down with battens, before cutting off any excess plastic. Gather up the surplus plastic at the ends of the cloche. Bury it in the soil or peg it down with pins and battens, using the same method as on the sides of the cloche.*

Greenhouses

*Owning a greenhouse is the mark of a serious gardener. You can have a
simple, unheated greenhouse or a heated one. However, if you want to
cultivate tender plants in a climate that is too cold to support them,
an unheated greenhouse will not keep them warm enough.*

Lean-to greenhouse
(below) *This spacious greenhouse makes the most of the
area immediately adjacent to
the wall of the house, so that
the large structure does not
impose on the yard.*

Keeping a greenhouse heated to
the right temperature and
ensuring that it has sufficient ventilation in hot weather requires
fairly diligent attention, so it is not
a job for the faint-hearted or those
with strict time limits. However, if
you are a committed gardener, a
greenhouse can be an invaluable
tool that opens up new opportuni-
ties which would otherwise be
impossible in your climate.

Unheated greenhouses work in
the same way as a cloche or cold
frame (see pages 218–221), except
that they are bigger and permanently sited. They are most useful
for sowing seeds in mid- to late
spring in order to get a head start on
the weather; by the time all danger
of frost has passed, the plants are
already well established and therefore less vulnerable. This enables
you to enjoy various vegetables and

salad crops much earlier in the
season than they would be made
available in stores or at times of the
year when they are expensive to
buy. A greenhouse will also enable
you to ripen crops or encourage
ornamental plants to flower earlier
than they would if planted outside.
An unheated greenhouse is an ideal
place for growing plants such as
tomatoes, which in colder climates
often fail to ripen properly.

TYPES OF GREENHOUSES

Greenhouses are available in
various different styles and
materials, each with its own
advantages and drawbacks.

■ *Softwood frames need regular
painting, western red cedar
needs occasional treatment
with preservative.*
■ *Aluminum is maintenance free.*
■ *A traditional span roof is ideal
for vegetables at ground level.*
■ *Half-boarded or those on a low
wall are more economical to heat.*
■ *Lean-tos retain heat well.*
■ *A conservatory is similar to a
lean-to but generally more sturdy.*
■ *A plastic walk-in tunnel is
inexpensive but not a good
insulator, although ideal for
vegetables in summer.*

Choosing a greenhouse (right)
*Greenhouses can be elegant structures
in their own right. Here, the building
blends well with the plants.*

Choosing a greenhouse

You do not need a huge green-house. Very simple but highly practical greenhouses can be purchased in kit form; these are more than adequate for the purpose of raising a few vegetables and tender bedding plants from seeds each spring, and perhaps propagating a few plants for the house.

One of the most useful and economic greenhouses in terms of space is the lean-to. This type utilizes use of an existing wall as the back supporting structure, so as well as making the best use of the space (essential if you have a small yard), it can be placed in a sheltered area away from high winds.

Planning the greenhouse

You need to think carefully about where your greenhouse should be positioned. Orientate a free-standing greenhouse so that the ridge runs east to west. You will need to site it near an external water supply, as watering is one of the major preoccupations of any gardener growing plants under glass. Some kind of drainage system for water runoff is essential as well.

Ideally, the greenhouse should be equipped with lightweight staging on which trays of seedlings and plants can be stored, and there should also be an area dedicated to potting and transplanting.

USEFUL GREENHOUSE CROPS

These crops are for growing to maturity in the greenhouse. Most need artificial heat early in the year.

Eggplants

Climbing French beans (for early crops, unheated)

Capsicums (sweet peppers, chilis)

Cucumbers (greenhouse varieties)

Herbs (for winter to spring, unheated or heated)

Lettuces (winter or spring, unheated)

Tomatoes (greenhouse varieties)

Grapes (back wall of lean-to)

Melons

Peaches and nectarines (back wall of lean-to)

Strawberries (pot grown, gently forced for an early crop)

Large greenhouse (above) *This greenhouse has plenty of space in which to move about and ample staging for growing and displaying plants. It has ventilators to help reduce the temperature in hot weather.*

Harvesting

If you have gone to the trouble of growing your own fruits and vegetables, it is important that you get to enjoy eating them! Not only do you need to exercise care when harvesting the crop so that you do not damage the plants and the produce, but at times you will inevitably have a glut of fruits and vegetables and will need to know how to store them.

Storing apples (above)
Wrapping the apples individually will help prevent them from rotting.

While some smaller vegetables (such as onions and root crops) are harvested in their entirety by pulling up the whole plant, leaf and fruiting vegetables can be treated differently.

Some salad vegetables can be grown so that you either harvest the entire plant; or, opt for the "cut-and-come-again" method, whereby you simply cut off as many leaves as you need, allowing the plant to continue producing more leaves for the next cut. Leafy salad crops, such as argula, purslane, loose-leaf lettuce and lamb's lettuce, can all be treated in this way.

It is worth noting that most vegetables and fruits, especially those containing vitamin C, have their optimum vitamin content immediately after picking; they will lose vitamins in storage or in cooking so it pays to eat as much fresh and raw produce as you can to get the maximum benefit from it. This is one of the benefits of growing your own fruit and vegetables, because you have no way of knowing for sure how long commercially grown produce has been stored.

Harvesting lettuce (right)
Harvest lettuce by cutting through the stem as close to ground level as possible; remove the entire plant, before trimming away any unwanted outer leaves.

Storing onions (above) *Onions can be stored in a cool, dark, frost-free environment. Threading them into the leg of a pair of old panty hose and separating each onion with a knot is a very easy and effective method.*

Not all vegetables store well, nor do they all necessarily benefit from the same kind of storage conditions. Leafy green vegetables generally do not store well; root vegetables, peas, and beans can be kept more successfully. Store root vegetables in a cool, dark place or in a box of sand with a lid. Put onions on a rack to dry and then thread them together in strings so that they can be hung up.

Many vegetables freeze well, and for most gardeners this is the preferred method of storage. The chart opposite gives the harvesting time and storage method for most commonly grown crops. Some crops need to be blanched before freezing. This involves boiling them rapidly for a very short time before cooling quickly and bagging them for the freezer.

THE VEGETABLE HARVEST

The chart below shows the length of growing season, approximate yield per square yard, and suitability for freezing for some of the principal vegetables you are likely to grow.

Vegetable	Yield (lbs. per sq. yd.)	Length of growing season (weeks)	Suitable for freezing
Argula	1	12	no
Beets	4½	26	yes
Broad beans	9	28	yes
Broccoli	4½	45	yes
Brussels sprouts	3½	52	yes
Carrots	4½	26	yes
Cauliflowers	10	24	yes
Celery	9	36	yes
Chinese cabbage	3½	16	yes
Cucumbers	6½	20	no
Eggplants	11	30	yes
Garlic	4½	40	no
Lettuces	3½	20	no
Leeks	4½	36	no
Onions	3½	32	no
Peas	6½	28	yes
Peppers	3½	28	no
Radishes	1	6	no
Runner beans	8	20	yes
Spinach	3½	36	yes
Sweet corn	2	20	yes
Tomatoes	5½	24	no
Zucchini	4½	20	yes

STORING CHIVES

It is easy to keep herbs fresh by freezing them to create herbal ice cubes.

Storing potatoes (above) *Potatoes can be stored in a cool, dark, frost-free place, but they need plenty of air circulation. A woven basket lined with straw is an ideal storage container. Make sure that light is kept out.*

1 *Wash the chives and use a sharp kitchen knife to chop them into 1–1½ in. lengths.*

2 *Place small bunches of the chopped chives into each cell of an ice cube tray, before filling the tray up to the brim with water and placing it in the freezer overnight.*

3 *Once frozen, the blocks of chives are ready for use, or they can be stored loose in plastic bags until required. The ice cube tray can be used again.*

Lawns and groundcover

Groundcover

Covering the surface of the soil with plants is one of the easiest ways to look after your garden, because the layer of foliage suppresses weed growth, leaving you with very little to do. However, very large areas of groundcover can look less than exciting, so you will need to find ways to use groundcover plants attractively to help cut down on garden chores.

Groundcover plants (below, left to right)

bugleweed (Ajuga reptans); *red epimedium* (Epimedium × rubrum); *winter creeper* (Euonymus fortunei 'Emerald 'n' Gold').

Some of the most successful groundcovers are plants that spread by rhizomes (creeping underground stems), so that they rapidly establish a carpet of foliage. Be aware that this spreading carpet may not stop where you would prefer it to, and use these sometimes invasive plants in specific areas where they cannot run rampant (between an area of paving and a wall, for example).

Of the low, spreading groundcover plants grown principally for foliage, periwinkles are a good choice, particularly for an area in partial shade. There are two species, *Vinca major* (more inva-sive) and *V. minor* (the more deli-cate of the two). Both have ever-green foliage and pretty blue flowers. Another popular standby is Japanese pachysandra (*Pachysandra terminalis*), with whorl-like evergreen leaves.

The hardy cranesbills also make excellent groundcover; additionally, they have handsome foliage, along with the bonus of an attractive flowering display in early summer. *Geranium renardii* and bigroot cranesbill (*G. macr-orrhizum*) are both useful, although not spectacular. The deadnettle is another carpeting plant and the spotted deadnettle (*Lamium maculatum* 'Aureum') is particularly valuable as is bugle-weed. The cultivar 'Burgundy Glow' has red-flushed foliage and bright blue flowers.

For deep shade, ivy (*Hedera* spp.) is invaluable, rapidly cover-ing surfaces with its densely packed evergreen leaves. There are many forms of ivy with fascinating leaf shapes and varie-gations, although those with colored leaves, such as *H. helix* 'Buttercup', need exposure to sunshine in order to maintain their variegation.

You can cover the sides of paths with ribbon-like plantings

Combining materials (above) *Plants can work in harmony with hard materials to provide attractive groundcover. Here sculptural hostas combine with gravel and colorful heucheras to great effect.*

of groundcover plants. Low-growing shrubs like lavender cotton, lavender, and catmint are particularly useful for this. They can be trimmed annually to keep their size and shape in check.

One of the best ways to establish groundcover is to plant through a covering of black plastic. This will suppress weeds in the early stages. You can cover the surface of the plastic with bark mulch to make it look more attractive. The spacing of the plants will depend on what you are planting, but 12–18 in. between plants is a good general guide.

Although not listed as groundcover plants, many shrubs do sterling service in the garden in this role, particularly those with a spreading habit, such as some of the low-growing flaky junipers (*Juniperus squamata* cultivars) or the mound-forming David viburnum (*Viburnum davidii*). Taller shrubs with a spreading canopy will also play their part, casting dense shade over the area. This means that weeds will find it difficult to germinate underneath the canopy, so less weeding will be required.

Groundcover plants (below, left to right) *English ivy* (Hedera helix 'Goldstern'); *dwarf lilyturf* (Ophiopogon planiscapus 'Nigrescens'); *barrenwort* (Epimedium × youngianum 'Niveum').

Types of grasses

One of the most valuable plants for creating attractive groundcover and smothering weeds is the humble grass. In fact, there are many different kinds, often referred to as ornamental grasses, in addition to the varieties commonly used for turf.

Untamed grasses (right)

Ornamental grasses can be contained in neat pots or beds, or allowed to run wild to create a dramatic display.

Ornamental grasses include true grasses (Poaceae) and the sedge (Cyperaceae) and rush (Juncaceae) families. Grasses can be divided into three groups: annuals, biennials, and perennials. The most useful for the gardener are perennials, which carry on year after year. However, while a grass may be perennial in a warm climate, often it can only be grown as an annual in areas that are cooler, so keep this in mind, especially if you are looking for a low-maintenance solution. The tender fountain grass (*Pennisetum setaceum*) is one example.

Grasses can also be categorized by their habit: running or clumping. The running grasses, which spread by stolons above ground or rhizomes below the surface, tend to be invasive, but are useful for general groundcover. For the ornamental garden, the clump-forming grasses are the best to choose because they stay in position. These range from tiny varieties like the bear grass fescue (*Festuca glauca* 'Scoparia'), to the massive pampas grass (*Cortaderia selloana*). The colors vary from rich, bluish-greens, such as those of glaucus blue grass (*Poa glauca*), to bronze, gold and purplish-tinted ones.

To classify the habit of grasses, botanists also use more descriptive terms: tufted, mounded, upright, upright divergent, upright arching, and arching.

Where to grow grasses

You can plant grasses in a wide range of situations in the garden, from tiny species dotted around rock gardens to handsome, impressive feature plants in containers. Many grow well in damp soil and therefore make the perfect surround for a water feature, especially an informal pond. Grasses that originate from arid regions will do sterling service in a gravel garden, requiring little watering even in times of drought.

Maintaining grasses

In temperate climates, plant grasses in spring or fall. If you have to plant when the weather is warm, cut the grasses back to one-third of their size after planting and water regularly, although they cope better with drought than most plants—they will simply not grow as high or as strongly.

In their natural habitats, grasses are frequently subjected to summer fires, which actually benefit the formation of new growth. It pays to adopt a policy of cutting back your grasses in very early spring, just before the new season's growth emerges. This timing does not deprive you of the autumn seedheads, which can be a source of great delight, the rustling heads dancing in the low autumn light.

You can divide your grasses in late autumn or early spring—this takes some brute force and a very sharp saw or knife. After dividing and replanting, cut the foliage back by one-third to reduce moisture loss.

One of the virtues of grasses is that they are relatively pest and disease free, although mammals such as rabbits will feed on them.

Combining grasses (left)
Grow grasses of different heights and colors to create a layered effect with a range of heights and interesting forms.

Grass shapes (below)
Grasses come in a wide range of different shapes, from light and wispy to more solid and structural.

Meadows and natural effects

Although the beautifully manicured lawn is much revered by many aspiring gardeners, recent trends toward gardening based on ecological principles have led many more people to embrace the idea of the wild or semi-wild garden.

U nmowed grass or flowery grassland can be very attractive in the right place and is the ideal solution for an orchard or the farthest end of an otherwise neatly kept suburban garden. It offers the great bonus of providing a suitable habitat for wildlife, too. It is gratifying to think that in return for working less hard, you are actually benefiting the local flora and fauna! The distinguished entomologist Miriam Rothschild has long been an advocate of using native plants, on the basis that those with single flowers (unlike their highly bred, double-flowered cousins) are not sterile and therefore provide nectar.

If your taste lies in greater formality, in larger gardens you can use areas of uncut grass to edge more formal lawns or create a mown strip as a path through a flowery meadow. This not only helps to demarcate the wild from the cultivated, but also gives the whole area a more groomed appearance.

If you plan to give these natural areas of long grass a once-yearly trim, normally carried out in summer, then you can plant them up for a good display of spring-flowering bulbs, many of which will naturalize well in grassland. Among those that do well in these conditions are snowdrops, daffodils, crocuses, and fritillaries. The leaves of the bulbs will have died down by the time you wish to cut the grass in midsummer. If you remove the leaves, the bulbs will lose their food supply and you will have a diminished display the following year.

If you grow summer-flowering perennials in your long grass, the annual cut will have to wait until late summer (as would be done for a hayfield).

Planting bulbs in grass

Most bulbs should be planted in autumn, and it pays to use a bulb planter. This tool removes a plug of turf and soil, leaving a hole into which you then plant the bulb at the appropriate depth (most bulbs should be planted at twice their own depth). The soil plug is then replaced.

BULBS FOR GRASS

A number of bulbs will naturalize (grow well and spread) in grass. Among the best are:

Camassia

Colchicum

Crocus

Erythronium

Fritillaria

Galanthus

Leucojum

Muscari

Narcissus

Ornithogalum

Scilla

Meadow planting (left) *You could create a meadow using a relaxed style of planting in a corner or at the back of your garden. As well as looking good, it will attract the local wildlife.*

Early color (above) *These snowdrops will provide a burst of color when much of the garden is dormant.*

Using taller plants (left)
You do not have to limit yourself to planting low-growing bulbs in grass. Taller plants, such as these daffodils, blend well with longer grass.

Sowing a flowering meadow

To create a flower-rich grassland, you need to choose plants that are native to your area. Not only will they fare better, but they will look appropriate and serve the local wildlife effectively. A flower-rich seed packet will contain a mixture of tough but slow-growing grasses and a selection of broad-leaved perennials. The climate, the condition, and structure of the soil, and moisture levels will determine what grows well. Generally speaking, the poorer the soil, the wider the range of flowering plants that will succeed, so there is no need to fertilize the area.

PLANTING BULBS IN GRASS

The easiest way to plant bulbs in grass is using a bulb planter. Do not plant the bulbs in regimented rows, but scatter them to achieve a natural "wild" effect.

1 *Scatter a handful of the bulbs to achieve a natural look. Plant them where they land.*

2 *Twist the bulb planter into the ground to the desired depth and, still twisting, pull it out again.*

3 *Place the bulb in the hole in an upright position, but do not press it down too firmly.*

4 *Place some of the plug around the bulb until level with the top. Add the remainder and press into place.*

Creating a lawn

If you wish to create a lawn, you will need to prepare the area thoroughly. Remember that a lawn is a long-term project and often a major feature within the garden. Keeping this in mind, it is essential to prepare the soil well before laying the lawn. It is worth putting in the effort from the start to ensure a successful and lasting result.

Before you can lay any lawn, whether you choose seed or turf, you need to make sure that the surface is properly prepared. Your first task is to remove any perennial weeds (see pages 148–149) and any stones on your site. Then it is important to ensure that the area is level. Lawns are notoriously difficult to mow if they are uneven (hence the need for a smooth surface), so putting in the work now will make it easier later.

Leveling the ground

There are various ways to level the ground, the method you use depending on the size of the area. For large areas, the simplest solution is to knock wooden pegs (on which height markers have been indicated with black pen) into the ground, each to the same depth. You can then run string between the pegs at the desired height and adjust the soil surface so that it is level with the string. If you decide to lay turf on the area rather than sow seed, remember to allow roughly 2 in. on top of the desired height to account for the thickness of the turf.

Drainage

Another factor to consider when planning a new lawn is drainage. Lawn grasses grow best on well-drained, light soil. If your garden is waterlogged and the soil generally composed of heavy clay, you will have to consider draining the area first, and you should also incorporate generous quantities of sand and organic matter into the soil itself. Soils that are very light will benefit from the addition of plenty of bulky organic matter to maximize their water-retaining properties.

A simple soakaway system using clay pipes works well to alleviate waterlogged sites (see pages 202–203). Normally, these pipes are laid at intervals of 16½ ft., leading to a gravel-filled soakaway. How closely the drains are spaced will be determined by the local climate and the water table. In areas of heavy rainfall, you will need to position the pipes closer together—in most cases, this should be around 10 ft. apart.

GRASS ROOTS

Not only does grass make a dense mat of foliage above the ground, but beneath the soil there is an even denser mass of fibrous roots. The roots spread rapidly, but in order for them to penetrate to their maximum depth, they need a regular and plentiful supply of moisture.

On light soils, it is important to make sure that you have watered long enough for the water to penetrate to the lower layers of the soil. Shallow watering encourages plant roots to remain near the surface, making them more susceptible to drought.

Drainage (above) *Tackle any potential drainage problems in the area before you sow or lay your lawn. A soakaway system will help if drainage on your site is very poor.*

For areas of the garden such as a lawn,
general care and maintenance are so much
easier if the site is level or has a gentle slope.

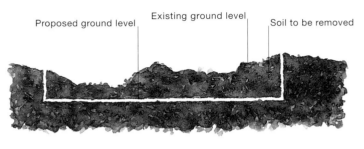

Proposed ground level   Existing ground level   Soil to be removed

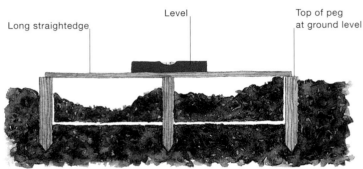

Long straightedge   Level   Top of peg at ground level

1 *Mark out the area with canes and a clearly visible garden line.*

2 *Using a hammer, knock wooden pegs into the soil at 6½ ft. intervals.*

3 *Use a level and a 6½ ft. long, straight-edged board to make sure the tops of the wooden pegs are at the same level.*

4 *Rake the soil between the upright pegs until the same amount of each peg is visible. Check that the level of the soil is consistent as before.*

Preparing the ground

Once you have leveled the ground and dealt with any drainage issues on your site, you will need to firm the surface in preparation for the seed or turf. This is best done by treading it down, more than once if possible. You can do this simply by walking on the ground, making sure you have covered the whole area.

Once it is firm and level, rake over the ground to create a fine tilth. After raking, leave the area fallow for a few weeks, then hoe off any weed seeds that have germinated during this time. Finally, apply a specially formulated lawn fertilizer. Check the instructions carefully to ensure you follow the recommended rate of application.

PREPARING THE GROUND

Carry out your preparation work a few weeks in advance of sowing
or laying the turf to give the ground a chance to settle.

1 *First, rake the area to a fine tilth, removing any weeds or large stones from the site. Break up any large clods of soil as you go.*

2 *Walk across the lawn area, applying pressure with your heels to firm the soil and reduce settling later. Rake again to remove the footprints and level the soil.*

Sowing or laying?

You can either sow a new lawn from seed or you can lay turf.
Turf produces instant results but seed is cheaper; therefore, in large
gardens, it is probably the better option. In smaller gardens, turf may
be the better choice.

Seed is the practical option for repairing small bare patches in a lawn. For larger areas, you can replace sections of turf or reuse existing turf in combination with sowing seed (see page 241).

Sowing seed

Try to sow a new lawn at the most propitious time of year, when the grass seeds will germinate fast and grow quickly. Normally, early fall is the best time, when the soil is still warm. If you sow seed in summer, you will have to water the area frequently.

It is important to get the application rate right for the type of grass you are using. The fescues and bent grasses (*Agrostis*) that are normally used for lawns are sown at half the rate of tougher perennial rye grasses. If you sow too thinly, the lawn will take longer to establish; if you sow too thickly, the seedlings will compete with each other for the available light and nutrients. The seed supplier will give recommended rates. Large areas are best sown by machine, which dispense the seed evenly. Sowing by hand is fine for smaller areas.

Preparing to sow

You need to mark out the area to be sown in squares of around 6½ ft. so that you can sow each one before moving on to the next. Work out the quantity of seed for each area; using a cup or small pail, scatter the seed in one direction and then back again in the other direction to cover the whole area.

After sowing, lightly rake the surface to cover the seed, and then water it regularly to stimulate germination. Once the seedlings reach about 2 in. in

SOWING A LAWN

Seed takes longer to establish as a lawn than turf, but if sown in the spring or autumn it will produce a good-quality result.
You can select a grass seed mixture to suit your purpose, while specialist turf has to be ordered well in advance.

1 *Rake the prepared soil again to form a finely tilled seed bed, removing any large stones and using the rake to break up any remaining lumps of soil.*

2 *Mark out the area into equal squares. Weigh out the seed for each square, then sow the seed evenly, half in each direction. Lightly rake the area.*

3 *Apply the seed by sowing it evenly with your hand at about knee level. This allows the seed to disperse evenly as it travels outward.*

height, you can cut the lawn to roughly half this height with a rotary mower.

Laying turf

A new lawn can be laid from turf in almost any season, except during frost periods, droughts, or very wet weather. Buy good-quality turf, in good condition, from a reputable source. It will normally be sold to you in small rolls, about 1 ft. wide by 3 ft. long; high-quality, golf-course-quality turf comes in smaller units of about 1 ft. square. Make sure that you estimate the area correctly when you order, to save waste and unnecessary expense.

Organize the ordering and delivery of the turf at a convenient time, since ideally it should be laid the day it is delivered. If you do have to store the turf for more than a few days before using it, unroll and lay it surface up, in a shady place and cover with plastic sheeting. Water the turf if you keep it like this for more than 48 hours.

Lay the turf as you would create a brick wall—with staggered joins. Use the nearest straight edge as a guide and work in rows across the area. Butt each new piece of turf flush with its neighbor.

When you have laid all the turf, tamp it down well with the back of a rake, or use a small roller if you have one. This will get rid of any air pockets. Finally, spread some sandy loam soil, which will help to seal the gaps. If you are laying the turf in dry weather, make sure you water it well immediately after laying, and continue watering daily until it becomes established.

To edge the lawn, lay a garden hose or a string between pegs to mark out a curved border, and a plank or similar edge for rectangular shapes. A half-moon blade is ideal for cutting edges.

Storing turf (above) *Do not store turf in rolls for more than two or three days, or the grass inside the rolls will turn yellow due to a lack of light.*

LAYING TURF

Turf provides an almost instant effect, although it may be several weeks before it is fully stable. Ideally, turf should be laid in the fall. However, if the soil is too wet to work on in autumn, the turf can be laid in the spring.

1 *Starting from one corner, lay the first row of turf alongside a plank or length of twine pulled taut to get a neat, straight edge.*

2 *From the same corner, lay the second row at right angles to the first. Set each piece like bricks in a wall, so the joints are staggered.*

3 *Work from a flat board to avoid damaging the turf by walking on it; firm the turf into place. Push the joints together tightly.*

4 *Spread a dressing of sandy loam over the turf and brush or rake it into any gaps to prevent the edges from drying out and shrinking.*

Lawn maintenance

Like all other living parts of your garden, lawns need to be well maintained in order to look their best. As well as cutting your grass to the desired length, it is also important to know how to deal with weeds, feed your lawn, and repair any damage that may occur.

Creating a large area of lawn may seem the ideal way to achieve a low-maintenance garden. To a certain extent, this is true; however, you will still have to put in some hard work to keep your lawn looking as neat and healthy as when you first laid it.

Mowing

The first and most obvious job that must be carried out is mowing. You should never allow your lawn to grow more than about 1½ in. long. There is a wide choice of mowers available, from simple hand-operated machines to large ride-on tractor-style versions suitable for the largest lawns. The hand-operated cylinder mower undoubtedly gives the finest finish, with the handsome stripes reminiscent of a golf course. Rotary mowers do the job more quickly and easily, but without the finish. Hover mowers work quickly and are ideal if your ground is uneven, but they do not cut closely.

If you want a smartly striped finish, start in the center of the lawn and mow away from the house, returning toward the house for the next stripe. Finish one side, and then return to the center cut, starting at the farthest end from the house.

Finishing edges

No lawn will look even half decent unless the edges are neatly finished off. A half-moon blade will cut through the turf neatly. Run a line with pegs and string to ensure a neat edge. Every time you mow, you will need to trim the lawn edges with lawn shears or an electric edger.

ACTION OF CYLINDER/ROTARY MOWER
The style of lawn you choose
should influence the type of mower you buy
to keep your grass neatly trimmed.

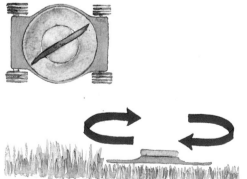

Rotary mowers cut with a scything action. Use these for informal lawns.

Cylinder mowers cut like scissors. They are useful for formal, low-cut lawns.

above *The cylinder action enables this type of mower to cut very close to the ground, creating a neat, well-finished effect.*

CREATING A PATH

If your lawn is the main route from one part of the garden to another, such as the vegetable plot, it is worth thinking in advance about creating a path through it.

The best form to choose is one of stepping stones that are sunk slightly below the level of the grass (1 in. below the surface). This not only prevents the grass wearing unattractively on your chosen route through it, but ensures that the mowing operation is seamless, as you can simply run the mower over the stones.

Mowing strip (above) *Creating a boundary strip of hard landscaping materials, such as brick, eliminates the need for trimming lawn edges.*

Concrete and groundcover path (above) *This decorative path features hexagonal slabs of concrete set into a background of close-cut groundcover.*

Lawn path (above) *A path across a wide expanse of lawn minimizes damage to the grass. Choose the most direct route to encourage people to use the path.*

Lawn edging (above) *Often, after the lawn has been cut, a fringe of grass is left growing out over the edge of the lawn. This can be removed with a pair of edging shears, which cut the grass flush with the edge of the lawn.*

Mown path through long grass (above) *Here, different lengths of grass have been used to create a beautifully edged path through an orchard. The longer grass provides a suitable underplanting for the trees.*

fertilizer supplies a much-needed boost of nutrients. Some fertilizers release their nutrients very slowly, so always read the packet information.

If broad-leaved perennial weeds do take hold, apply a dose of selective weedkiller that targets broad-leaved plants, following the manufacturer's instructions. However, if you do not wish to add chemical preparations to your lawn you will have to remove the inevitable weeds by hand. A sharp knife does the job more efficiently than other tools.

Repairing holes

Even a lawn that is well cared for can encounter some wear and tear. Most lawns are not purely ornamental and are subjected to some degree of use—they may even be a favorite play area for children and pets. Even the daily process of walking up and down

Formal stripes (above)

Many people aspire to a traditional, elegantly striped lawn. However, maintaining this effect requires a lot of care and attention on the part of the gardener.

Maintaining lawn health and vigor

In order to prevent the lawn from becoming either patchy or infested with broad-leaved weeds, carry out a fairly regular program of feeding and pay special attention to the removal of weeds.

Most lawn grasses need regular scarifying. This involves punching holes into the earth to enable oxygen to reach the roots of the grass. You can do this with a garden fork or a purpose-made hollow-tined spiker, which will make the job less arduous. Periodically, apply a top dressing of sand and fertilizer to your lawn. The sand will help to improve the drainage, and the

RAKING

If the lawn feels soft and spongy to walk on, it is usually due to a layer of dead grass clippings or "thatch" that has formed on the soil surface. If allowed to remain, this layer may harbor pests and diseases, as well as weed seeds.

1 *Use a rake to remove the thatch from your lawn. A spring-tined rake is ideal for dragging out the layers of dead material that have accumulated.*

2 *The raking must be vigorous enough to "comb" the soil surface, so that the roots of the grass plants are broken and "pruned" sufficiently to encourage new root growth.*

3 *Remove all the waste and dispose of it away from the lawn. This prevents any pests, diseases, or weeds that may be in the waste from infecting your lawn.*

SPIKING OR SCARIFYING A LAWN

For lawns growing on poorly drained or compacted soil, it is important to allow more air to penetrate around the roots to let them breathe. The easiest way to do this is to make a series of puncture holes, which will enable oxygen to enter the soil quickly.

1 *Press the tines of a hollow-tined spiker into the lawn to about 6 in. The next time the tines are inserted, fresh soil will displace the soil already there and leave it on the grass.*

2 *After an area has been spiked, the soil "cores" can be removed and small heaps of fine topsoil can be brushed or raked into the holes left by the hollow-tined spiker.*

3 *As an alternative, if you have a small garden you can use a simple garden fork to make the holes over the lawn area.*

the garden and tending to your beds and borders can eventually take its toll.

Luckily, if your lawn does become damaged, there are steps you can follow to repair it. If you have bare areas of lawn, you can either use new turf to repair them, or if the area is small, you can sow some grass seed. It is important to make sure that you choose the same type of grass as your existing lawn. If you use seed, laying a sheet of plastic wrap, secured at the corners, over the new area may encourage the new seeds to germinate.

REPAIRING A LAWN

Damaged lawns can be repaired by simply replacing a section of turf, or by lifting and turning the damaged turf and then resowing the problem area.

1 *Using a spade, remove the damaged section of lawn. Cut an area the same size as the new piece of turf.*

2 *Lay the new section of turf by hand, butting it flush with the adjacent edges.*

3 *Tamp down the new turf well, and water it in. Avoid walking on the area for a few days.*

Alternative lawns

A lawn does not have to consist of grass plants. In fact, the original lawns were made up of low, spreading plants that could recover quickly if they were walked upon; they could also tolerate close clipping.

Plants that have fragrant or aromatic leaves are often used for alternative lawns, as the crushed leaves release a pleasant aroma as you walk over them, creating a wonderful effect on summer evenings. The soft, spreading cushions of lush foliage also often have the advantage of acting as an insect repellent.

Traditionally, plants such as wild thyme (*Thymus serpyllum*) and Roman chamomile (*Chamaemelum nobile*) were popular as lawns until reliable, mechanical grass cutters became available, making it possible to manage a grass lawn more easily. This type of aromatic lawn has regained popularity in recent years, with gardeners looking for lawns that need less maintenance but still provide attractive groundcover and complement the other plants within the garden. However, it should always be remembered that plants like thyme and chamomile are not as hard-wearing as grass plants and will not recover from heavy use as easily as a grass lawn.

The preparation for a non-grass lawn is almost identical to the steps you would take to prepare for a grass lawn, in that the soil needs to be cultivated, graded, and leveled in the same way. Ideally, preparation should begin much earlier than planting, in order to allow several generations of weed seedlings to germinate and be killed by hoeing or spraying. This will prevent them from being a problem as the lawn becomes established. The main difference with a non-grass lawn is that this type of lawn cannot be created quickly—it must be planted, especially if the non-flowering form of chamomile (*Chamaemelum nobile* 'Treneague') is used, as growing from seed is not an option.

Laying out a chamomile lawn (right) *Planting a lawn is very different from sowing grass seed or laying turf. Large numbers of small plants have to be positioned and planted individually over a large area.*

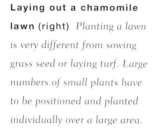

MAKING A CHAMOMILE LAWN

1 *Start by raking level the site for the lawn, firstly using a large rake to break down any large lumps of earth, then a smaller rake with fine teeth to leave a smooth, even finish. Finally, remove any stones.*

2 *Mark out the area using a length of twine. This will mark the boundaries of the lawn and act as a planting guide for the position of the outer rows of plants.*

3 *Start by putting the outer row of plants in first, gently firming each plant into the soil to help them to establish quickly—loose planting often leads to poor establishment due to drying out.*

4 *Plants that have lots of stems and form clumps can be carefully divided into two sections to increase the number of plants and help the lawn to thicken up quickly.*

5 *If the plants have become long and straggly, clip them with a pair of garden shears. They will need to be trimmed anyway and it is much easier to do this while they are still in the nursery tray. Also, clipping will make them branch from the base and spread along the soil.*

6 *Once planting is finished and all the plants are firmed into position, water the whole area with several cans of water or use a garden hose.*

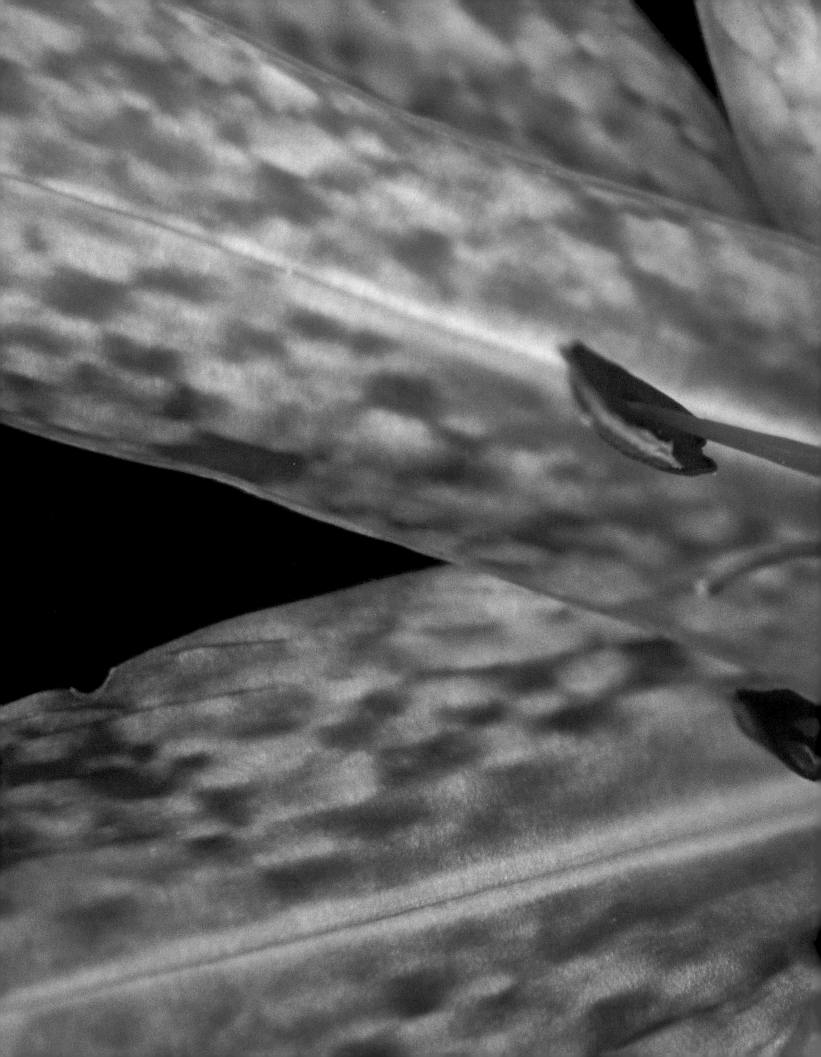

Plant directory

Trees

There is a very wide range of trees to choose from, but for most of us with small gardens, the major issue is how big they will grow. Another factor to keep in mind when making a choice is whether you want your tree to provide some kind of screening. If you do, it is best to go for an evergreen, which will do the job all year round; a deciduous tree will provide an effective screen for only half the year.

It is always worth looking for trees that offer a variety of attributes: attractive autumn leaf color, berries, or perhaps fragrant or abundant flowers, such as those of ornamental cherries or magnolias. The color and structure of the foliage is important, too. You can find a wonderfully diverse range of leaf forms and types, ranging from the needle-like leaves of conifers to the heavily dissected leaves of some Japanese maples, most of which also provide a spectacular autumn display of color. Hawthorns (*Crataegus*) are good year-rounders, offering pretty flowers in spring, abundant rich green summer foliage and brilliantly colored fruits and good leaf color in autumn. They are also relatively small, so they are good candidates for restricted spaces.

Be aware that trees must not be planted too close to buildings, because the roots can be invasive. Willows (*Salix*) are notorious in this respect. Equally, fast-growing trees, such as some species of cypress (*Chamaecyparis*), while useful for providing quick screening effects, can become too tall for their situation unless pruned.

Pruning of large trees is best left to the experts, both from a safety point of view and to ensure that the tree is not damaged in the process.

Acer palmatum f. *atropurpureum*
Japanese maple

H 15 ft. S 15 ft.

A slow-growing, deciduous Japanese maple with attractive reddish-purple foliage in spring and summer, turning to fiery red in autumn. The palmate leaves, deeply divided into 5–7 lobes, are borne on red stems. It forms a round-headed, spreading tree; it can be grown in a container, where its size will be restricted. It needs protection from cold, drying winds, which can scorch and curl the delicate leaves. Clusters of small flowers appear in spring, followed by reddish, winged fruits in autumn. Prune lightly in autumn to remove dead or damaged wood. Propagate by sowing seeds in autumn as soon as they are ripe.

Ailanthus altissima
Tree of heaven

H 80 ft. S 50 ft.

Ultimately reaching the size of a woodland tree, the deciduous tree of heaven is a specimen for a large garden. It has striking large, pinnate leaves, which open reddish-green and age to mid-green. The young shoots are red-bronze and covered in minute hairs; the bark is gray and deeply fissured. Greenish-white flowers are borne in large clusters in summer, followed by red-brown, winged fruits. Male and female flowers occur on separate plants; both are needed for fruits to form. Pruning hard every year will keep the plant as a bush, but it may sucker. Propagate by sowing ripe seeds in autumn or spring or by potting suckers.

Aralia elata 'Variegata'
Japanese angelica tree

H 30 ft. S 30 ft.

The Japanese angelica tree is a clump-forming, deciduous tree with spiny stems which sucker freely. Its leaves are up to 4 ft. long and doubly pinnate, being divided into about 80 small, oval leaflets, each with an irregular creamy-white edge. In autumn they turn to shades of orange and yellow before falling. During late summer and autumn, showy clusters of creamy-white flowers form at the tips of the shoots, followed by round black fruits. Prune out all surplus suckers and any shoots that revert to plain green. Propagate by grafting in winter or by rooting suckers.

Arbutus unedo
Strawberry tree

H 20 ft. S 20 ft.

The strawberry tree is an extremely handsome small evergreen tree or large shrub with peeling, red-brown bark and glossy, dark green foliage. In autumn, it produces clusters of hanging white or pink-tinged flowers, followed by knobbly, spherical fruits. These ripen to a glowing scarlet by the following autumn and are edible. The form f. *rubra* has dark pink flowers, while 'Elfin King' is much more compact at 6 ft. tall and 5 ft. wide. Grow in a border or as a specimen in a container, pruning only if absolutely necessary. Propagate by sowing seeds as soon as they ripen or by taking semi-ripe cuttings in summer.

Chamaecyparis pisifera 'Filifera Aurea'
Sawara cypress

H 30 ft. S 12 ft.

An unusual slow-growing conifer with peeling, rust-brown bark and slender, drooping, whip-like young shoots. The foliage matures as flattened sprays. It is a glorious golden yellow all over, making this an ideal specimen for a conifer planting or container, although it does need room to spread. It has tiny male cones in spring and small, angular female cones that mature from green to brown in the first fall. Sawara cypress will grow in all soils but prefers neutral to slightly acid conditions. Grow it in full sun to maintain the color—it will turn greenish in shade. Prune only if absolutely necessary and do not cut into old wood. Propagate from semi-ripe cuttings taken in late summer.

Crataegus
Hawthorn

H 25 ft. S 25 ft.

An attractive deciduous tree, the hawthorn has dull mid-green leaves and thorny shoots. It is colorful in spring when it produces clusters of single or double flowers about ½ in. across in creamy white, or light- or dark-pink, such as *C. laevigata* 'Paul's Scarlet'. In autumn, these are followed by round to oval red fruits and plants like *C. persimilis* 'Prunifolia', have attractive leaf colors. Most hawthorns are hardy, resilient plants that tolerate wind, coastal salt, pollution, and any position except a waterlogged soil. Prune only to maintain the health and shape. Propagate by budding in summer or grafting while the plant is dormant in winter.

Eucalyptus gunnii
Cider gum

H 30–60 ft. S 15–30 ft.

The evergreen cider gum is one of the best known eucalypts, and one of the hardiest. It is grown for its juvenile leaves, which are much prized by flower arrangers. They are rounded and blue on young plants, sickle-shaped and gray-green on mature trees. Pruning hard every spring will encourage a multi-stemmed plant with 4–5 shoots of about 5 ft. tall. This also has the benefits of maintaining the juvenile foliage and controlling the size of the plant. With age, the blue-gray bark becomes greenish-white, peeling off in long strips to reveal new gray-green bark, sometimes shaded pink. Small, creamy-white flowers are borne in summer on mature trees. Propagate by sowing seeds in spring.

Ilex aquifolium
English holly

H 30 ft. S 10 ft.

The English holly forms a pyramid-shaped shrub or tree with gray bark and prickly, glossy evergreen leaves. There are many forms, some with more prickles or with leaf variegations in silver or gold. Small white- or pink-tinted flowers are produced in spring, followed (on female plants) by bright, shiny berries of red or yellow, according to the variety. Male and female plants are both needed for berries to form. English holly is attractive as a specimen but can also be used as a strong hedge. Prune only to maintain the health or shape of the plant. Propagate species by sowing seeds in fall (germination may take 3 years); take semi-ripe cuttings of forms.

Magnolia grandiflora 'Exmouth'
Southern magnolia

H 20–40 ft. S up to 30 ft.

A large but fairly slow-growing evergreen magnolia with dense, glossy foliage of a rich dark green. The underside of the leaf is paler green with a covering of rusty-red hairs. In late summer and autumn, striking large, cup-shaped, creamy-white flowers with purple centers are produced, each about 10 in. across. Southern magnolia can be grown as a freestanding specimen, either in a border or a large container, or it can be trained against a wall, where it provides attractive coverage throughout the year. Prune only to maintain the health and shape of the plant. Propagate by taking semi-ripe cuttings in late summer.

Prunus serrulata 'Kiku-Shidari'
Oriental cherry

H 10 ft. S 10 ft.

An ornamental cherry also sold as 'Cheal's Weeping', this is a lovely deciduous tree for color in a small garden. In spring, as the bronze new leaves are emerging, the branches are covered with double bright pink flowers that are about 1½ in. across and borne in dense clusters. It has a second flush of color in autumn as the tapering, mid-green leaves turn to shades of orange and red before being shed. Remove dead or damaged wood in summer to avoid infection by silver-leaf disease, which causes the branches to die back. Propagate by budding in summer or grafting when the plant is dormant in winter or early spring.

Prunus subhirtella 'Autumnalis Rosea'
Higan cherry

H 20 ft. S 20 ft.

This flowering cherry forms a wide-spreading, deciduous tree. The toothed leaves are bronze in spring as they emerge, mature to dark green, and turn a glorious butter yellow in autumn before they fall. The attraction of this tree is that the small, semi-double pink flowers are produced in clusters throughout the fall, winter, and early spring, whenever there is a period of mild weather. Prune to remove dead or damaged shoots, and do it in summer to avoid the risk of infection by silver-leaf disease, which makes the branches die back. Propagate by budding in summer or grafting while the plant is dormant in winter or early spring.

Pyrus salicifolia 'Pendula'
Willow-leaved pear

H 15 ft. S 12 ft.

An ornamental form of pear, this deciduous tree forms a tangled mass of weeping branches. The long, pale green, willow-like leaves have a felt-like covering of hairs when they are young, giving them an attractive silvery-gray coloring; this felting disappears as the leaves age. Pretty creamy-white flowers are produced in clusters of 6–8 in spring and are followed in late summer by small green, pear-shaped fruits. The shape of this plant can be improved with regular pruning in late spring after flowering to reduce the number of shoots and control their direction of growth. Propagate by budding in summer or grafting in winter.

Rhus typhina
Staghorn sumac

H 6 ft. S 10 ft.

This is a small deciduous tree with velvety red shoot tips resembling antlers. In spring, erect clusters of red flowers are produced on the shoot tips. It suckers freely and may become invasive if these are allowed to develop. The main season of attraction is autumn, when the long pinnate leaves turn from dark green to fiery shades of red, orange, and gold before they fall. The form R. t. 'Dissecta' has finely dissected, lacy-looking leaves and yellowish flowers up to 8 in. long, followed by hairy, dark red fruits. May be hard pruned in spring to produce large leaves. Propagate by digging up rooted suckers when they are dormant.

Robinia pseudoacacia 'Frisia'
Black locust

H 30 ft. S 15 ft.

This variant of the black locust is a quick-growing, deciduous tree that can sucker freely. Its young shoots have wine-red spines, and the bark of the trunk becomes deeply furrowed as the plant ages. The leaves are pinnate and change from golden-yellow as they emerge to greenish-yellow in summer, then orange-yellow in autumn. Fragrant, white, pea-like flowers are produced in long, hanging clusters in summer, followed by brown seedpods. Black locust can be pruned hard in early spring each year to control the size and produce larger leaves, or in late summer or autumn (to avoid excessive bleeding) to maintain health. Propagate by grafting in winter.

Sorbus hupehensis
Mountain ash

H 25 ft. S 25 ft.

A pretty deciduous tree with pinnate, blue-green leaves that turn red in autumn before they fall. Pyramidal clusters of white flowers in late spring are followed in summer by hanging clusters of round, pink-flushed white berries. Like other members of the rowan group, this is tolerant of atmospheric pollution and makes an excellent choice for a city garden. Variants include var. *obtusa*, whose berries ripen to a dark pink. S. 'Joseph Rock' is a popular choice for city gardens, because it has a more upright habit and the leaves color well in autumn, turning shades of red, purple and orange. The berries are yellow. Most species of rowan thrive in well-drained soil, in full sun or dappled shade. *S. aria*, the whitebeam, does well on dry, chalky soil. Prune mountain ash in late winter or early spring only to remove any dead or damaged wood. Propagate by taking softwood cuttings in early summer or by grafting in winter.

Taxus baccata
Yew

H 30 ft. S 25 ft.

The common yew is a dense, heavily branched evergreen plant with peeling, reddish-brown bark and needle-like leaves of a glossy deep green. It will tolerate shade, dry conditions, and atmospheric pollution, making it useful in cities and beside roads. Yellow male cones are produced in spring and female plants produce shiny, red fruits in autumn. The numerous forms include 'Dovastonii Aurea' (spreading, golden), 'Fastigiata' (upright, green), and 'Standishii' (compact, upright, golden). Yew may be pruned quite hard to maintain its shape, which makes it useful for hedging and topiary. Propagate by sowing seeds as soon as they ripen (species only) or by taking semi-ripe cuttings in summer.

Shrubs

Shrubs are the backbone of any garden. Their varied forms, growth habit, leaf shapes, and flowers are essential elements in their design, and so their choice needs careful consideration. Too many evergreens can create a gloomy and static effect, but a few should be planted to provide structure and form in the winter months, when perennials have died down and deciduous shrubs are reduced to skeletons.

Whether they are deciduous or evergreen, it pays to select shrubs with variously colored and textured foliage. The choice is vast—from dark glossy leaves to fine almost silvery ones; from plain dark leaves to brilliantly variegated ones. By making a diverse selection, you will create a permanent feeling of light and life in your garden, complementing the flowering plants.

Height and shape are crucial considerations; again, aim for variety. Include a few taller-growing shrubs to provide shelter and screening, add medium-sized ones to flesh out the back of borders and provide focal points in the plan and, finally, pick smaller ones to beef up the planting in perennial borders or make low-growing hedges.

Many shrubs are ideal for hedging. You can choose from quick-growing but more labor-intensive evergreens to flowering shrubs, which provide a less solid but more visually exciting screen.

Pruning is of major importance if flowering shrubs are to perform as they should. When done properly it will encourage the maximum number of flowers to form; get the timing wrong and you could lose a flower display.

Aucuba japonica
Japanese laurel

H 6 ft. S 6 ft.

An attractive, evergreen shrub, tolerant of shade, moisture, pollution, and salt winds. Its glossy, oval-shaped leaves are mid-green with a few teeth at the edges. Variegated forms include the female *A. j.* 'Crotonifolia', with bright yellow-splashed leaves and small purple-red flowers in spring followed by large, bright red berries that last into the winter as long as a male form such as *A. j.* 'Crassifolia' is growing nearby. Prune lightly in spring to maintain the shape. Propagate by seed sown in autumn or semi-ripe cuttings in summer.

Berberis thunbergii 'Atropurpurea'
Japanese barberry

H 3 ft. S 3 ft.

A densely branched, deciduous shrub with angular, red-brown stems set with very sharp spines. A row of these plants makes a good boundary hedge to discourage intruders. The rounded leaves are dark reddish-purple or bronze-purple and turn a glorious fiery red in autumn before they fall. Clusters of red-tinted, yellow flowers appear in spring, followed by glossy red fruits in autumn. It tolerates regular pruning in spring after flowering. Remove a quarter of the old growth to the base to promote new shoots. Propagate by taking soft-tip cuttings in spring or semi-ripe cuttings in summer.

Buddleia davidii
Butterflybush

H 10 ft. S 10 ft.

This butterflybush is a large, quick-growing deciduous shrub that will thrive in any well-drained soil. The large, pointed leaves are borne on long, arching shoots and are mid-green, edged with yellow as they emerge, aging to cream and white. Full sun brings out the best color in the leaves. In summer, butterflies are attracted to the fragrant, rich red-purple flowers, which are borne on spikes up to 12 in. long. Prune hard in early spring. Propagate from hardwood cuttings in winter.

Buxus sempervirens
American boxwood

H 10 ft. S 10 ft.

A slow-growing, bushy evergreen plant that can easily be clipped to form different topiary shapes. It is useful as a foil to more brightly colored plants or as a specimen in its own right, in the border or a container. Its small, tough, oval leaves are a glossy dark green, and it produces masses of tiny, star-shaped, yellowish-green flowers in spring. Variegated forms are often lower-growing. They include 'Elegantissima' (white-edged leaves), 'Latifolia Maculata' (compact, with bright yellow young foliage, maturing to dark green with yellow markings), and 'Marginata' (yellow-edged leaves). 'Suffruticosa' is slow-growing and compact, making it particularly good for topiary. Propagate by taking semi-ripe cuttings in summer.

Camellia x *williamsii* 'Donation'
Camellia

H 15 ft. S 8 ft.

An evergreen shrub with attractive glossy, oval leaves on pale brown stems. In spring it produces wide, semi-double pink flowers with golden centers. As these may be spoiled by wet or frosty weather, the plant will benefit from some shelter or the warmth of a wall. Camellias are suitable for growing in containers, especially if the native soil is alkaline, as they need acidic conditions. Watering must be consistent, otherwise the flower buds may be shed before they open. Pruning is not necessary. Propagate by taking semi-ripe cuttings in summer (with at least 1 in. of woody stem at the base). Use rooting hormone and provide bottom heat, such as with an electric propagator.

Choisya ternata
Mexican orange flower

H 5 ft. S 5 ft.

The Mexican orange blossom is a compact evergreen shrub with glossy, aromatic, palmate leaves produced in whorls on green, woody stems. Dense clusters of small white, musk-scented, star-shaped flowers appear in late spring and again in late summer and fall. 'Sundance' rarely flowers but has bright yellow foliage (this may scorch in intense sunlight and turns lime-green in partial shade). C. 'Aztec Pearl' is compact, with long, thin, dark green leaflets and pink-tinted white flowers. Grow in any well-drained soil or a container and prune only to remove damaged shoots. Propagate by taking semi-ripe cuttings in late summer.

Cordyline australis 'Torbay Dazzler'
Cabbage tree

H 3 ft. S 3 ft.

An evergreen, spiky-leaved perennial, the cabbage tree will eventually grow to resemble a woody-stemmed, palm-like tree. It is an architectural plant, and it makes a good individual specimen, either in a border or container. The arching, lance-like leaves are striped and edged with creamy-white and may be up to 3 ft. long. The sweetly fragrant and cup-shaped flowers are produced in long clusters in summer on mature plants and are followed in hot years by round, white berries. Propagate by removing offshoots as soon as they have good roots. These can be planted right away or potted until they are required.

Cornus alba 'Spaethii'
Tartarian dogwood

H 10 ft. S 10 ft.

The tartarian dogwood is an upright deciduous shrub, ideal for planting in a mixed border or beside a pool. It is grown for its slender, rich red stems, which are particularly striking in winter, when the plant gives a welcome splash of color. The leaves are bronzed as they open, then mid-green and pointed, with a bright blotch of yellow around the edges. They turn to red and orange before falling in autumn. The white flowers are produced in flat heads during summer. The young stems have the best color—to give the most colorful display, prune the plant hard every spring. Propagate by taking hardwood cuttings in autumn (or late winter as the shoots are pruned).

Cotinus coggygria
Smoke tree

H 10 ft. S 10 ft.

The smoke tree is a deciduous shrub with rounded, mid-green leaves. In autumn these turn to shades of orange and red before falling. Fluffy-looking, heavily branched plumes of tiny fruits appear in summer, maturing from pinky-purple to smoky-gray and producing the misty appearance that gives rise to the plant's common name. Grow it in a mixed border. The form 'Royal Purple' has leaves of rich, dark, reddish-purple that turn red in autumn, and 'Notcutt's Variety' has burgundy-colored foliage and purplish-pink fruiting panicles. These purple-leaved variants are an excellent choice for the back of a border, introducing height as well as color to the planting. 'Flame' is taller, to 20 ft. high, with light green leaves that turn orange-red in autumn. Prune hard each spring to increase leaf size, or only lightly to maintain the shape and health of the plant. Propagate by taking softwood cuttings in spring.

Cytisus x *praecox* 'Allgold'
Broom

H 4 ft. S 5 ft.

A compact, deciduous shrub with arching, green shoots and tiny leaves that grows to form a dome-shaped mound. In spring it produces a bright show of color when it is smothered in pea-like, dark golden-yellow flowers. This is a useful plant for the front of a mixed border or in a container, rock garden, or raised bed. It is very tolerant of its site and will survive in an exposed or coastal position. Broom will grow in most soils, even poor ones, but it prefers acid soil. Prune only to remove any dead or damaged shoots. Propagate by taking semi-ripe cuttings in late summer.

Elaeagnus x *ebbingei*
Ebbinge's silverberry

H 10 ft. S 10 ft.

An attractive, hardy, and reliable evergreen shrub that is tolerant of coastal exposure and has a spreading habit and scaly, golden-bronze shoots. The leathery, broadly lance-shaped leaves are metallic-green above and silvery-green beneath. In the autumn and winter, small, highly fragrant, white, bell-like flowers are produced beneath the leaves. The fragrance is often noticed before the flowers are seen. Variegated cultivars include 'Gilt Edge' (yellow-edged leaves) and 'Limelight' (silvery new shoots and lime-green to yellow leaf markings). Remove any shoots that revert to green on a variegated plant, otherwise they will take over. Propagate by taking semi-ripe cuttings in summer.

Euonymus fortunei 'Emerald Gaiety'
Wintercreeper

H 2 ft. S indefinite

A low-growing, bushy evergreen shrub grown for its brightly marked foliage rather than its greenish-white flowers, which are small and insignificant. The oval, leathery leaves are bright green and edged with white, which flushes mid-pink in winter. The stems trail as groundcover but will scramble up to 5 ft. high, if given some support. It is tolerant of a range of conditions, although the leaf markings may be affected in deep shade. Plant it as a low hedge, in a border, at the base of a wall, or in a container, among other plants as groundcover or as a specimen. Prune in spring if necessary to maintain shape. Propagate by taking semi-ripe cuttings in late summer.

Euphorbia characias subsp. *wulfenii*
Milkweed, spurge

H 4 ft. S 4 ft.

This is an unusual upright plant for a mixed border. It is normally categorized as an evergreen shrub, but it has shoots that develop and die back over two years (biennial). The woolly, purple-tinted stems are produced in clusters, with elongated, gray-green leaves. The flowers have reduced male and female parts in a yellowish-green structure called a cyathium surrounded by a green involucre (single bract). They are borne in dense, rounded clusters at the tops of the stems from early spring and should be removed, because they fade if seeds are not required. Cut all flowered stems back to the base after flowering. Propagate by division in spring.

Exochorda x *macrantha* 'The Bride'
Pearlbush

H 6 ft. S 10 ft.

This compact deciduous shrub has arching stems and grows to form a rounded mound of mid-green leaves. In late spring and early summer, it disappears under a covering of beautiful saucer-shaped, white flowers up to 1 in. across and borne in clusters of 6–10. It is ideal in a border or as a single specimen and can be grown in a container. Prune annually after flowering to remove flowered shoots back to a strong pair of buds, and on established shrubs, remove about a quarter of the growth back to the base of the plant to promote new shoots. Propagate by taking softwood cuttings in summer.

Fatsia japonica
Japanese fatsia

H 10 ft. S 10 ft.

An evergreen spreading shrub that can reach a considerable size in the right conditions. It prefers shelter from cold winds, which can damage the large, glossy, 7–11 lobed, dark green leaves, but it will tolerate both coastal exposure and pollution. It is a wonderful plant for introducing a tropical feel to the garden and will grow happily in a container, which will keep the size under control. The creamy-white flowers are borne in spherical clusters on branching shoots in autumn and are followed by black fruits. Prune in spring only to remove old flower heads and any damaged shoots. Propagate by sowing seeds indoors as soon as they ripen in autumn or take semi-ripe cuttings in summer.

Hamamelis x *intermedia* 'Pallida'
Witch-hazel

H 12 ft. S 12 ft.

A spreading shrub with ascending branches grown for its spidery winter flowers and glorious autumn color. The oval leaves are matte-green in summer turning to yellow in autumn. In mid- to late winter, small, fragrant flowers appear in clusters on the bare shoots. Each has 4 crumpled, strap-like, sulfur-yellow petals surrounding a red center. They are fairly frost-resistant, but flowering may pause during a really cold spell. Grow in a mixed border or woodland setting, and prune only to maintain the health of the plant. Propagate by layering in spring, grafting in winter, or budding in summer.

Kolkwitzia amabilis
Beautybush

H 10 ft. S 10 ft.

The beautybush is a deciduous suckering shrub that will grow almost anywhere, but benefits from shelter in spring as the leaves emerge. It has long, arching stems with peeling bark and pointed, mid-green leaves. In late spring and early summer it produces clusters of bell-shaped, 5-lobed flowers, pale to rose-pink outside and marked with yellow and orange in the throat. These are borne in huge quantities all over the plant, making a spectacular display of color. Prune annually after flowering: Remove flowered shoots to a strong bud and, on established plants, cut off a quarter of the shoots completely to encourage growth from the base. Propagate by taking softwood cuttings in summer.

Magnolia stellata
Star magnolia

H 10 ft. S 12 ft.

This magnolia is an attractive deciduous shrub with a spreading growth habit and gray stems. The star-like flowers start as furry buds in late winter, opening in early or midspring to reveal pure white flowers 5 in. across with golden centers and up to 15 petals. Opening before the long, mid-green leaves start to emerge, these become pink-tinted as they age. This magnolia will benefit from protection in spring, as the flowers may be damaged by late frosts; it is ideal for growing as a specimen in a border or in an ornamental container. It should not require pruning unless it is damaged. Propagate by taking semi-ripe cuttings in late summer or by layering in spring.

Prunus laurocerasus 'Otto Luyken'
Common cherry laurel

H 3 ft. S 5 ft.

The common cherry laurel is a leafy evergreen shrub that will grow almost anywhere. It has a compact habit and long, glossy, dark green leaves that make it a useful foil to the brighter colors of summer in the border, once it has finished flowering. Small, cup-shaped, and creamy-white, the flowers are borne in upright spikes on the shoot tips in spring and are followed by round fruits that ripen from red to black. It may have a second flush of flowers in autumn. Prune after flowering, if any shoots need removing to improve shape. Propagate by taking semi-ripe cuttings in late summer.

Rhododendron yakushimanum
Rhododendron

H 6 ft. S 6 ft.

A beautiful compact evergreen shrub that remains attractive even when the flowers finish. Grow it in a shrub border, woodland garden or container. The young leaves are covered with cinnamon-colored felting on both sides; this is lost off the upper side as the leaf ages, but the underside retains a thick, red-brown covering. In midspring, trusses of up to 10 bell-shaped flowers appear, dark pink in bud, opening rose-pink, and fading to white, so that all three colors may be present at the same time. Prune only to remove faded flowers. Propagate by taking semi-ripe cuttings in late summer or by layering in spring.

Ribes sanguineum
Winter currant

H 6 ft. S 6 ft.

The winter currant is a deciduous shrub with alternate, 3- to 5-lobed leaves and bell-shaped, pink to reddish flowers, borne in hanging clusters in spring. The leaves are highly aromatic—some people find the scent unpleasant. The variety 'Pulborough Scarlet' has flowers of dark red with a white eye, while those of 'Tydeman's White' are pure white. The flowers are sometimes followed by round, red or black fruits. Winter currants are perfect for a mixed or shrub border. Propagate by rooting semi-ripe cuttings in late summer or hardwood cuttings in fall or winter.

Rosa 'Fru Dagmar Hastrup'
Rose

H 3 ft. S 3 ft.

This is one of the rugosa group of roses, which are typified by their
upright, densely thorny stems and heavily fragrant flowers. It forms
a rounded deciduous plant with a spreading habit and coarse-looking,
heavily veined, mid-green leaves that turn butter-yellow before they fall
in autumn. In summer it produces single, shallowly cup-shaped, pale
pink flowers up to 3 in. across with a delicious scent of cloves. These are
followed in autumn by attractive rounded, dark red hips. Plant this rose as
a low hedge or in a mixed border. Prune only to remove old hips and any
dead or damaged shoots. Propagate by taking hardwood cuttings from late
autumn to early winter.

Rosa xanthina 'Canary Bird'
Rose

H 10 ft. S 10 ft.

A densely branched deciduous shrub rose with
arching, reddish-brown shoots and grayish-
green leaves. This is one of the earliest roses
to flower and is spectacular in spring, when
the branches are covered with single, fragrant
blooms up to 2 in. across. These are a rich
bright golden yellow and have a raised center of
golden stamens. There may be a second flush
of flowers in summer, and any hips that form
are rounded and brown- or maroon-red. 'Canary
Bird' is ideal grown against a fence, where the
flowers will enjoy the added protection. Prune
after flowering to remove dead or damaged
wood. Propagate by taking hardwood cuttings
from late autumn to early winter.

Rosmarinus officinalis 'Miss Jessopp's Upright'
Rosemary

H 6 ft. S 5 ft.

This is a form of rosemary that grows with a strong, upright habit, as the name suggests. Grow it in a mixed border or herb garden, or as a hedge. The evergreen blue-green foliage is strongly aromatic and very useful in both cooking and herbal treatments. Each leaf is narrow and leathery, an adaptation to resist moisture loss in the hot Mediterranean regions from where the species originates. In late spring and early summer, small, 2-lipped, blue flowers are produced along the stems, sometimes with a second flush in autumn. Prune annually after the first flowering, especially if the foliage is to be harvested. Propagate by taking semi-ripe cuttings in summer.

Sambucus racemosa 'Plumosa Aurea'
European red elderberry

H 10 ft. S 10 ft.

This variety of the European red elderberry is grown for its spectacular foliage. It is a vigorous plant, suitable as a specimen in a border, where its long, arching stems have room to grow. The finely cut, deciduous leaves are bronze as they emerge, opening to a bright golden yellow. Their color is better when the plant is grown in full sun, but the hot sun of midday in summer may cause some scorching. Clusters of creamy-yellow flowers are borne in spring, followed in late summer or autumn by shiny, round, red fruits. Prune hard annually, reducing stems to 2–3 buds, to maintain a good show of foliage. Propagate by taking hardwood cuttings in winter.

Skimmia x *confusa* 'Kew Green'
Skimmia

H 3 ft. S 5 ft.

A slow-growing, evergreen, aromatic shrub that forms a compact dome shape. It is an ideal plant for a border or container and tolerates shade, atmospheric pollution, and even some neglect. The thick, leathery, mid-green leaves are oval, ending in a pointed tip and carried on stocky, green stems. In spring, small, fragrant, star-like, creamy-white male flowers are borne in dense clusters up to 6 in. long. Male and female flowers occur on separate plants, so this is an ideal pollinator for a female variety. It needs no regular pruning—only trim to improve shape if necessary. Propagate by taking semi-ripe cuttings in summer.

Viburnum x *bodnantense* 'Dawn'
Bodnant viburnum

H 6 ft. S 5 ft.

A spectacular upright deciduous shrub for winter color, this plant produces its clusters of rich pink flowers on bare stems continuously from late autumn until early spring, although it will pause in periods of severe weather. On a warm, calm day, the sweet fragrance will carry some distance from the plant. As the flowers fade, the coarse-looking leaves begin to emerge, bronze-green at first, aging to dark green. This viburnum is ideal for the back of a border, but it should be accessible so that the fragrance can be appreciated. Prune only to remove dead or damaged stems. Propagate by taking softwood cuttings in summer.

Viburnum plicatum
Japanese snowball viburnum

H 10 ft. S 12 ft.

This deciduous viburnum makes a spreading bush with large clusters of white, saucer-shaped flowers in spring. The leaves turn a rich reddish purple in autumn. There are several popular and attractive cultivars, including 'Grandiflorum', with particularly large white flowers, and 'Mariesii', which has a distinctly layered shape with the branches held in tiers. Viburnums grow well in sun or partial shade. You can propagate from softwood cuttings in summer.

Weigela florida 'Variegata'
Old-fashioned weigela

H 6 ft. S 6 ft.

A compact deciduous shrub with arching shoots, ideal for growing in a border or container. The tapering, oval leaves are gray-green, edged with creamy-white, and they hold their color better in a well-lit position, although the intense sun at midday in summer may cause some scorch. Tubular flowers of a deep rose pink are produced along the stems in early summer. In addition to this variegated weigela, there are many other choices, including the attractive bronze-leaved 'Foliis Purpureis', which has deep pink flowers that are whitish inside. 'Eva Rathke' is slightly smaller, to 5 ft. tall, with dark crimson flowers. A different species, *W. praecox*, which grows taller, to 8 ft., has dark green leaves and fragrant pink flowers with a yellow throat. The stems of weigelas grow one year and flower the next, after which they can be cut back hard to ensure continued production of flowering wood. Propagate by taking semi-ripe cuttings in late summer or hardwood cuttings in winter.

Climbers and wall shrubs

Few plants give you such good value for your money as climbers. From a very small area of ground space, they produce yards of foliage and flowers, to cover or enhance walls, sheds, and trees. Wall shrubs are ordinary shrubs that lend themselves to being trained against a wall, where they benefit from the protection. Some, such as flowering maple, have fairly thin stems that need support.

The choice of climbers and wall shrubs is vast, and the plants featured below are just a small selection. We all have particular favorites—among the most popular are climbing roses and clematis—but some of the less flashy performers do sterling work in covering large and boring expanses of wall or fence. Those that are evergreen (such as some clematis and all firethorns) will do the job all year round as a bonus.

Scent is an important factor in making a choice; many climbers are generous in this respect—nothing quite beats the sweet fragrance of roses or honeysuckle wafting in through a bedroom window in summer. It is also worth trying to plan for color or interest over more than one season, so pick some that flower in winter or spring, such as winter jasmine, and others, such as firethorn, that provide brilliant displays of berries in the fall.

The speed of growth of some climbers does mean that you may well have your work cut out controlling them, and you may have to supply an ever increasing network of wires on which to train the errant stems. Since the weight of a vigorous climber in full flower is considerable, the support and the support system must be sufficiently strong.

Abutilon megapotamicum
Flowering maple

H 6 ft. S 6 ft.

A graceful spreading shrub with semi-evergreen, mid-green leaves, which may be entire or up to 5-lobed, on arching stems. The attractive showy flowers are produced singly or in small groups along the shoots from summer to autumn. They are bell-shaped with a red calyx, yellow petals, and prominent purple stamens. The form 'Variegatum' has bright yellow-splashed leaves. It will grow well against a warm wall, where it will benefit from the protection; in very cold areas, it may be kept in a container so that you can protect it from frost during the winter by moving it indoors or into a sheltered corner. Prune by cutting back old flowered shoots to 2–3 buds in early spring. Propagate by taking softwood cuttings in summer.

Akebia quinata
Chocolate vine, five-leaf akebia

H 30 ft. S 15 ft.

The chocolate vine is a semi-evergreen, twining climber with palmate leaves of mid-green that are tinted bronze as they emerge. The vanilla-scented flowers appear in spring, in rich maroon to chocolate brown. Male and female flowers are borne within the same cluster; small male ones at the tip and larger female ones at the base. Long, sausage-shaped purple fruits will be produced in a hot summer, if there is a second plant nearby to cross-pollinate. Grow chocolate vine against a warm wall or over a pergola. Prune after flowering, if necessary, to maintain the shape. Propagate by layering in spring, taking semi-ripe cuttings in summer or sowing seeds as soon as they are ripe.

Campsis x *tagliabuana* 'Madame Galen'
Trumpet creeper

H 30 ft. S 15 ft.

This vigorous deciduous trumpet creeper grows well on a sunny wall, fence, or pergola, where it supports itself using aerial roots. It produces pinnate, dark green leaves which turn golden-yellow in autumn. Showy trumpet-shaped, orange-red flowers open in clusters of up to 12 on the shoot tips from midsummer until the first frosts. Tie young shoots to the support until the aerial roots take hold—it may take 2–3 years for this plant to establish in position. Prune by cutting back all sideshoots in late winter. Propagate by taking semi-ripe cuttings in late summer or root cuttings in winter.

Ceanothus 'Autumnal Blue'
California lilac

H 6 ft. S 6 ft.

This California lilac is a bushy evergreen shrub clothed with glossy, dark green, finely toothed leaves. From late summer into the fall, it produces masses of beautiful china-blue flowers in open, fluffy-looking spikes up to 3 in. long. It is ideal for growing against a warm wall, where it will give year-round coverage and will benefit from the protection against damaging frosts and cold winds. It is tolerant of most soils except shallow chalk, which may cause yellowing of the leaves, and it responds well to regular light pruning to keep it in shape. Propagate by taking semi-ripe cuttings in summer.

Clematis armandii
Evergreen clematis

H 12 ft. S 10 ft.

An attractive woody climber, this is one of the few evergreen clematis; it is ideal for growing against a wall or fence, because it needs shade over its roots. The glossy, leathery leaves are divided into 3 leaflets. They are up to 6 in. long and tend to be tinted bronze as they emerge, aging to a rich dark green. In early spring, fragrant, saucer-shaped, white flowers are produced in dense clusters. 'Apple Blossom' has white flowers tinted with pink, and 'Snowdrift' is pure white. After flowering, prune back flowered stems to a strong pair of buds to encourage flowering wood for next year. Propagate by taking semi-ripe cuttings in late summer.

Clematis 'Etoile Violette'
Clematis

H 12 ft. S 5 ft.

This clematis is a member of the viticella group, and it flowers toward the end of the season, during late summer and autumn. It is a deciduous, semi-woody climber with slightly hairy leaves divided into 3 leaflets; it is ideal for growing against a wall or over a pergola, as long as its roots can be shaded. Held on slender, nodding stems, its flowers are single and saucer-shaped; they are violet-purple with bright yellow anthers in the center. Prune in spring before the plant starts into growth, cutting back to strong buds about 8 in. above ground level. Propagate by taking softwood cuttings in summer or by serpentine layering in spring.

Clematis 'Nelly Moser'
Clematis

H 6 ft. S 3 ft.

This is a fairly compact deciduous clematis that will grow in almost any position, as long as the roots are shaded. It is happy in a container and will even tolerate growing against a shady wall, as long as it has some shelter from cold winds. In early summer, it produces huge flowers of up to 6 in. across; they are pale pink with a darker central stripe and red anthers. There will often be a second flush of flowers in late summer and these tend to be paler in color. Trim back the shoots by a third to a strong pair of buds in late winter or early spring. Propagate by taking softwood cuttings in summer or by serpentine layering in spring.

Humulus lupulus
Hop

H 10 ft. S 10 ft.

The hop is a self-supporting, hardy, herbaceous perennial climber with thin, bristly, twining stems. The equally bristly, deeply lobed green leaves have toothed edges. In summer, insignificant flowers are produced, followed in autumn by clusters of fruit (hops). The dried stems and flowers can be used for indoor arrangements. It will tolerate partial shade and a north-facing aspect, although the spring growth may be a little delayed. The form 'Aureus' is a soft golden-yellow throughout, but may scorch in full sun. Prune down to 4 in. every spring to allow the new growth room to expand. Propagate by semi-ripe cuttings in June and July.

Rosa 'Albertine'
Climbing rose

H 15 ft. S 12 ft.

Raised in France in 1921, this strong-growing
deciduous rambling rose is one of the most
reliable ever produced, and it is ideal against
a wall, trellis, or fence. The young growths
produce copper-brown leaves, later glossy,
mid-green, on arching, red-thorned, dull red
shoots. The fragrant salmon-pink summer
flowers, becoming paler with age, are fully
double and about 3 in. across. Pruning involves
cutting out the old flowered shoots immediately
after flowering and removing any suckers that
may originate from the rootstock of a grafted
plant. These need to be removed at their base
or they will dominate the top variety. Propagate
by taking hardwood cuttings in late autumn.

Rosa 'Mermaid'
Climbing rose

H 20 ft. S 20 ft.

A vigorous but slow-growing deciduous climbing rose that will thrive
against a wall or pergola. The stiff stems are reddish-brown with sharply
hooked thorns and glossy, dark green leaves, which are bronze-tinted as
they emerge. During summer and autumn it produces single, flat flowers
up to 4 in. across that are glowing primrose yellow. These will persist
into winter (as will the foliage) if the weather is mild and the plant is
sheltered. For 2 years after planting, prune only to remove damaged
shoots, then prune each spring to reduce the main shoots back to the
support and the sideshoots back to 3–4 buds. Propagate by grafting
in winter or budding in summer.

Perennials, annuals, and bulbs

The major flowering plants in the garden are those that are mostly ephemeral, producing an often fleeting, but nonetheless welcome, display of color. It is important, when selecting from this group, to think strategically so that you achieve as long a season of interest as you can by growing a range of plants to perform at different times of the year. It pays, too, to plan your color schemes so that those plants that do flower at the same time complement each other as much as possible. Fashions for color themes tend to wax and wane, but, generally speaking, it is best to create harmonious schemes of toning colors; alternatively, go for contrasting schemes with fully saturated, strong colors. What tends to look most odd is when one or two brilliantly colored flowers scream out from an otherwise soft-hued display.

For spring color, bulbs are invaluable, and there is a wide choice that will take you through from early to late in the season, and some, indeed, for summer and autumn, too. Perennials come into their own in early summer and last through to late summer, after which their seedheads may provide an attractive ghostly display in autumn and winter. Annuals are usually fast-growing and quick to come into flower. Blooming at various times over the summer depending on the type, they die after flowering.

Remember to consider the foliage of perennials and annuals when planning your planting, as the leaves will be part of the display for a great deal longer than the flowers. Some, like crocosmias and irises, have handsome linear leaves; others have rounded, soft leaves, like those of lady's-mantle and geraniums.

Achillea filipendulina 'Cloth of Gold'
Fernleaf yarrow

H 5 ft. S 2 ft.

A clump-forming semi-evergreen herbaceous perennial, this yarrow grows well in a sunny, mixed, or herbaceous border. It has hairy, pinnate, light green leaves which look slightly ferny and grow in a rosette at the base. Bright golden-yellow, daisy-like flowers are borne in flattened clusters, up to 4 in. across, on tall, leafy stems. These flower heads are produced from early summer until the autumn frosts begin and may be cut and dried for indoor use. Remove the faded flower heads, if they are not needed, to encourage further flowering. Propagate by dividing in spring.

Achillea millefolium 'Cerise Queen'
Yarrow

H 2 ft. S 2 ft.

Once established, this form of yarrow spreads by underground rhizomes and can be invasive. It is an ideal perennial for a large border, where it can be allowed space to grow, or for a container, which will keep the growth under control. It has divided, ferny, mid-green leaves on upright stems, and bright cerise-pink, daisy-like flowers with white centers. These are produced from early summer until the autumn frosts begin. Cut down the old flower stems each spring to prepare for the new growth, and propagate by division, also in spring.

Calendula officinalis
Pot marigold

H 12 in. S 12 in.

This marigold is a compact, quick-growing annual with multiple stems and lance-like, hairy, aromatic foliage. Throughout summer and autumn it produces daisy-like single or double flowers in shades of orange and yellow with darker centers. Use it for an added splash of color at the front of a border, or in a container or windowbox. Deadhead regularly to prevent it from setting seed and to ensure a continuous succession of flowers. Any seeds that do form and are shed are likely to grow next year. Propagate by sowing seeds outside in their final growing positions in late spring.

Calluna vulgaris
Scotch heather

H 18 in. S 18 in.

A group of low-growing, bushy evergreen shrubs, known collectively as heathers. They have small, hairy leaves laid flat and overlapping along tough, woody stems. Leaf colors include shades of green, gray, yellow, red, or orange, often changing shade in winter after a frost. Small, bell-like flowers are carried in spikes on the tips of shoots from mid-summer until late-autumn. They may be white or shades of pink or red. Grow in the border if conditions permit, or in a container where the soil can be adjusted to suit. Prune in spring to remove faded flowers. Propagate by cuttings taken in the autumn after flowering has finished.

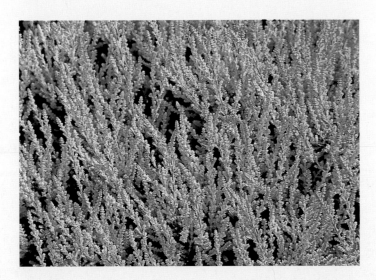

Camassia leichtlinii
Large camas

H up to 4½ ft. S 4 in.

An attractive bulbous perennial producing upright, narrow, strap-like leaves up to 2 ft. long. In late spring, tall flower spikes bear star-shaped, creamy-white flowers in loose clusters at their tips. Forms include: 'Semiplena', with semi-double flowers, and subsp. *suksdorfii* 'Blauwe Donau', which has violet-blue flowers. Plant the bulb 4 in. deep in autumn in a well-drained position, and mulch to protect it from frost over winter. It will grow well in a container, kept in a frost-free spot in winter. Propagate by removing offsets during late summer while the bulb is dormant.

Campanula lactiflora 'Prichard's Variety'
Milky bellflower

H 30 in. S 2 ft.

The milky bellflower is a pretty upright herbaceous perennial that is ideal for a border, as it tends to need staking as it grows. It has thin, long-oval, toothed, mid-green leaves and spikes of open bell-shaped, dark purple-blue flowers from early summer through to autumn. It will self-seed easily, although the flower color of the seedlings may vary from that of the parents. Regularly deadhead as flowers fade to prevent the plant from setting seed and to encourage more flowers to form. Propagate by division in spring or autumn or basal cuttings in spring.

Canna x *generalis* 'Bengal Tiger'
Calla lily

H 5 ft. S 2 ft.

An unusual and highly striking herbaceous, rhizomatous perennial grown for its exotic-looking foliage and flowers. It will add a colorful, tropical touch to the garden and can be grown in a border or a container. Borne on tall, dark red-purple stems, the large, dramatic leaves are blade-shaped and light or yellowish-green with pronounced bright yellow veins. The tubular flowers are a glowing orange, flaring out as 3 wide petals, and are carried on an upright spike in summer and early autumn. In frost-prone areas, lift the rhizome or bring the pot indoors over winter, and put it outside again after the danger of frost has passed. Propagate by division in spring (each piece needs a growth bud).

Colchicum autumnale
Autumn crocus
H 6 in. S 3 in.

This crocus-like plant is ideal for growing under trees and shrubs or in grass. It is a vigorous cormous perennial that produces long, strap-like leaves and large, showy, goblet-shaped flowers. It flowers in autumn without leaves (which appear in spring), producing its blooms as many other plants are starting to die down. The flowers are pale purple-pink with wide-spreading sepals and golden stamens. The form 'Alboplenum' has double white flowers, while 'Pleniflorum' has large, double lilac-pink flowers. Plant 4 in. deep in summer or early autumn; if they are in a container, repot every 4–5 years during summer, dividing if they are becoming congested. Propagate by dividing dormant corms in summer.

Convallaria majalis
Lily of the valley
H 9 in. S 12 in.

The lily of the valley is a beautiful rhizomatous perennial that will thrive in a shady spot beneath other plants or in a container. It is low-growing and spreads as ground cover. Broad, oval basal leaves surround an upright flowering stalk bearing pretty hanging, bell-shaped, white flowers in spring. Plant it in pots to be brought into a cool room or greenhouse for flowering, where the sweet fragrance can be fully appreciated. The form 'Albostriata' has white-striped leaves; 'Flore Pleno' has double flowers, and var. *rosea* has pale pink flowers. Propagate by dividing the rhizomes in autumn when the leaves have died, but do not allow them to dry out.

Cosmos
Cosmos

H 30 in. S 18 in.

This genus includes both perennials and annuals. They are grown for their saucer or bowl-shaped flowers, which appear in a range of colors from white, pink, and red to maroon, depending on the species or cultivar; they can be planted in a mixed or annual border or in containers on a patio. *C. atrosanguineus*, chocolate cosmos, earns its name from the chocolate scent of its rich, velvety, chocolate-colored flowers. It is a spreading, tuberous perennial which will survive for many years in milder areas; it is likely to be killed off by winter frost, unless given a thick protective mulch. The mid- to dark green foliage is divided and borne on reddish stems. Throughout summer and autumn, the saucer-shaped, dark red-brown flowers are produced singly on tall stems. Garden cosmos (*C. bipinnatus*) is an annual, available as cultivars with white, pink, crimson, and even striped flowers. The Sensation Series has larger flowers, while those of the dwarf Sonata Series are much smaller. Deadhead regularly to help ensure a succession of flowers. Propagate perennials, such as chocolate cosmos, by taking basal cuttings in spring, and annuals by sowing seeds, also in spring.

Crocosmia
Crocosmia, montbretia

H up to 3 ft. S 3 in.

Crocosmia is a clump-forming perennial that grows from individual corms and will thrive in a border, where it will gradually spread from the new corms that develop. The leaves are long and lance-shaped with prominent ribs or pleats. From mid- to late summer, tall, slender stems bear funnel-shaped flowers in spikes that open toward the tip as they grow and are good for cutting for indoors. Forms include 'Lucifer', which is tall and sturdy with fiery red flowers. *C.* × *crocosmiiflora* 'Jackanapes' has bicolored, dark orange and yellow flowers, while *C.* × *c.* 'Norwich Canary' has golden-yellow flowers. Plant 3–4 in. deep in spring and propagate by dividing the clumps, also in spring.

Crocus
Crocus

H 4–8 in. S 2 in.

These small, autumn-, winter-, or spring-flowering cormous perennials are perfect for growing around shrubs, in short grass, or in a rock garden. They have slender leaves, often with a white stripe, and the flowers, 4 or more per corm, are goblet-shaped in white or shades of yellow, blue, or purple, and plain or striped. Snow crocus (*C. chrysanthus*) flowers are golden-yellow with a striped maroon reverse (late winter to early spring). Dutch crocus (*C. vernus*) and its hybrids flower in shades of white ('Jeanne d'Arc'), blue ('Queen of the Blues') or purple ('Purpureus Grandiflorus') in spring. Plant 3–4 in. deep in autumn. Propagate by dividing in summer.

Cyclamen
Cyclamen

H 3 in. S 14 in.

Cyclamens are tuberous perennials that grow best in the shade of trees or shrubs, giving color during fall, winter, or spring, when the other plants are bare; they are lying dormant in summer. They produce rounded, heart-shaped leaves with markings of contrasting green or silver. The nodding flowers are on slender, upright stems and have 5 reflexed petals. Baby cyclamen (*C. hederifolium*) produces pink flowers in autumn before the leaves, and Persian violet (*C. coum*) has compact flowers of white, pink or red from late winter to early spring. Plant 1–2 in. deep in early autumn. Propagate by sowing seeds as soon as they are ripe.

Dahlia
Dahlia

H up to 3 ft. S 2 ft.

There are about 30 species of dahlia and some 20,000 cultivars grown for exhibition, cutting, or simply admiring in the garden. Showy and resilient, these tuberous perennials range from bedding to border varieties. They are classified by flower form: anemone, ball, cactus, decorative, miscellaneous (including orchid, peony, and star), pompon, semi-cactus, single, and waterlily. Colors range from white to maroon to yellows, pinks, oranges, and reds. Sow seeds of bedding dahlias in spring; take basal shoot cuttings from tubers of border dahlias in spring or divide them into pieces, each with a shoot. In frost-prone areas, lift tubers in autumn, shorten stems to 6 in., then overwinter them in dry sand.

Dianthus chinensis
China pinks

H up to 28 in. S up to 12 in.

The China pinks are lovely bushy, sun-loving plants that prefer alkaline conditions and grow to form cushion-like mounds of silver-gray foliage. They are short-lived evergreen perennials; they are usually grown as annuals from seeds each year and are ideal for placing at the front of a mixed border or in a container. Silver-gray stems carry narrow, spiky, gray- to mid-green leaves and delicately clove-scented single flowers, in clusters of up to 15, in summer. The flowers are up to 3 in. across, with heavily fringed petals, and may be white, pink, or red. Sow the seeds in situ in spring or take cuttings from non-flowering shoots in summer.

Eschscholzia californica
California poppy

H 12 in. S 6 in.

The California poppy is a pretty sun-loving annual (or short-lived perennial) which grows quickly from seeds sown in situ to produce its brightly colored flowers in summer. It has finely divided, ferny foliage of gray- or green-blue. The flowers, which close up in dull weather, consist of 4 paper-thin petals unfurling to produce a shallow cup shape around a golden center. They are good for cutting and come in shades of red, orange, peach, yellow and cream. Long seed pods follow the flowers. California poppy will grow in even quite poor soil, in a border or pot. Forms are available with double, semi-double, or ruffled flowers.

Felicia
Blue daisy

H up to 2 ft. S up to 2 ft.

The daisy-like summer flowers of felicias are generally blue, making these plants an interesting addition to the garden for bedding or in containers. *F. amelloides* is a small, bushy, tender sub-shrub, usually grown as an annual, with deep green leaves and flower shades from pale to deep blue: 'Read's Blue' is mid-blue, 'Read's White' is pure white, and 'Santa Anita' is rich blue. *F. amoena* (also treated as an annual) has bright blue flowers; 'Variegata' has cream-variegated leaves. *F. bergeriana*, the kingfisher daisy, is a creeping annual with bright blue, yellow-centered flowers. Propagate annuals from seeds in spring; take tip cuttings of tender perennials in late summer and overwinter indoors.

Helianthus
Sunflower

H up to 15 ft. S up to 2 ft.

The daisy-like annual sunflower comes in all shapes and sizes with summer flowers in all shades of yellow. Shorter ones are suitable for small gardens or containers; taller ones are best grown against a warm wall for support and shelter. They have coarse, heart-shaped leaves, hairy stems, and flowers with outer ray florets (usually yellow) and inner disc florets (yellow, brown, or purple). *Helianthus annus* 'Teddy Bear' is compact 3 ft. with deep yellow double flowers up to 5 in. across. *H. a.* 'Music Box' is a branched variety to 30 in. tall with flowerheads 4–5 in. across, ray florets of pale yellow to red (including bicolors), and dark brown disc florets. 'Sunspot' has large yellow flowers, 10 in. across, on a plant of only 2 ft. high. Mountain sunflower (*H. × laetiflorus*) is a perennial sunflower that grows to about 6 ft. It has long, dark green leaves; from late summer to early autumn, it produces bright yellow flowers about 5 in. across with a central disc of small florets. *H. a.* 'Lemon Queen' is a popular cultivar of 5 ft. high. Its pale yellow flowers have slightly darker central discs. Perennial sunflowers are ideal for growing in a mixed border. Propagate annuals by sowing seeds in situ in spring; divide perennials in spring.

Hyacinthus orientalis
Hyacinth

H 8–12 in. S 3 in.

Hyacinths are bulbous perennials, usually grown in containers, with highly scented, waxy flowers in spring. These are bell-shaped, single or double, and come in many colors in clusters of up to 40 on a single, broad, upright stem, amid bright green, strap-like leaves. Among the best are 'Blue Jacket' (single, navy-blue), 'City of Haarlem' (single, primrose-yellow), 'Delft Blue' (single, powder-blue), 'Gipsy Queen' (single, orange-pink), 'Hollyhock' (double, crimson), 'L'Innocence' (single, white), and 'Pink Pearl' (single, pink). Plant with the tip of the bulb 1–1¼ in. below the surface of the compost in autumn. Propagate by removing small offsets in summer when the bulbs are dormant.

Impatiens
Impatiens

H up to 12 in. S up to 2 ft.

The reliable impatiens flower throughout summer, preferring shelter and partial shade in a border or container. They are tender perennials, usually treated as annuals, and they bloom from a young age, producing clusters of spurred, 5-petaled blooms on brittle, succulent stems, also bearing lush, fleshy foliage. Busy Lizzie (*I. walleriana*) comes in many seed mixes with flowers of purple, red, salmon, pink, and white. The New Guinea hybrids are larger and have leaves splashed yellow or bronze-red. Their flowers are generally single in white and shades of purple, red, pink, and mauve. Propagate by sowing seeds in spring or taking softwood cuttings in spring or summer.

Iris
Bulbous iris

H up to 2 ft. S up to 12 in.

Bulbous irises have lance-shaped leaves and flowers without beards (hairs on the petals) from late winter to midsummer, depending on the variety. There are 3 groups: Juno with colorful falls (pendent petals) and small standards (upright petals); Reticulata with blue, white, or red-purple flowers; and Xiphium with blue, lavender, yellow, or white flowers. Species include Danford iris (*I. danfordiae*, yellow) and dwarf iris (*I. reticulata*, violet-blue). *I. magnifica* (pale lilac) flowers in midspring. *I. latifolia* (blue, violet, or white) and Spanish iris (*I. xiphium*, blue, white, or yellow) flower in early summer. Plant in autumn at twice the depth of the bulb. Propagate by division or by separating offsets in autumn.

Lathyrus odoratus
Sweet pea

H up to 6 ft. S up to 18 in.

The sweet pea is a favorite garden annual, available as a tall-growing climber for a wigwam in the border or against a fence, or in a dwarf form, bred for growing in containers and hanging baskets. In summer, clusters of usually heavily fragrant, wavy-edged flowers are produced in white and shades of pink, red, and blue. Some are bicolored or have a picotee edging, and all are ideal for cutting for bringing indoors. The many cultivars have been developed for different characteristics. Old-fashioned cultivars were selected primarily for scent: 'Quito', which has 4 small, strongly scented flowers per stem, is a typical example. Color has been important in modern breeding programs, and flowers are available in an ever-increasing range: the Spencer cultivars are among the most popular. They are vigorous, growing to 6 ft. Sweet peas usually climb by means of tendrils; however, the dwarf Snoopea Group has no tendrils, reaches only 2 ft. high, and can be used as ground cover. Propagate by sowing seeds in autumn or early spring.

Lobelia erinus
Trailing lobelia

H 3 ft. S 12 in.

This striking herbaceous perennial grows to form a clump of unusual, dark bronze-purple stems. The glossy, red-purple leaves are up to 4 in. long and lance-shaped with toothed edges. During the late summer and into the autumn, tall spikes of bright scarlet flowers are produced, each 2-lipped and tubular with reddish-purple bracts. This plant needs a moist position to grow well, and is ideal in the soil at the edge of a pond or stream, or in a moist border. It is short-lived and should be propagated from bud cuttings in the summer to ensure that it is not lost.

Muscari armeniacum
Grape hyacinth

H 8 in. S 2 in.

The grape hyacinth is a dwarf bulbous perennial with long, narrow, fleshy leaves. These begin to grow in autumn, then spread and separate as flower buds appear. The spiky flower heads are produced in spring over a period of several weeks and are densely packed with tiny, bell-shaped, deep blue flowers. Among the many forms are 'Argaei Album' (white flowers), 'Blue Spike' (large, double blue flowers), and 'Heavenly Blue' (bright blue). Grow grape hyacinths in drifts around shrubs, in a rock garden, or in containers. Plant 4 in. deep in autumn. Propagate by regular division of large clumps in midsummer when they are dormant to keep the plants healthy and prevent congestion.

Narcissus
Daffodil

H 4–24 in. S 2–6 in.

There are hundreds of varieties of these spring-flowering bulbs, ideal for growing around shrubs, under deciduous trees, in grass, and in containers. They have narrow, strap-like leaves and flowers with an inner trumpet or cup and an outer row of petals. Flower shades include yellow, white, orange, cream, and pink; the blooms may be solitary or clustered, single or double, and have varying lengths and shapes of cup or trumpet. They range from dwarf types of 4 in. high, to tall varieties reaching 2 ft. Plant the dormant bulbs at 1½ times their own depth in autumn. Deadhead after flowering and remove brown foliage during midsummer. Lift and divide every 3–5 years, once the foliage has died down.

Nicotiana x *sanderae*
Sander's tobacco

H 10–24 in. S 12–18 in.

This ornamental relative of tobacco is a multi-branched and stout-stemmed plant that grows as an annual, a biennial, or sometimes a short-lived perennial, according to the conditions; it is usually treated as an annual for summer bedding, borders, or containers. The wavy-edged leaves form a basal rosette, from which the tall flowering stem rises. The individual flowers have a tube about 2 in. long, flaring into a wide trumpet shape with 5 rounded lobes. They are available in white and shades of red, pink, purple, and even lime-green. Compact forms, such as Domino Series, are ideal for a container. Grow from seeds in spring.

Osteospermum
African daisy

H 12–24 in. S 12–24 in.

There are many forms and hybrids of osteospermums in a wide range of colors. All form rounded, dome-shaped mounds of gray- to mid-green foliage as they grow, producing wide, daisy-like flowers on slender stems throughout summer and autumn. The flowers are generally single and come in white or shades of cream, orange, yellow, or pink, often with a contrasting center and occasionally with unusually crimped, spoon-shaped petals ('Whirlygig'). 'Buttermilk' has solitary large, pale yellow flowers that are darker yellow on the reverse side, while 'Tresco Purple' has purplish-green stems and, for a long season from spring to autumn, bears dark purple flowers that are white on the reverse side. It is small, growing to just 6 in. tall. African daisies are excellent for containers. They may be grown as annuals but are perennial in frost-free areas. Sow seeds in spring or take semi-ripe cuttings in late summer to overwinter indoors.

Papaver croceum
Iceland poppy

H 12 in. S 6 in.

The Iceland poppy is a hairy-leaved perennial, often grown as a biennial, suitable for a border or container. It flowers in summer, producing solitary bowl-shaped, usually single flowers, with long, golden stamens, on tall, slender stems, followed by seed heads. Attractive seed selections include 'Garden Gnome' (compact, red, salmon, orange, yellow and white), 'Meadow Pastels' (large flowers in white and shades of red, orange, and yellow), and 'Champagne Bubbles' (large flowers in pastel shades of bronze, apricot, yellow, and pink). The larger blooms are suitable for cutting but need shelter from cold winds, which will spoil them. Sow seeds in spring.

Pelargonium
Geranium

H 6–24 in. S 6–24 in.

The geraniums grown for garden display are mainly evergreen perennials. Geraniums are often confused with cranesbills, which are part of the genus Geranium. Geraniums are valued for their bright attractive summer flowers and/or scented foliage. They are ideal for growing in borders or containers. There are various forms with different characteristics. Regal geraniums are bushy with thick, branching stems, hairy, toothed, palm-like leaves and large, showy flowers in white, pink, salmon, orange, red, or purple. Scented-leaf geraniums have smaller flowers and finely cut, toothed or lobed, aromatic foliage—scents include lemon, peppermint, orange, lime, or balm. The very well known zonal geraniums have smooth, succulent stems and large rounded leaves. The flowers may be single, semi-double, or double, in white and shades of orange, pink, red, purple, and occasionally yellow. Trailing geraniums have ivy-like foliage and single or double flowers in white or shades of purple, red, pink, and mauve. Propagate by taking softwood or semi-ripe cuttings from non-flowering shoots in early or late summer. Keep frost-free over winter.

Phlox drummondii
Annual phlox

H 4–24 in. S 12 in.

The half-hardy annual phlox is grown for its brightly colored flowers and makes a good summer bedding or patio container plant. Single or double, in white or shades of purple, red, pink, or lilac, the blooms are carried in dense clusters, up to 3 in. across, on the tips of the shoots from midsummer to early autumn. The plants have an upright habit and narrow, strap-like leaves of mid- to light green in pairs on slender, green stems. Available forms include named cultivars, such as 'Chanal' (rich pale pink, double), and mixed color seed collections, such as 'Tapestry' (fragrant flowers in a wide range of colors). Deadhead regularly for continuous flowering. Sow seeds in early spring.

Primula
Primrose, auricula, polyanthus

H 8 in. S 8–12 in.

Primroses, auriculas, and polyanthus are perennials with basal rosettes of leaves and flaring, funnel-shaped flowers. They are ideal for bedding and containers. Auricula (*P. auricula*) has clustered, deep yellow, red, or purple flowers, with a yellow center, on a stout stem above the foliage. English primrose (*P. vulgaris*) bears solitary pale yellow flowers on short, slender stems amid the foliage. *Polyanthus* hybrids have primrose-shaped flowers in clusters on a stem above the foliage. They are maroon, red, orange, yellow, pink, white, or blue. Propagate by sowing seeds in spring or dividing in autumn.

Rudbeckia
Coneflower

H 10–36 in. S 12–36 in.

A group of annuals, biennials, and perennials with daisy-like flowers in summer and autumn. The flowers are in shades of yellow, orange, and red with brown or green centers and are good for cutting. Sow annuals and biennials in spring. They include black-eyed Susan (*R. hirta*) cultivars 'Becky Mixed' (dwarf, large flowers in yellows and oranges), 'Goldilocks' (double and semi-double, golden-yellow), and 'Kelvedon Star' (golden-yellow with rich brown markings). Perennial forms are propagated by division in spring. They include *R. fulgida* var. *sullivantii* 'Goldsturm' (large, golden flowers) and *R.* 'Herbstsonne' (vigorous, to 6 ft., bright yellow with green centers).

Salvia
Sage

H 12–60 in. S 9–24 in.

Sage is a large genus of annuals, biennials, perennials, and shrubs, distinguished by their striking colorful, 2-lipped flowers in summer and autumn. Most sages have aromatic foliage, including garden sage (*S. officinalis*), which is used in cooking. Annual sages are used for bedding or containers, while perennials make good border plants. Bedding annuals include scarlet sage (*S. splendens* 'Blaze of Fire' and 'Red Arrow'), both with bright red flowers. The annual painted sage (*S. viridis* 'Claryssa') is dwarf and bushy, with brightly colored bracts of purple, pink, or white. *S. farinacea*, mealy sage, is a perennial, usually grown as an annual. It has deep lavender-blue flowers in terminal spikes from summer to autumn. *S. f.* 'White Porcelain' has white flowers. The perennial salvia (*S. nemorosa*) has long, mid-green leaves and violet-purple or white to pink flowers, in dense terminal racemes. *S. n.* 'Ostfriesland' has dark violet-blue flowers, while 'Lubeca' has violet flowers with purplish bracts that remain on the plant after flowering. Among the blue-flowered forms are gentian sage (*S. patens*), a tuberous perennial with hairy leaves, and sapphire sage (*S. guaranitica*), a tender sub-shrub with long, deep blue flowers. Sow seeds of annuals and perennials in spring; divide perennials in spring and take semi-ripe cuttings of shrubs in late summer.

Tropaeolum majus
Climbing nasturtium

H 5 ft. S 5 ft.

This is a climbing or trailing half-hardy annual with rounded, light green leaves, sometimes marked with white splashes. The long-spurred, broadly trumpet-shaped flowers, about 2 in. across, are borne throughout summer and autumn in shades of yellow, cream, orange and red, often with a contrasting splash in the throat. They are edible and look very colorful in a salad. There are many seed mixes available, including 'Climbing Mixed', the semi-trailing Gleam Series, and the dwarf Whirlybird Series. Grow in containers, hanging baskets, or at the front of a border. Propagate by sowing seeds indoors in spring, or outdoors once the risk of frost has passed.

Tulipa
Tulip

H 8–20 in. S 4 in.

Tulips are spring-flowering bulbs that are ideal for growing in containers or borders. The wide range of species and hybrids are classified according to botanical characteristics and time of flowering. The flowers may be single or double, goblet- or star-shaped, fringed or smooth-petaled, rounded or long and slender. Flower shades include white, yellow, pink, red, orange, and purple to almost black. 'Purissima' is a popular white-flowered tulip, while 'Queen of Night' is diametrically opposed with deep maroon, almost black flowers. Striped tulips have long been a collector's curiosity: 'Carnaval de Nice' is a double-flowered hybrid with red-striped, white flowers, while 'Flaming Parrot' has yellow-and-red striped, fringed petals. Low growers are usually *T. kaufmanniana* hybrids (waterlily tulip), such as 'Giuseppe Verdi' (yellow-and-red striped flowers), and *T. greigii* hybrids such as 'Red Riding Hood' (red flowers). *T. praestans* is taller at 12 in. and bears clusters of up to 5 orange-red flowers. Deadhead after flowering and allow to die down. Plant new bulbs in autumn 4–6 in. deep. Propagate by division when the bulbs are lifted after flowering.

Verbena bonariensis
Verbena

H 6 ft. S 18 in.

A tall, clump-forming perennial with stiff, upright stems that branch regularly and bear a few rough, wrinkled leaves. Flattened flower heads of slightly scented purple flowers are produced throughout summer and autumn, until they are stopped by the frosts. This is an ideal plant for the center or back of a border, where it may need staking to keep it from leaning over. It self-seeds profusely, and the seedlings can be lifted for planting elsewhere, or the plant may be divided in spring. Cut the growth down each spring, as it regrows from the base.

Viola cornuta
Horned violet

H 6 in. S 16 in.

A spreading evergreen perennial with stems that are flat at first, then turn upwards. It has glossy, oval leaves, with toothed edges, and slightly fragrant flowers during spring and early summer. These are about 1½ in. across, with 5 widely separate petals of lilac to violet. The lower petals have white markings and thin, slightly curved spurs. White, yellow, pink, and red forms have been bred. Horned violet is ideal under other plants in a border or permanent container. Grow from seeds sown in spring or as soon as they are ripe, or divide established clumps in spring (after flowering) or autumn.

Viola Delta Series
Pansy

H 8 in. S 10 in.

This series of colorful pansies is compact and robust, with larger than usual faces. It is one of many in the *Viola × wittrockiana* group of cultivars. They bring color to gardens, containers, and bedding schemes throughout the year, even during winter. They have been bred to be tolerant of most conditions and will flower continuously as long as they do not set seed. They have a bushy, spreading habit with evergreen, heart-shaped leaves and flowers up to 4 in. across. These are available in white and shades of purple, blue, bronze, maroon, pink, orange, and yellow, often with a darker colored eye, color splashes, or petals of different colors. Many seed mixes are available, including 'Can Can Mixed' (full, ruffled, and wavy petals). Sow seeds any time except midsummer. In the Delta Series, 'Azure Wing' has light petals and a deep mauve face; 'White Rose' has a mauve and white face.

Viola tricolor
Heartsease

H 5 in. S 6 in.

The heartsease or wild pansy is a small, tuft-forming annual, biennial, or short-lived perennial for a border or container. It has toothed, heart-shaped leaves and pretty 3-colored flowers during spring, summer, and autumn. Of the 5 petals, the upper 2 are dark purple or violet, the central 2 paler purple, and the bottom one yellow streaked with violet. The colors are not definite—the middle petals may be almost white or as dark as purple. The form 'Bowles' Black' is very deep violet with a yellow eye. Heartsease is short-lived (from seeds sown in spring), but it sets seeds easily and may be invasive.

Zinnia
Zinnia

H 10–24 in. S 12 in.

A group of tender, bushy annuals with branched stems, mid-green, lance-shaped leaves, and colorful, daisy-like flowers. They are excellent for summer bedding or containers and good for cutting. Z. *elegans* is upright and bushy with broad-petaled, purple flowers. Its forms include the Thumbelina Series (dwarf, single or semi-double, magenta, red, pink, or yellow) and 'Envy' (lime-green). 'Profusion Cherry' is a dwarf variety with cherry-red flowers. Z. *haageana* is bushy with bright orange flowers. Its forms include 'Persian Carpet' (small, semi-double and double, single and bicolors, in shades of purple, red, brown, orange, and yellow). Deadhead regularly to prolong the flowering period. Sow seeds in spring.

Bamboos, grasses, and ferns

As gardeners have become increasingly sophisticated in their tastes, bamboos, grasses, and ferns have experienced an unprecedented upsurge in popularity. Whereas once only brightly colored flowers sold well in garden centers, the architectural merits and low-maintenance qualities of this group of plants are now much more appreciated. Although botanically different from each other, they are used in gardens for similar reasons: to add a note of calm and stability in plantings.

Bamboos make useful screening plants and are good subjects for containers, with the added bonus that the containers will keep their more invasive tendencies in check. Their stems, known as canes, come in various colors, including striped forms and black ones. Dividing up the length of the canes are nodes, which can also be decorative.

The related grasses can be used to punctuate the more ebullient flowering borders, providing a sense of form and scale. Some are invasive, so it is generally best to choose the clump-forming ones, which do not send out long runners. Grass flowers are called spikelets, and they are followed by seed heads, which are of particular value in autumn, when perennial flowers are dying down. There are many different forms of grasses, some small, some of giant proportions, and you can find species that thrive in damp soil, and others that do well in dry conditions.

Ferns are ideal subjects for shrub borders, for growing under trees, and for woodland-style gardens, as many of them do particularly well in shade. Their handsome fronds (leaves) can take many forms, from almost flat and ribbon-like to curled and finely divided.

Asplenium scolopendrium
Hart's tonguefern

H 18–28 in. S 2 ft.

The hart's tonguefern is a ground-dwelling evergreen that spreads by short rhizomes. It produces upright, shuttlecock-like crowns of glossy, leathery leaves, up to 16 in. long and sword-shaped, with a wavy edge and a thick, green-brown rib running down the center. The lush foliage is an excellent foil for more brightly colored plants, or to create a woodland effect in a shady corner. There are many forms of this fern, each exhibiting slightly differing characteristics, including 'Crispum', which has very wavy, almost frilly, edges to its mid-green fronds. Propagate by division or by sowing spores in spring.

Dryopteris filix-mas
Male fern
H 3 ft. S 3 ft.

The deciduous or sometimes semi-evergreen male fern thrives in shade, but will tolerate some brighter light. It forms a shuttlecock-shaped clump of lance-shaped, deeply cut fronds, reaching up to 3 ft. high; it is a wonderfully architectural plant, ideal for a shady corner in the border or a container. Cultivated forms include 'Grandiceps Wills', which is a truly striking plant with a broad, heavy crest at the tip of each frond, and 'Crispa Cristata', which has crested fronds and pinnae (the leaflets that make up a frond). The Linearis Group has a more delicate appearance. 'Linearis Cristata' is so called because the pinnae and the frond tips are crested. *D. affinis*, the golden male fern, is very similar to *D. filix-mas* and is distinguished by a dark spot where the pinnae join the midrib. *D. a.* 'Crispa Gracilis' is a dwarf form, growing to just 12 in. tall. It is evergreen with twisted pinnae. Propagate by division in spring or by sowing spores as soon as they are ripe.

Sinarundinaria nitida
Fountain bamboo
H 10 ft. S 5 ft.

The fountain bamboo is a slow-growing evergreen that is ideal for a wood-land garden, shrub border, or as a container plant. It forms a dense clump of dark purple-green canes; each is 1/8 – 3/8 in. thick and may reach 10 ft. or more tall (depending on its position or the size of the container it is growing in). The canes are covered in a grayish powder at first, becoming lined purple-brown, with white below the nodes, as they age. Purple branchlets are produced in the second year, arching as they grow until finally they look as if they are cascading like water. Dark green, finely tapered leaves flicker gently in even the lightest breeze, giving a constant movement. Propagate by dividing clumps in spring.

Matteuccia struthiopteris
Ostrich fern, shuttlecock fern

H 5 ft. S 3 ft.

The deciduous ostrich fern is grown for its attractive fronds, which are arranged like a shuttlecock in 2 distinct rings. The outer ring consists of sterile, pale yellow-green fronds, which arch elegantly and are up to 5 ft. long. The inner ring has shorter, fertile, dark greenish-brown fronds, which appear in late summer and last over winter. Both types of frond are deeply cut and broadly spear-shaped with a blackish-brown midrib. This fern likes slightly acid to neutral soil and prefers to grow in very moist conditions, such as the edge of a pond, but should never be waterlogged. Propagate by division in late spring or sow spores as soon as they are ripe.

Milium effusum 'Aureum'
Golden millet grass

H 12 in. S 12 in.

This semi-evergreen perennial grass forms a loose mound and spreads slowly in a border or container. Every part of the plant is a rich golden yellow, from the soft, smooth leaves through to the flowers and seed heads. However, direct midday sun may scorch the leaves, and they turn lime-green if the plant is growing in deep shade. The leaves are strap-like and up to 12 in. long. Flowering starts in midspring and continues until late summer; delicate golden spikelets, up to 12 in. long, are so light that the tiny flowers dance in the gentlest of breezes. Propagate by division or by sowing seeds in spring.

Phyllostachys nigra
Black bamboo

H 10–15 ft. S 6–10 ft.

The compact, clump-forming black bamboo has hollow canes up to 15 ft. tall, although their height may be restricted by their position in the garden or the size of the container the bamboo is growing in. The young canes are green, turning shiny black as they age, with a groove to one side and a white, waxy powder below the nodes. The leaves are lance-shaped, dark green, and up to 5 in. long. This elegant plant does well in a large container (which will restrict both growth and spread) and is useful grown as a windblock to protect other plants or to shelter a seating area. Propagate by division in spring.

Sasa veitchii
Kuma-zasa

H 3 ft. S indefinite

An attractive low-growing bamboo that has smooth, purple canes and is tolerant of a wide range of conditions, including deep shade. It spreads by rhizomes and can be quite invasive in the open garden, but it does well in a large pot, plunged into the border, to restrict it. The glossy, mid-green leaves are a broad, oval-lance-shape and make a wonderful rustling sound as the wind disturbs them. The leaf edges tend to wither during winter, giving each leaf a beige edging. Propagate by division in spring, keeping the youngest parts of the rhizome and discarding the oldest.

Stipa
Feather grass

H 2–6 ft. S 1–4 ft.

There are several garden worthy species in this genus. Giant needle grass (*S. gigantea*) is a densely tufted, evergreen perennial grass that is particularly striking when in flower. It has thin, rolled, mid-green leaves, growing up to 28 in. long and arching over. Tall, purple-green flower spikes, up to 6 ft. high, are produced in summer, bearing silver, bristly spikelets. These turn golden-yellow as they ripen, giving rise to the common name golden oats, because they closely resemble panicles of oats. The dry flower heads rustle in the slightest breeze and look particularly effective when grown against a dark background to highlight their color. Other attractive species include Mexican feather grass (*S. tenuissima*), which is only 2 ft. high. It is deciduous, forming dense tufts of bright green, slender leaves and greenish-white, feathery flower apanicles that ripen to buff and tremble in the lightest of breezes. *S. calamagrostis* is also deciduous with arching, bluish-green leaves and long, purplish-tinted, silvery, slightly drooping flower panicles. It grows to 3 ft. high. Propagate by division in spring or autumn, or sow seeds in spring.

Herbs

Herbs are among the easiest plants to grow in your garden and the most rewarding, providing both culinary and medicinal benefits, not to mention the attractive and often aromatic foliage. Most herbs are small, hardy, or half-hardy perennials, although a few are shrubs or trees, including rosemary (*Rosmarinus officinalis*) and sweet bay (*Laurus nobilis*), and one or two are tender; these are treated as annuals in colder climates and include the popular herb sweet basil (*Ocimum basilicum*).

The majority of herbs prefer a sunny spot and well-drained soil, because quite a few originate from the Mediterranean regions of Europe. You can grow many of them very successfully in containers, including windowboxes.

The following list is just a small selection of some of the best culinary herbs available, but there are hundreds that you can choose from, and many have a range of varieties offering interesting leaf colors and forms.

Herbs are ideal plants for growing in containers, and you can grow a good selection of the smaller ones, such as thyme, parsley, basil, chives, and marjoram, in a windowbox, for example.

You can dry many of the herbs for use in cooking, in particular thyme, parsley, bay, sage, rosemary, and mint. Simply snip off 4 in. sections of shoot and hang up in a warm, dry place for a month or so. You can then use these for a bouquet garni in winter cooking, such as soups and stews.

Allium schoenoprasum
Chives

H 12 in. S 12 in.

This hardy perennial bulb is grown for its delicately onion-flavored leaves, which are useful in salads and as an addition to soups and egg dishes. It has attractive rounded heads of light purple flowers in summer. Grow clumps of chives 12 in. apart in light, well-drained soil or in a container. In a sheltered site, they will continue to grow well into the winter. Propagate by dividing clumps in spring.

Anethum graveolens
Dill

H 5 ft. S 12 in.

A hardy annual, dill has fern-like leaves and large decorative umbels of yellow flowers in summer. It is best grown in a sunny position in light soil. Both the leaves and seeds are used in cooking; the flower heads and seeds are used to flavor pickles, while the leaves have an aniseed flavor. Dill is an excellent aid for digestion. Propagate by sowing seeds in midspring.

Coriandrum sativum
Coriander, cilantro, Chinese parsley

H 2 ft. S 4 in.

Coriander is a hardy annual with divided, pungent leaves and very
aromatic seeds. One of the oldest known herbs in cultivation, it is a
staple ingredient in Asian cooking, where it is used to flavor curries
and pickles. It is thought to greatly aid digestion. Sow seeds in situ in
spring in a sunny, sheltered spot. Thin seedlings to 12 in. apart. Water
copiously in summer.

Laurus nobilis
Sweet bay

H 10–40 ft. S 10–30 ft.

Originating from the Mediterranean region, this hardy evergreen tree
has aromatic, shiny, dark green, oval leaves and fares best in a sunny,
well-drained site. The small spring flowers are followed by black berries.
The leaves are used to flavor soups and stews—they are one of the classic
ingredients of bouquet garni. There is also a golden-leaved form 'Aurea'.
Bay can be clipped to form standards or pyramids. Propagate by taking
semi-ripe cuttings in summer.

Mentha
Mint

H 4–36 in. S 18 in. to indefinite

Mint is a vigorous perennial with slightly hairy, mid-green leaves that
are very aromatic when crushed. The flowers are white or pinkish-mauve
and appear in summer. Mint will cope well with partial shade but needs
a lot of moisture. It can be invasive if not controlled by growing it in
a container. There are many types, including creeping ones, such as
pennyroyal (*M. pulegium*) and those with differently flavored leaves—
M. spicata (spearmint) and *M. suaveolens* (apple mint) to name but two.
Propagate by division in spring or autumn.

Origanum majorana
Sweet marjoram

H 18 in. S 8–12 in.

Grown as an annual in temperate climates, this evergreen sub-shrub has aromatic leaves and small white, pink, or mauve flowers in summer. The leaves are used for soups, stuffings, and sauces. *O. onites*, pot marjoram, is a hardy sub-shrub with pink or white flowers and similarly aromatic leaves. There is also wild marjoram, *O. vulgare*, which is hardier than sweet marjoram, with pink flowers and leaves that are less heavily aromatic. Its golden form 'Aureum' is a popular cultivar and has small yellowish-green leaves. Grow marjoram in a herb garden, mixed border, or container. Propagate by sowing seeds in late spring or divide perennials in autumn.

Petroselinum crispum
Parsley

H 8–12 in. S 8–12 in.

Parsley is a biennial with deeply cut, tightly curled leaves that are rich in vitamins A, B, and C and trace elements. It is used to flavor soups, stews, and salads. 'Moss Curled' is a tall cultivar with very tightly curled leaves, while var. *neapolitanum*, also known as 'Italian', is flat-leaved with a pungent flavor. With the added benefit of fleshy, edible roots, var. *tuberosum*, Hamburg or turnip-rooted parsley, has less highly flavored leaves. Parsley is generally grown in a herb garden, but is also suitable for containers. Propagate by sowing seeds in midspring (pouring boiling water over the sown seeds hastens germination).

Rosmarinus officinalis
Rosemary

H 5 ft. S 5 ft.

This frost-hardy, evergreen shrub has needle-like, waxy, highly aromatic leaves and mauvish-blue flowers in early summer. The leaves are used to flavor roasts, grills, and potato dishes. There are many different forms of rosemary, some with pink flowers and some that are low-growing or sprawling. Upright forms can be trained as small standards, which look very effective with lower-growing herbs planted underneath. All rosemaries need a position in full sun and well-drained soil. Propagate by taking semi-ripe tip cuttings in summer.

Salvia officinalis
Garden sage
H 2 ft. S 2 ft.

Garden sage is a shrubby evergreen perennial,
native to the Mediterranean region, with highly
aromatic, felted leaves and purple-blue flowers
in summer. The leaves are used particularly for
pork and offal dishes and to make stuffings.
A purple-leaved form, 'Purpurascens', is widely
grown, while 'Kew Gold' has bright golden
leaves. Grow sage in a herb garden or in patio
containers. The colored-leaved varieties make
good front-of-the-border plants. Sage needs
little pruning, apart from tidying up in early
spring. Propagate by taking soft basal cuttings
in spring or semi-ripe tip cuttings in late
summer; sow seeds in spring.

Thymus vulgaris
Garden thyme
H 6–12 in. S 15 in.

Garden thyme is grown in containers or herb gardens for its aromatic,
small evergreen leaves, used to flavor soups, stews, and stuffings. It bears
small, usually mauve flowers in summer. There are many other species
in this wide-ranging genus. The more tender bush varieties are native
to Mediterranean regions. Creeping, hardier forms occur naturally in
temperate climates. *T. × citriodorus*, known as lemon-scented thyme,
has lemon-scented leaves and pink flowers, while the cultivar 'Aureus'
has golden-variegated leaves. 'Silver Queen' has whitish variegation.
Thyme needs well-drained soil and a sunny position. Propagate by
sowing seeds in spring or taking semi-ripe tip cuttings in late summer.

Fruit

Homegrown fruit is delicious but requires more careful cultivation than most vegetables and herbs. Not only are fruit trees and bushes more prone to pests and diseases, the feeding and watering is more demanding. However, new disease-resistant varieties are being bred and are worth looking out for. Some, such as strawberries, raspberries, currants, blackberries, and apples produce good yields without too much trouble.

Unfortunately, most varieties of fruit are more difficult to grow than vegetables, although a few, such as strawberries, raspberries, currants, blackberries, and apples, are relatively easy. Strawberries have the advantage of fruiting well in containers. Blueberries need acid soil but also do well in containers; if you live in an alkaline area, they are not beyond your reach, because you can plant them in containers filled with acidic compost.

The range of fruit trees available is expanding, and there are special ones that have been bred on dwarfing rootstocks so that they are suitable for small spaces. Most of the more tender stone fruits, such as peaches, are quite difficult to grow in colder climates but can be encouraged to fruit against a sunny, sheltered wall, for example. With fruit trees, a good harvest relies on correct pruning, which encourages the maximum number of flower buds and, subsequently, fruit.

To ensure that your crop does not fall prey to birds, you may need to cover the tree or bush with fine netting once the fruit starts to swell. A high potassium feed will help to ensure good yields.

Fragaria x *ananassa* cultivars
Hybrid strawberry

H 6 in. S 1 ft.

These herbaceous perennials are easy to grow, and they propagate themselves by sending out runners (long stems) with new plants at the tips. To obtain a long season, choose cultivars from each fruiting season: early, such as 'Elvira', mid-season, such as 'Cambridge Favourite', and late, such as 'Domanil'. Reaching about 12 in. high with a similar spread, strawberries do best on well-drained soils and crop for about 3 years. Plant them 18 in. apart in rows 2 ft. apart, either in a raised bed or on slightly raised ridges. Mulch the plants with straw once the fruits start to form. Alternatively, plant them through black plastic. Water well, especially once the fruits form.

Malus domestica cultivars
Apple

H 21 ft. S 15 ft.

Apple trees bear copious quantities of fruit if cultivated and pruned properly. Popular cultivars include the culinary 'Bramley's Seedling' and the dessert 'Cox's Orange Pippin'. Most apples are not self-fertile and therefore need a compatible pollinator (check compatibility when buying). Plant trees in late autumn or early winter in well-manured soil. Water them from the time they blossom. For apples that fruit from spurs (clusters of buds along the stems), prune in winter, reducing the main leaders by a third of the current season's growth and sideshoots back to 4–5 buds. Other apples carry fruits on the shoot tips and need renewal pruning (cutting back some of the old fruited shoots to their bases) each year.

Prunus avium cultivars
Sweet cherry

H 21 ft. S 15 ft.

Sweet cherries are among the most delicious fruit you can grow. The trees are vigorous and are usually grafted onto dwarfing rootstocks to make them more manageable in small gardens. Choose a self-fertile cultivar such as 'Stella'. Cherries need a sunny site and deep, moisture-retentive soil; they do well trained as fans against a wall or fence. Plant them in late autumn, giving each tree a good 20 ft. of space around it. Feed trees with plenty of organic matter and make sure that they are well watered in dry periods. Net the fruit as it forms. Prune fans after fruiting, cutting back sideshoots to 3 leaves.

Prunus persica cultivars
Common peach

H 16 ft. S 10 ft.

Peaches, with their wonderful slightly furred skin, are a bit more difficult to grow than sweet cherries, because the flowers are susceptible to frosts. Grow the trees as fans in a sunny position against a wall or fence with wires for training. Provide deep, moisture-retentive soil and plenty of space around each tree (as for sweet cherries). Peaches are self-fertile, but pollination can be improved by dabbing each flower with a brush, transferring the pollen in the process. Peaches produce fruit on the previous season's growth, so when fruiting is over, cut out fruited sideshoots and tie in young replacement shoots. If necessary, protect flowers from frosts with a plastic sheet.

Prunus domestica cultivars
European plum

H 16 ft. S 13 ft.

Plums are prolific, producing a good yield off a single tree, and they are easier to grow than other member of the *Prunus* family. 'Victoria' is a well-known performer and very widely grown. In small gardens, choose dwarf bush forms. Ideally, grow more than one to improve pollination chances. Plant trees in deep, fertile soil. Make sure they are well fed and watered regularly. You may need to thin the crop if it is especially heavy, because the boughs may break under the strain. Pruning consists of thinning out overcrowded branches and keeping the remainder to about 5 ft. long. Plums are susceptible to silver-leaf disease, which causes the branches to die back; pruning in late summer reduces the possibility of an attack.

Ribes nigrum cultivars, *R. rubrum* cultivars
Black currant, red currant
H 4 ft. S 4 ft.

Currants are grown for their black, red, or white fruits. Bushy shrubs of about 5 ft., they do well in a sunny, open, but sheltered site. Plant them in autumn in deep, moisture-retentive soil, spaced about 5 ft. apart. They crop the first season after planting but will fruit more vigorously the following year. Mulch heavily with organic matter in spring and water regularly once the fruits form. Prune in autumn or winter to create an open framework—with black currants, remove a quarter of the 2-year-old wood each year; with red currants, cut back sideshoots to 1 bud. Black currants are usually ready to harvest in midsummer; white and red currants ripen a few weeks later.

Ribes uva-crispa var. *reclinatum* cultivars
Gooseberry
H 3 ft. S 3 ft.

The green, yellow, or red fruits of gooseberries are used for desserts . The larger, sweeter, red fruits can be eaten raw, others need to be cooked. Mature gooseberry bushes will reach about 4 ft. in height. Plant them from autumn to early spring, about 4 ft. apart with 5 ft. between rows. They need fertile, well-manured soil to crop well. Prune the bushes to create an,open framework, cutting back main stems by about a half. Remove very old stems and any that are overcrowded or crossing. Retain all strong, young shoots. Harvest early gooseberries for cooking; later, as they ripen, they are suitable for desserts.

Rubus fruticosus cultivars
Blackberry
H 5 ft. S 10 ft.

Although in nature blackberries are fiercely prickly shrubs, thornless cultivars, such as 'Oregon Thornless', have now been bred with larger than usual sweet fruit. Plant the canes at least 10 ft. apart in autumn. Mulch well with organic matter and water regularly once the fruits start to form. Blackberries need a strong support system, so train the stems along wires attached to stout posts and tie the shoots into the horizontal wires to expose the maximum number of stems to the sun and encourage heavy fruiting. Blackberries are vigorous and require ruthless pruning— after fruiting, cut all old fruited canes to soil level; trim back the main leaders of young canes by up to 5 ft. a year if necessary.

Rubus idaeus cultivars
Raspberry
H 6 ft. S 3 ft.

Raspberries are cane-forming shrubs that produce heavy crops in summer or autumn, according to the cultivar. They prefer well-drained, very fertile soil and a sheltered position, ideally in full sun. They grow to about 6 ft. high and need to be supported with stakes and wires. Plant canes from autumn to early spring, 18 in. apart in rows 6 ft. apart. Mulch with straw or organic matter to control weeds. Trim to 9 in. after planting. In subsequent years, prune summer-fruiting raspberries after fruiting by cutting all fruited canes to soil level; for autumn-fruiting cultivars, cut all canes to soil level in late winter.

Vaccinium corymbosum
Blueberry
H 3 ft. S 4 ft.

Blueberries are deciduous shrubs producing blue berries in late summer; the early cultivar 'Bluecrop' has large, pale blue berries. They need acidic soil and cool, moist conditions. They will tolerate partial shade but will crop more vigorously in full sun. A mature bush grows to about 4 ft. high. Plant bushes between autumn and early spring, roughly 5 ft. apart. Add peat to the soil to raise the acid level if necessary, or grow plants in containers of acidic compost. Mulch with well-rotted manure in early summer. Blueberries do not require pruning until they are 3–4 years old, when some of the oldest shoots should be cut back to soil level in autumn. Harvest in late summer.

Vegetables

There is a wide range of vegetables that you can grow in your garden. Some vegetables are much easier to grow than others, including beets, turnips, zucchini, carrots, lettuce, radishes, and broad beans. Choose from among these easy-to-grow varieties if you are planting vegetables for the first time.

Vegetables contain a wide range of vitamins and minerals, and some plants are very rich in a particular nutrient. For example, pulses, such as beans and peas, are a rich source of vitamin B, while peppers, potatoes, and tomatoes all contain high levels of vitamin C. It is now thought that antioxidants found in many of the green leafy vegetables that you can grow in your garden, such as broccoli and cabbage, help to protect against cancer.

Grow vegetables successively, where possible, planting a few seeds per week or fortnight, so that you extend the harvesting season and avoid a glut of one type of crop at any particular time. You can store root vegetables for several months by keeping them in a cool, dark place. Freezing is another option, but you will need to blanch the vegetables (boil them for a minute or two) beforehand.

Most vegetables need a sunny site and good, humus-rich soil. To achieve maximum yields, till the soil well and keep it well fed. Water the plants regularly.

A range of pests and diseases will attack your crops. Minimize these by choosing disease-resistant varieties and by looking after your plants well throughout the year.

Allium porrum
Leek

H 2 ft. S 6 in.

A close relative of onions, leeks are among the hardiest vegetables, over-wintering even in very cold climates. The long stem, known as the shank, is the edible part, and leek plants are grown in deep holes to encourage this to grow white (blanched). Leeks prefer light, open soil that is high in nitrogen. Sow the seeds in the open in early spring in drills 12 in. apart. Transplant the seedlings when they are roughly 6 in. tall, planting them into deep, narrow holes created by a dibber, at spacings roughly 8 in. apart, in rows 12 in. apart. Harvest leeks from early autumn onward; leave them in the ground until they are needed.

Allium
Onion, shallot, garlic

H 6 in. S 6 in.

Onions (*Allium cepa*), shallots (*Allium ascalonicum*), and garlic (*Allium sativum*, zone 8) all need rich soil. Plant sets (immature bulbs) in autumn (a period of cool weather helps promote strong growth); garlic is best planted in spring. Sow onion seeds in early spring in drills ½ in. deep and 12 in. apart, and thin seedlings to 6 in. apart. Plant garlic cloves at about their own depth, shallots ½ in. deep, 6 in. apart in all directions. Harvest the bulbs when the leaves turn yellow and keel over. Lift them with a garden fork and allow them to dry naturally before storing in a cool, dry, frost-proof place. To make strings of bulbs, leave 6 in. of leaf above the bulb and loop this around a doubled-over piece of string.

Apium graveolens var. *dulce*
Celery, celeriac

H 2 ft. S 6 in.

Celery is grown for its crisp, succulent leaf stalks; choose self-blanching varieties, which are easier to grow than those that need blanching. Celeriac is grown for its edible bulb-like stem, in the same way as celery. Provide an open, sunny site with deep, fertile soil. Sow the seeds indoors in early spring, planting the seedlings out in late spring, when they have developed 4–5 true leaves. Leave about 10 in. between plants. Water regularly. Both celery and celeriac are ready for harvesting about 6 months after sowing—from early autumn. Remove the base leaves from celeriac in early autumn and mulch with straw to protect from frosts. Remember that celery will only survive light frosts.

Beta vulgaris
Beet

H 8 in. S 6 in.

Beets are extremely rich in minerals and vitamins. Good cultivars include 'Detroit 2 Crimson Globes', 'Burpee's Golden' (yellow flesh), and 'Chioggia Pink' (pink and white flesh). Plant in rich but not freshly manured soil in slightly raised rows. Sow in situ about 4 weeks before the last frosts (soak the seeds in cold water for 12 hours to increase germination). Sow ½ in. deep and 2 in. apart, with 12 in. between rows. When the seedlings are 2 in. tall, thin to 4 in. apart. Keep the plants weed-free and mulch to conserve moisture. Liquid feed every 2 weeks for tender roots. Harvest roots as soon as they reach their full size, twisting off tops to prevent bleeding. Beets can be stored in sand for 6 months.

Brassica oleracea var. *gemmifera*
Brussels sprouts

H 2 ft. S 1 ft.

These very hardy vegetables produce edible flower buds that form tight sprouts in the leaf joints on the main stalk. Brussels sprouts need well firmed, alkaline soil to do well and to discourage club root, so you may need to add a little lime to your soil when digging it over. Sow the seeds from mid- to late spring, and then transplant the seedlings to their final planting positions once they are 6 in. tall, roughly 2 ft. apart in all directions. Firm the soil well. Harvest from early autumn to midspring. Compost the remaining stalks at the end of the season.

Brassica oleracea var. *italica*

Broccoli

H 3 ft. S 2 ft.

There are two types of broccoli: sprouting broccoli and calabrese. Sprouting broccoli, a biennial to 3 ft. high, has two forms: purple and white. Sow the seeds in late spring to give a crop the following spring. Calabrese, a green-sprouting broccoli, is not as hardy and is usually sown from spring to early summer, to crop some 12–14 weeks later. Modern F1 varieties include 'Corvet'. Broccoli prefers alkaline soil, so add lime to yours if it is acidic. The soil should be high in nitrogen but not freshly manured. Sow seeds in 6 in. pots and plant out 2 ft. apart when 3–4 true leaves have developed. Water the plants well, particularly just after transplanting and again when the heads form.

Brassica oleracea var. *capitata*

Cabbage

H 18 in. S 1 ft.

In cool climates you can grow and harvest cabbages all year round—sow summer and autumn cabbages from early spring to early summer, winter cabbages in late spring, and spring cabbages in late summer to overwinter for the following spring. There is a large range of varieties of all types—choose to suit your likes and needs. All cabbages prefer alkaline soil that is firm and high in nitrogen. Sow the seeds of all types ¾ in. deep and transplant the seedlings to 12 in. apart all around for spring cabbages, 6 in. or so farther apart for summer and winter cabbages.

Brassica oleracea var. *botrytis*

Cauliflower

H 18 in. S 1 ft.

Cauliflowers divide into groups, depending on the time of harvest. Winter cauliflowers can be grown only in mild or frost-free areas but summer and autumn cauliflowers can be grown anywhere. Like cabbages, cauliflowers prefer alkaline soil with medium nitrogen. Sow the seeds ¾ in. deep from early spring to early summer, depending on the variety. Transplant seedlings to 2 ft. apart all around. Alternatively, sow them in small pots and plant out when 3–4 true leaves have developed. Water the plants well, particularly after transplanting and when the heads begin to form. Protect the white curds from sun or frost by wrapping the leaves over them. Harvest when the curds are fully developed.

Brassica rapa var. *rapifera*
Turnip

H 8 in. S 6 in.

This hardy, fast-growing crop is regarded as a winter vegetable, but from an early sowing you can harvest it from summer onwards; cultivars like 'Tokyo Cross' are quick to mature and very tasty. Turnips prefer light soil that is high in nitrogen and do best in slightly alkaline conditions. Sow the seeds in drills 12 in. apart from late spring through to midsummer. Thin to 6 in. apart when the plants reach 2 in. high. Make sure they are regularly watered to prevent forked roots or bolting (producing flowers and seeds at the expense of roots). Harvest turnips by gently pulling up plants when the roots have swollen to the size of a golf ball. Young turnips have the best flavor.

Capsicum annuum var. *grossum*
Sweet pepper

H 3 ft. S 18 in.

There are many varieties of this fruiting vegetable: you can choose cultivars to produce red, yellow, green, orange, or even bluish-black fruit. Grow them in deep, well-cultivated soil or in growing bags—for best results, grow them in a greenhouse. Sow the seeds in individual pots in warmth in midspring. Plant seedlings roughly 2 ft. apart; plant outdoors only after the last frosts. Stake each plant and pinch out the growing point when it reaches 2 ft. high. Give a high-potassium feed once fruits start to form, and keep moist and humid, if possible. The peppers are ready to harvest about 3 months after planting out.

Capsicum annuum var. annum Longum
Chili pepper

H 1 ft. S 18 in.

Grow these fiery, tapering peppers in the same way as sweet peppers—in rich soil or in growing bags. For best results, grow under glass. Sow the seeds in pots indoors in midspring. Plant outdoors after the last frosts, spacing them about 2 ft. apart and providing a stake for each plant. Pinch out the growing point when it reaches 2 ft. high. Feed with a high-potassium fertilizer once fruits start to form, and keep moist and humid. The easy-to-grow cultivars, such as 'Apache', are ready about 3 months after planting out—the riper the chilies, the more fiery they taste. If they are not ripe by the first frosts, pull up the whole plant and hang it upside down indoors, somewhere warm, and the fruits will continue to ripen.

Cucumis sativus
Garden cucumber

H 3–10 ft. S 18 in.

Outdoor cucumbers are easier to grow than their indoor counterparts, because they are less susceptible to pests and diseases, but they do require temperatures above 50°F. They do well in growing bags. Some cultivars are low-growing and bushy, others trail and can be trained up wire netting; 'Burpless Tasty Green' is a favorite. Sow the seeds in midspring in individual pots in warmth. Once the seedlings are large enough to handle, harden them off gradually and plant at intervals of about 3 ft. Train trailing cucumbers up string or netting, keeping them in place with loose ties. Trim back the sideshoots as the main stems grow. The fruits are ready to harvest in late summer, about 12 weeks after sowing.

Curcurbita pepo
Zucchini

H 12 in. S 6 in.

Zucchini, which are younger versions of marrow squash, are quick and easy to grow; they are ready for eating 6–8 weeks after sowing. Squashes require similar cultivation and take about 16 weeks to grow. Zucchini cultivars include 'Ambassador' (dark green) and 'Gold Rush' (yellow); for squashes, try 'Tivoli' (large, creamy-golden, and cylindrical with spaghetti-like flesh). All like fertile soil. Sow the seeds in pots in warmth about 2 weeks before the last frosts are expected (soak them overnight to help germination). Plant out the young plants 3 ft. apart (more for trailing varieties). Water copiously. Regular picking encourages a continuous crop.

Cynara scolymus
Globe artichoke

H 6 ft. S 4 ft.

The globe artichoke is a handsome perennial plant with deeply divided, silvery foliage. The heart of the flower and the green, fleshy outer parts of the bud are edible once boiled. 'Green Globe' is the most popular variety. Grow globe artichokes in well-manured soil, raising them from seeds or rooted suckers taken from the parent plant in spring. Sow the seeds in small pots, 3 to a pot, under cover about 6–8 weeks before the last frosts. Thin out the plants to one per pot and plant them out, spacing them at least 24–30 in. apart, in late spring or early summer. Feed and water well in dry weather. Harvest the flower buds in summer when they are about the size of an orange.

Daucus carota subsp. *sativus*
Carrot

H 1 ft. S 6 in.

As well as the traditional orange form, there are white, yellow, or even crimson carrots. Round-rooted varieties are the easiest to grow and quick to mature. All carrots need well-prepared soil that is deep, rich, and stone-free. Avoid using fresh manure shortly before planting, as this leads to forked roots. Sow the seeds from early spring (the earliest sowings under cloches) and make successional sowings for a contin-uous supply. Thin out to 1 in. apart when the seedlings are about 2 in. high. Thin again a few weeks later to 3 in. Keep moist to prevent the roots from splitting, and mulch around the crowns to avoid their turning green. Harvest as soon as the carrots are large enough.

Foeniculum vulgare var. *azoricum*
Florence fennel

H 2 ft. S 18 in.

Florence fennel produces a large, succulent "bulb," consisting of swollen leaf bases, above ground. Its distinctive aniseed flavor is loved by some, loathed by others. 'Zefa Fino' is a popular cultivar. Fennel requires well-drained, but moisture-retentive soil with plenty of organic matter introduced the season before sowing. Raise the seeds in modules in warmth in early spring. Harden off young seedlings and plant out when the first 2 true leaves have developed, after the last frosts. Plant with about 12 in. between the plants all around. Once the bulbs start to form, mound up earth around them to avoid windrock. They are ready to harvest from late summer on, roughly 15 weeks after sowing.

Lactuca sativa
Garden lettuce

H 9 in. S 9 in.

The most popular salad vegetable, lettuce comes in several forms: cos, semi-cos, butterhead, loose-leaf, and crisphead. The loose-leaf forms bolt (form flowers and become bitter) less readily than the others and cope well with most growing conditions. Sow the seeds in drills about 12 in. apart in succession from early spring to midsummer. Thin seedlings to 12 in. once the plants form 2 true leaves. Water well at all times, but particularly as the plants start to mature. Lettuces take about 12 weeks to reach maturity: Loose-leaf lettuces are usually harvested using the cut-and-come-again method (picking a few leaves at a time); with other types, cut off the whole head.

Lycopersicon esculentum
Garden tomato

H up to 5 ft. S 18 in.

There are many cultivars of tomato for growing under glass or outdoors. The outdoor bush tomatoes are among the most popular; they are ideal for patio containers and do not require staking, unlike tall or cordon tomatoes. Sow seeds in pots in warmth in early to midspring. Plant seedlings 18 in. apart each way—if they are to go outdoors, wait until after the last frosts and harden them off first. Provide plenty of water. Mulch with straw and apply a high-potassium feed every 2 weeks. For tall cultivars, allow 5–7 trusses (flower clusters) to develop, then pinch out the plant's growing tips. Remove sideshoots as they develop, along with any leaves that shade the fruits. Pick the fruits as they ripen.

Pastinaca sativa
Parsnip

H 6 in. S 6 in.

These hardy root vegetables overwinter well when left in the ground. They do best in deep, fertile soil; remove large stones from the bed to ensure long, straight roots. Shorter-rooted cultivars can be grown in containers. Sow the seeds in drills in the open in early spring and thin the seedlings to 4 in. apart once they are 2 in. tall. Do not allow them to dry out, otherwise the flesh will become woody and the plants may develop forked roots. Parsnips are ready for harvesting from midautumn onward—leave them in the ground until they are needed.

Pisum sativum
Garden pea

H up to 3 ft. S 18 in.

As well as peas for shelling, you can grow snow and sugar peas (*P. s.* var. *macrocarpon*), which are eaten whole when they are young. Those for shelling are grouped according to the length of growing time they require: earlies, second earlies, and main crops. Sow peas in drills about 24 in. apart and 8 in. wide. Space them 2 in. apart and 2 in. deep. Make sure they do not dry out. Once the crop emerges, support it with twiggy pea sticks or wire netting. Make sure the plants are well watered, particularly after flowering. The earliest peas are ready to harvest 8 weeks after sowing; second earlies and main crops take 10–12 weeks. Harvest the pods regularly to encourage further flowering and more pods.

Phaseolus and *Vicia* spp
French bean, runner bean, broad bean

H 18in–6 ft. S 12 in.

The most popular beans are French beans (*Phaseolus vulgaris*), runner beans (*P. coccineus*), and broad beans (*Vicia faba*). French and runner beans are frost tender, but broad beans are hardy and can even be sown in autumn for an early crop the following year. All beans require sun, humus-rich soil, and plenty of water. Sow French and runner beans outdoors from midspring to early summer, broad beans in autumn or spring. Plant broad and French beans 6 in. apart in rows 12 in. apart. Space runners 6 in. apart in double rows, 2 ft. apart. Train runners up poles. A mid-season dressing of seaweed extract will improve the growth rate. Harvest beans while they are young and tender.

Solanum melongena var. *esculenta*
Eggplant

H 3 ft. S 2 ft.

Eggplants require a warm climate to produce their blackish-purple fruits, so they are usually grown under glass. They need deep, fertile soil. Sow the seeds in midspring, potting up the seedlings. Plant out the young plants as soon as the first flowers start to open—if they are to go outdoors, wait until after the frosts have passed. Space them 30 in. apart and stake their stems. Pinch out the growing points soon after planting. Feed with a high-potassium fertilizer every 2 weeks once the fruits begin to develop. Harvest 3–4 months after planting. Do not leave the fruits on the plant; otherwise, the flesh will become bitter.

Solanum tuberosum
Irish potato, white potato

H 2 ft. 6 in. S 18 in.

There is a huge variety of potatoes in different shapes, colors, textures, and flavors. Earlies are ready in early summer; main crops produce larger potatoes from late summer on; second earlies mature in between. All require a deep soil that is rich in organic matter. Buy tubers in late winter and put them in a warm, light place to develop shoots. Plant them out from early to midspring (according to type), 6 in. deep and 12 in. apart in rows 3 ft. apart. When they are 8 in. high, mound the soil around them to prevent the tubers from turning green. Harvest early potatoes as soon as the flowers start to open. Main crops are ready much later and can be stored in a cool, dark place for several months.

Glossary

A

Acid   Type of soil in which the pH value is less than 7.

Air layering   A method of propagation by which a plant is induced to form new roots from a cut or nicked shoot pegged onto a stem above ground level.

Alkaline   Soil with pH value of more than 7.

Annual   A plant that completes its growing cycle from seed to flower in one season.

Aquatic   Plant that grows happily in water, either free-floating or anchored in the soil.

B

Bare-root   Plants sold with the soil removed from their roots.

Base dressing   Fertilizer or compost applied to the soil before planting or sowing.

Biennial   Plant that completes its growing cycle from seed to flower over a two-year period.

Blanch   To exclude light from the stems of certain vegetables in order to improve flavor and remove bitterness.

Bolt   Said of a plant that produces flowers and seed prematurely.

Brassica   A member of the cabbage family.

C

Calyx   The outer whorl of green segments that enclose a flower bud.

Central leader   The upright stem of a tree or bush.

Chlorophyll   The green pigment in a leaf that absorbs light and allows photosynthesis to occur.

Cloche   A portable glass or transparent plastic structure used for protecting crops or warming soil prior to planting.

Cold frame   Similar to a cloche but usually permanent, with wood or brick sides.

Compost   Either a potting medium or organic, bulky, rotted matter used to fertilize the soil.

Cordon   A plant grained to one main stem by pruning, used for fruit production.

Corm   An underground bulb-like storage organ.

Crop rotation   A method of planting crops in a new area of soil each year to prevent the buildup of soil pests that attack certain crops, such as potatoes.

Crown   The base part of a perennial plant where roots and stem join. The crown of frost-sensitive plants often needs protection.

Cultivar   A cultivated variety as oppposed to a naturally occuring variety of plant.

Cutting   A portion of a plant, root, stem, leaf, or shoot from which new plants can be propagated.

D

Deadheading   Removal of spent flowers to encourage new blooms to form.

Deciduous   Plant that sheds its leaves in the fall.

Divison   A method of propagating or controlling plants by dividing them into sections, taking a portion of stem and new shoot with each section.

Dormancy   State of plant when growth ceases. This usually occurs during winter, because it is triggered by low light levels.

Double digging   A deeper than normal form of digging, in which the soil is cultivated to two spades' depth as opposed to a single spade's depth, which is normally used.

E

Espalier   A plant trained with a vertical central leader and tiers of side shoots horizontally on either side.

F

F1 hybrids   The first generation of plant bred from two selected pure-breeding parents. Seed from Fl hybrids will not come true (see glossary entry on page 313).

Falls   The lower petals of plants such as irises.

Family   The name for a group of plants that combine related genera.

Fibrous   Of roots that are fine and branching.

Force To induce any plant to grow faster than nature intended, usually by increasing temperature or light.

G

Genus or genera Category of plant in which a group of related species are linked by common characteristics.

Grafting A method of propagation in which the stems of two different plants are bound together so that they fuse to create one plant.

H

Half hardy Said of a plant that can survive some degree of frost for short periods but is not fully hardy (see below).

Hardy Said of a plant that is impervious to frost.

Heel A strip of bark removed with a cutting.

Herbaceous A nonwoody plant, such as a perennial.

Humus Organic residue of decayed matter.

Hybrid The offspring of genetically different parents.

L

Lateral A side growth arising from a shot or root.

Layering A method of propagation by which a plant is induced to form new roots from a cut or nicked shoot pegged down to the soil (see also air layering).

Lime Mineral made up of calcium, which makes soil more alkaline.

M

Mulch A layer of material applied to the soil surface to suppress weeds or reduce moisture loss.

N

Neutral Soil with a pH value of 7.

O

Offset A young plant that arises by natural reproduction, usually from bulbs.

Oxygenator A plant that lives in water and releases oxygen into the water. Essential for pond life.

P

Peat Humus-rich organic matter formed in wet soils.

Perennial Any plant that survives for more than two seasons, commonly applied to plants that die back in winter and grow again from their roots in spring.

PH A measurement of acidity or alkalinity in the soil.

Pinch out The removal of the growing tip of a plant.

Pricking out Transferring young seedlings to their final growing position.

Pruning A method of removing parts of shrubs and trees in order to increase or decrease vigor, and to improve flowering or fruiting.

R

Remontant Plant that flowers twice in one year.

Rhizome A creeping, swollen underground storage organ.

Runner A spreading stem that runs above ground, rooting at its nodes to produce new plants.

S

Shrub A woody-stemmed perennial plant, branching at the base. A tree normally has one single main stem.

Species A category of plant, in which several characteristics are shared, within a genus.

Spur A short branch bearing flower buds.

Stopping To pinch out to prevent further growth.

Succulent A plant with thick, fleshy leaves that store water.

Sucker A shoot that arises below the soil or below the graft union on grafted plants.

T

Tap root A root with a single downward-growing main root.

Tender A plant that is vulnerable to any frost damage.

Topiary The art of clipping evergreens into geometric shapes.

Transplanting Moving a plant from one position to another.

True Term used in breeding to describe plants that have the same characteristics as the parent plants.

V

Variegated Used to describe leaves with various color markings, usually white or yellow.

Variety A naturally occuring variant of a plant.

Index

Entries in *italics* refer to illustrations.

A

Abutilon megapotamicum, 264, *264*

Acanthus mollis, 20

Acer palmatum f. *atropurpureum*, 33, 246, *246*

Achillea filipendulina 'Cloth of Gold', 270, *270*

    A. millefolium 'Cerise Queen', 270, *270*

acidic soils, 16–17, 40–1, 46–7, *47*

Actinidia kolomikta, 99

African daisy, 283, *283*

Ailanthus altissima, 246, *246*

air layering, 131

Ajuga reptans, 228, *228*

Akebia quinata, 264, *264*

Alchemilla mollis, 271, *271*

alkaline soils, 16, 40–1, 46–7

Allium, 37, 85

    A. christophii, 271, *271*

American boxwood, 194, 253, *253*

Anemone hupehensis 'Hadspen Abundance', 271, *271*

annuals, 270–89, 111

Antirrhinum, 103

aphids, 166, *166*

apples, 298, *298*

Aralia elata 'Variegata', 247, *247*

arbors, 89

Arbutus unedo, 247, *247*

Artemisia 'Powis Castle', 272, *272*

Asplenium scolopendrium, 290, *290*

Aster amellus 'Veilchenkönigin', 272, *272*

Aucuba japonica 'Crotonifolia', 252, *252*

autumn, 20, 85

B

bamboos, 83, 290–3

bare rooted plants, 109

basal cuttings, 127

basil, 212

baskets, 67, 78–9

bay, 213, 295, *295*

beans, 206, 207, *207*

beautybush, 258, *258*

beet, 303, *303*

Bellis perennis 'Pompette', 272, *272*

Berberis thunbergii 'Atropurpurea', 252, *252*

black bamboo, 292, *292*

black locust, 250, *250*

blackberries, 208, 300, *300*

blackcurrants, *209*, 300, *300*

blackjack, *146*

blue daisy, 279, *279*

blueberries, 301, *301*

bluecrown passionflower, *113*, 268, *268*

borders, planning, 82–3, 90–1

boron deficiency, *50*

botrytis, 168, *168*

breeding plants, 36–7

broad beans, 310, *310*

broccoli, 304, *304*

broom, 255, *255*

brushwood cutters, 73

brussels sprouts, 303, *303*

Buddleia davidii 'Harlequin', 253, *253*

bulbs, 270–89

    naturalizing, 232, *233*

    planting, 110

butterflybush, 253, *253*

Buxus, 96, 97

    B. sempervirens, 20, 194, 253, *253*

C

cabbage tree, 254, *254*

cabbages, 206, 304, *304*

cactus, *26*

Calendula officinalis 'Fiesta Gitana', 273, *273*

California lilac, 265, *265*

California poppy, 278, *278*

calla lily, 274, *274*

Calluna vulgaris 'Firefly', 273, *273*

Camassia leichtlinii, 273, *273*

Camellia × williamsii 'Donation', 253, *253*

Campanula lactiflora 'Pritchard's Variety', 274, *274*

Campsis × tagliabuana 'Madame Galen', 99, 265, *265*

canker, 168, *168*

Canna 'Phaison', 33

    C. × generalis 'Bengal Tiger', 274, *274*

carrots, 308, *308*

carrying sheets, 67

catalogs, 21

caterpillars, 166, *166*

cauliflower, 304, *304*

Ceanothus 'Autumnal Blue', 265, *265*

celeriac, 303, *303*

celery, 206, 303, *303*

Chaenomeles speciosa, 98

chalk, 44

Chamaecyparis lawsoniana 'Green Hedger', 96

    C. pisifera 'Filifera Aurea', 247, *247*

chamomile, 212–13, 242

cherries, 299, *299*

chicken manure, 51

chili peppers, 306, *306*

China pinks, 278

Chinese parsley, 295, *295*

AUTHOR'S ACKNOWLEDGMENTS

Thanks to Steve and Val Bradley for the projects and contributions to text, Marcus Harpur and Mark Winwood for their photography, Corinne Asghar for editorial work, Ruth Hope for the design, Amanda Patten for her illustrations, and Iain Macgregor, Anna Osborn, and all at Murdoch Books for their help.

PHOTOGRAPHER'S ACKNOWLEDGMENTS

Marcus Harpur is very grateful to the following gardens, owners and designers who very kindly allowed him to photograph their work for this book.

Gordon Gardiner, London; RHS Hampton Court Palace Flower Show, 2001, 2000; Lee Jackson and Naila Green (Corporate Gardens), Design; Christopher Masson, Design, Wandsworth, London; Wyken Hall, Suffolk; RHS Chelsea Flower Show, 2001; Andy Sturgeon, Design, London; Jason de Grellier Payne, Design, London; Mr & Mrs Timothy Easton, Bedfield Hall, Suffolk; Walton Poor, Dorking, Surrey; Mr & Mrs P McPherson, Sussex; Jill Cowley, Park Farm, Essex; Mr & Mrs Henry Bradshaw, Norfolk; The Abbey Gardens, Malmesbury, Wilts; Beth Chatto Gardens, Elmstead Market, Essex; Paul Dyer, Design; The Really Interesting Landscape Company, Design; Pensthorpe Waterfowl Park, Fakenham, Norfolk; Andy Rees, Design; RHS Wisley, Surrey; Dr & Mrs NCW Harpur, Ixworth, Suffolk; Old Rectory, Sudborough, Northants; Cressing Temple, Braintree, Essex; Chenies Manor, Buckinghamshire; Saling Hall, Essex; Ballymalloe Cookery School, Shanagarry, Co. Cork, Ireland; Wickham Place Farm, nr Witham, Essex; Congham Hall Hotel, Norfolk; Jonathan Baillie, Design, London; Geoff Whiten, Design, Wales; Mrs MP Giblin, Good Easter, Essex; Julia Scott, The Walled Garden, Worcester; Jorn Langberg, Hillwatering, Suffolk; Tom Stuart-Smith, Design, London; The Garden in an Orchard, Norfolk; Katie Howlett for her very kind assistance and Mary Harpur for her continuing forebearance.

ISBN 1-57145-821-2

Library of Congress Cataloging-in-Publication Data available upon request.

Printed in China.

2 3 4 5 06 05 04 03 02

Commissioning Editor: Iain Macgregor
Editors: Sarah Widdicombe, Jo Weeks and Corinne Asghar
Designer: Ruth Hope
Managing Editor: Anna Osborn
Design Manager: Helen Taylor and Sarah Rock
Photo Librarian: Bobbie Leah
Photography: Marcus Harpur and Mark Wi nwood
Illustrations: Amanda Patten
CEO: Robert Oerton
Publisher: Catie Ziller
Production Manager: Lucy Byrne